DR. LEE ANN B. MARINO, PH.D., D.MIN., D.D.

MINISTRY SCHOOL BASIC TRAINING

BE ALL THAT YOU CAN BE IN GOD'S ARMY
(A Guide For Lay Membership)

MINISTRY SCHOOL BASIC TRAINING

BE ALL THAT YOU CAN BE IN GOD'S ARMY
(A Guide For Lay Membership)

DR. LEE ANN B. MARINO, PH.D., D.MIN., D.D.

Published by:
Righteous Pen Publications
www.righteouspenpublications.com

All rights reserved. No part of this book may be reproduced or transmitted in any form or by any means, electronic or mechanical, or information storage and retrieval system without written permission from the author.

Unless otherwise noted, all Scriptures are taken from *the Holy Bible, New Living Translation* copyright © 1996, 2004, 2007 by the Tyndale House Foundation. Used by permission of Tyndale House Publishers, Inc., Carol Stream, Illinois 60188. All rights reserved.

All Scriptures marked AMPC are taken from *The Amplified® Bible, Classic Edition.* Copyright © 1954, 1958, 1962, 1964, 1965, 1987 by The Lockman Foundation. Used by permission. (www.Lockman.org)

All passages marked GW *are a copyrighted work of God's Word to the Nations.* Quotations are used by permission. Copyright 1995 by God's Word to the Nations. All rights reserved.

Cover and interior photos in the public domain.

Book classification: 1. Nonfiction > Religion > Christian Life > Spiritual Growth

Copyright © 2020, 2025 by Dr. Lee Ann B. Marino.

ISBN: 1-940197-60-0
13-Digit: 978-1-940197-60-9

Printed in the United States of America.

So Paul, standing before the council, addressed them as follows: "Men of Athens, I notice that you are very religious in every way, for as I was walking along I saw your many shrines. And one of your altars had this inscription on it: 'To an Unknown God.' This God, Whom you worship without knowing, is the one I'm telling you about.

"He is the God Who made the world and everything in it. Since He is Lord of heaven and earth, He doesn't live in man-made temples, and human hands can't serve His needs—for He has no needs. He himself gives life and breath to everything, and He satisfies every need. From one man He created all the nations throughout the whole earth. He decided beforehand when they should rise and fall, and He determined their boundaries.

"His purpose was for the nations to seek after God and perhaps feel their way toward Him and find Him—though He is not far from any one of us. For in Him we live and move and exist. As some of your own poets have said, 'We are His offspring.' And since this is true, we shouldn't think of God as an idol designed by craftsmen from gold or silver or stone.

"God overlooked people's ignorance about these things in earlier times, but now He commands everyone everywhere to repent of their sins and turn to Him. For He has set a day for judging the world with justice by the man He has appointed, and He proved to everyone Who this is by raising Him from the dead."
(Acts 17:22-31)

TABLE OF CONTENTS

	Preface..	1
1	The Kingdom of God is Within You!..	1
2	The Kingdom of God is Around You!..	23
3	The Kingdom of God is Among You!..	75
4	The Essentials of Our Faith..	105
5	Offering What You've Received..	129
6	Receiving Guidance From God's Military Leaders.....................	149
7	Be a Radical Giver!..	189
8	You're a Soldier in the Army of the Lord................................	211
9	Taking Our Place in History...	231
10	Jesus: First, Last, and Best...	257
	About the Author...	283

~ PREFACE ~

Ministry School Boot Camp: Training for Helps Ministries, Appointments, and Beyond was the first book I wrote to reach the status of a personal best-seller. This was surprising to me at the time, as I wrote the book in response to a need that existed in one of our ministries. One of our leaders needed to train someone in her ministry to assist in ministry activities. Not being sure where to start, I offered to do it and sat down to pen what would become my first major seller. All over the world, people embraced the contents of *Ministry School Boot Camp*: training members interested in service, lay leadership, and greater participation. In Apostolic University, the text became a primer for our Seminary program. In Bible colleges around the United States, *Ministry School Boot Camp* became an important text for educating future leaders in church in the right and proper way.

About three years ago, it became evident a new installment was needed in the continuing series that became a wide phenomenon. Rather than a primer for lay leadership and service, we needed a book that could be used by the average ministry or church member who wasn't preparing or planning on future church service. It was important to have a work that addressed common issues as pertain to general membership: Kingdom understanding, Bible study, interactions with others, relationships, everyday spiritual living, giving, and beyond, all in a manner that exhibits such as relevant and applicable for every average believer.

Ministry School Basic Training serves as that foundational work: suitable for every member in a church, from the newest Christian to those who need a great refresher course on the foundations of their faith and participation in this Kingdom we have as citizens of heaven. Wherever you are in your faith, dive right in – and through – to re-learn, learn something new, and grow in your faith as a child of the Most High God.

+ Apostle Dr. Lee Ann B. Marino, Ph.D., D.Min., D.D.
October 3, 2019

~ CHAPTER ONE ~
THE KINGDOM OF GOD IS WITHIN YOU!

IF you are a member of the Kingdom of God, I am overjoyed to call you my brother, sister, or sibling in Christ. This means that even though we've never met, and we may very well never meet this side of heaven, we have something very important in common: we are both a part of God's family, His Kingdom, and His purpose. We might not look at things the exact same way all the time, but we have that uniting factor in common. If we think about this awesome thing, it should change our perspective on life, our understanding of what it means to be, one to another, and what it means to belong to God.

If you don't already know about everything we are going to cover, don't feel bad. It's very possible you haven't been saved long enough to have knowledge of it all and it's also possible that you have never heard much about it. Sometimes we don't hear a lot about this aspect of our spiritual lives because ministers and believers in general might not be sure how to talk about it in a way that is understandable. We tend to think being in God's Kingdom means being all deep and super-spiritual and being super-spiritual means nobody can understand what we mean when we say certain things. Being Kingdom and being about the Kingdom doesn't mean that we must be really deep, or that nobody can figure out what we mean. It does mean, however, that we take the effort to learn about the things related to Kingdom living and mindset that we don't readily understand without some greater information.

Here we are going to do just that: look at a most foundational aspect of being a part of the Kingdom of God, which is understanding the Kingdom. If we don't rightly understand being in the Kingdom and what it means to be in the Kingdom, then we aren't going to know what it means when we talk about being "Kingdom."

Yes, being born again, saved, in the process of salvation, starting our process of discipleship, or whatever you want to call it is an awesome thing that can take us to great places in our lives and can change us from the inside out. The catch with salvation is that it is a process, and it is a transformation, as we trade in the precepts of one kingdom (the world) for an eternal Kingdom (the Kingdom of God). As we go along that way, we come to understand and learn about the Kingdom of God that is within us and is changing us. First, we accept it and it is within us; then we become a part of God's larger body, and it is around us; and then we learn to live with others, and it is among us. To get to this point, we must first learn about thing special thing we call "Kingdom."

BORN AGAIN AND IN KINGDOM

There are admittedly a lot of things that can feel very confusing if one tries to take on too many Bible subjects at once. If you are new to Bible reading (or sometimes even if you have read the Bible for many years) the Bible can feel contradictory or hard to understand. There are a couple of key things, however, that one can discover if they look over the Scriptures carefully. One is the centrality of Jesus Christ. No matter what you know of Christ before you come to knowledge of discipleship, you cannot deny His complete and total importance in the work of salvation history. Jesus has done something for us that we could not do for ourselves, and that makes Him essential to our faith. The second key thing you can see is the Kingdom of God. From the very beginning of time, God has desired to have a special relationship with His people, the people who He is able to call His own.

In Bible times, the Kingdom of God started as God called unique individuals away from what they knew, what was comfortable for them, what they identified with, and who they knew to launch them into an entirely new place. In this new place, they were forced to start over again, to begin anew. This "forced" place wasn't a place of harm or abuse, but one where those individuals came to know God. It challenged them to start from the beginning and re-learn their entire way of being. They became new, living new lives and renewed and changed in their outlook.

This concept is the foundation for what we now classify as the "born again" experience. We come to find this place after we find ourselves in Christ, experiencing the walk of dying to sin and rising to new life (symbolized by our baptism in water). If we want to get right with God, we must start again at the beginning. Since we can't be literally born again from the womb, God must do something else, something new within us to "re-birth" us into this existence. Nothing like reincarnation and much cooler than the idea of having to endlessly come into being over and over again, God gives us the chance to be "reborn" in this lifetime, starting new.

Sounds impossible? It's not. It is better than anything we could imagine. Jesus Himself told us about this incredible experience in John 3:1-21:

There was a man named Nicodemus, a Jewish religious leader who was a Pharisee. After dark one evening, he came to speak with Jesus. "Rabbi," he said, "we all know that God has sent You to teach us. Your miraculous signs are evidence that God is with you."

Jesus replied, "I tell you the truth, unless you are born again, you cannot see the Kingdom of God."

"What do You mean?" exclaimed Nicodemus. "How can an old man go back into his mother's womb and be born again?"

Jesus replied, "I assure you, no one can enter the Kingdom of God without being born of water and the Spirit. Humans can reproduce only human life, but the Holy Spirit gives birth to spiritual life. So don't be surprised when I say, 'You must be born again.' The wind blows wherever it wants. Just as you can hear the wind but can't tell where it comes from or where it is going, so you can't explain how people are born of the Spirit."

"How are these things possible?" Nicodemus asked.

Jesus replied, "You are a respected Jewish teacher, and yet you don't understand these things? I assure you, we tell you what we know and have seen, and yet you won't believe our testimony. But if you don't believe Me when I tell you about earthly things, how can you possibly believe if I tell you about heavenly things? No one has ever gone to heaven and returned. But the Son of Man has come down from heaven. And as Moses lifted up the bronze snake on a pole in the wilderness, so the Son of Man must be lifted up, so that everyone who believes in Him will have eternal life.

"For this is how God loved the world: He gave His one and only Son, so that everyone who believes in Him will not perish but have eternal life. God sent His Son into the world not to judge the world, but to save the world through Him.

"There is no judgment against anyone who believes in Him. But anyone who does not believe in Him has already been judged for not believing in God's one and only Son. And the judgment is based on this fact: God's light came into the world, but people loved the darkness more than the light, for their actions were evil. All who do evil hate the light and refuse to go near it for fear their sins will be exposed. But those who do what is right come to the light so others can see that they are doing what God wants."

It seems that even in New Testament times, people sought out a way to "start again" with God. This reveals why we need something more than the movements people espoused in Old Testament times. The people sought God, they were sincere, and they made huge strides to start again, but it wasn't enough. We all know we can leave our homes, we can do different things, we can take a huge breath and try to reset, but our old ways, habits, and issues have a way of finding us. We can take ourselves out of a specific place, but it takes something spiritual to take those things out of us.

Nicodemus came to Jesus in honesty, recognizing things about both himself and Christ. He recognized there was something unique and special about Him, and that Jesus could reveal powerful truths to him that he couldn't find somewhere else. So, what does Jesus tell Nicodemus? Take everything you have and hide it somewhere? Amass more and more things to your name? Start a new job? Move to a whole different city? No! Jesus tells Nicodemus: we must be born again to see the Kingdom of God.

Whoa! Talk about getting an unexpected answer. All the things that we hold dear, all the things we think will make us happy, all the things that lead us along in this world are not the things that will help us see the Kingdom of God. To see the Kingdom of God, we must be "born again!"

In other words: if we want to be a part of God's Kingdom, we must start again spiritually. We must stand renewed, reborn, washed clean, and fresh, new before God, to see that Kingdom. We must be born of the Holy Spirit, receiving spiritual life, in a level and a way that no one can control, contain, or understand. God breathes life, it comes through the work of the Holy Spirit, and as we are renewed through the life and sacrifice of Christ, so that change comes through to us.

In our "born again" experience, we come out from everything we know, much like the people of old. The difference is that in our experience today, we do it in a spiritual sense. We come into the Kingdom through Christ because He is our King, having brought us into the Kingdom through His sacrifice on the cross. We don't have to be separated from God any longer, because Jesus made the way! God has now given us the ability to live by the Spirit and led in His transformative methods. We are now a part of this great Kingdom of God!

Now what?

Good question. You would be amazed how many people claim to be Christians, but do not have a solid understanding of what it means to be a part of God's Kingdom. As a result, they don't walk or live like they have undergone such a powerful transformation. They don't understand many key things about living in a Kingdom or about being a part of God's incredible system. This means they don't teach or talk about it in a way that everyone can understand. Here, we will get these powerful insights so you can truly be "all that you can be" in your spiritual life!

Kingdom Understanding

In times gone by, most societies were upheld by the principle that citizens didn't know what was good for them. They certainly didn't know enough to run a country or to have any idea what their rights should be, or so their governments led them to believe. Most citizens were uneducated and unable to read or write, which meant even if they felt they were getting a bad deal, they didn't have the skills to organize or move like they might have desired. In instances where they did revolt, the monarchies were often more powerful or other more powerful agencies came in to topple the citizens into a place of submission. It was often a rough life, and the poor often reaped the heaviest burden for political turmoil and upheavals. Because of obvious realities, people of old had to trust their leaders with their lives. They recognized their literal well-being rested in the decisions of leaders. Time and time again, they found their trust abused. They had no choice but to follow their leaders, but oftentimes found themselves overtaxed, sent to war, abused and mistreated, all because someone had power to take a seat of authority. Much of the time, there was nothing anyone could do to get such people out of power.

This means citizens of the old world knew something most of us today don't know: the governments and kingdoms of this world don't hold the answers we seek. While people fight all over the world to try and transform our political systems into structures they hope and believe will hold better answers for them (and often rightfully so), people of old knew their true hope was in God. They looked for the day when God would intervene on their behalf and end the suffering imposed by government leaders who took advantage of their positions and power.

Most of us in today's world don't live in governments with functioning monarchies. In nations where monarchies are present, they tend to be more ceremonial in position than governmental. Sometimes they impact politics or governances behind the scenes, but it is rare that a monarchy runs a nation front and center in modern times. Electoral process and democracies or republics of one form or another rule the world in which we live, and there are many reasons why these forms of government have taken center stage over the past two hundred years or so. Changing economic and political climates have caused citizens to rise and demand their interests have a voice in government leadership and affairs. Through revolts, revolutions, protests, and government overthrow, citizens worldwide have gained rights that people in times past did not have.

It sounds great that citizens are more involved with their government's advances and movements. We associate older governmental structures, such as monarchies or oligarchies, with oppression and economic poverty for the masses – and it is true that these things did exist under older forms of government and governmental regimes. As with all things, however, citizen revolt and its results are not quite as simple as all nations of the world live happily ever after now that the older governmental structures are gone. We now see the reality that nobody agrees on how to get things done and that people are easily and quickly divided by issues. Without formal government in place, many nations have seen the rise of rebel or terror groups that exploit the concept of order by imposing regimes of fear, death, sexual assault, and violence. While getting rid of one problem seems to be a good thing, it also brings with it many new problems.

If we are going to understand the Kingdom of God, we must first understand the basics of what a "kingdom" is and how a kingdom functions. Because we might never experience a functioning kingdom in our lifetime, we need to educate ourselves about kingdoms: how they work and what they do.

Kingdoms function as follows:

- Kingdoms center around a king or a queen, or another member of that specified royal family. The family holds its position due to its bloodline. Future monarchs are selected due to position in a royal family. The way such is selected does vary, but somehow, and some way, there is an established order to matters of succession (usually implemented when a monarch dies).

- Monarchs often rose to power through conquest, fame, inheritance, or power. The first kings acquired large plots of land through battle or purchase and then became part of the elite, with the top individual crowned as king. His heirs would then become successors for the same title. In some countries, there are still the descendants of these first monarchs, holding various positions and titles as part of royal families.

- Kings, queens, and other sovereign members of a royal ruling family are not in position by election. It doesn't matter if anyone wants them there or not. As history can testify, it can be very difficult to remove a monarch from their position.

- Kingdoms are set up to ensure the monarch's wishes, laws, edicts, and decrees are enforced. Government officials are positioned based on their loyalty to the monarch and their willingness to execute the monarch's wishes. Subjects must trust their governmental leaders, because in a monarchy, it is hard (if not impossible) to remove a ruler from power.

- Failure to support the king, queen, or other monarch may very well have resulted in exile from the kingdom or in death. Even today, it is considered taboo to speak out against a royal family member.

The reason we understand the Kingdom of God to be a Kingdom is because we serve an all-powerful, all-knowing God Who is not only just and fair, but He also knows the end from the beginning. We don't serve a King Who dominates us by force, makes us feel the same exact way about everything, or who threatens us with death if we slip up or have a bad day. We aren't servants of God because He is cruel and unrelenting. Our King leads His Kingdom by love, with love, and in love, and expects us to do the same:

"If you love Me, obey My commandments. And I will ask the Father, and He will give you another Advocate, Who will never leave you. He is the Holy Spirit, Who leads into all truth. The world cannot receive Him, because it isn't looking for Him and doesn't recognize Him. But you know Him, because He lives with you now and later will be in you. No, I will not abandon you as orphans—I will come to you. Soon the world will no longer see Me, but you will see Me. Since I live, you also will live. When I

am raised to life again, you will know that I am in My Father, and you are in Me, and I am in you. Those who accept My commandments and obey them are the ones who love Me. And because they love Me, My Father will love them. And I will love them and reveal Myself to each of them."

Judas (not Judas Iscariot, but the other disciple with that name) said to Him, "Lord, why are You going to reveal Yourself only to us and not to the world at large?"

Jesus replied, "All who love Me will do what I say. My Father will love them, and We will come and make our home with each of them. Anyone who doesn't love Me will not obey Me. And remember, My words are not My own. What I am telling you is from the Father Who sent Me. I am telling you these things now while I am still with you. But when the Father sends the Advocate as My representative—that is, the Holy Spirit—He will teach you everything and will remind you of everything I have told you. (John 14:15-26)

At the same time, we also understand ourselves to be a part of a Kingdom because if we are a part of God's Kingdom, we accept His rule in our lives. No, God does not come at us with force, but God is not just in our lives as some sort of fluffy marshmallow. God is our Sovereign, our Lord, our authority, our guide, and the One Who leads us rightly all the days of our lives. It is done in love, but that doesn't mean that God is any less a ruler with authority in our lives. If we are really with God, we receive His rule, and we respect those He sends out (His leaders) to maintain His order and grace in this Kingdom. As those who know His love, we trust Him. We trust that He has a rule of benefit for our lives, and we submit ourselves to His guidance and purposes for us. We have no reason to revolt, because we have found the true Leader Who is better and bigger and has the best and most powerful things for us in this life, and the next. He will never forsake us, nor mislead us. Now that we are in this place, we are never the same.

A Misunderstood Monarch

It's easy for us to think about the kings of the 1400s and 1500s when we think about "monarchy." The kings of those eras sat on big thrones and wore big, puffy, uncomfortable, and well, ugly clothing. While their kingdoms operated by the precepts we mentioned earlier, there were some differences between kingdoms in Biblical times and kingdoms in medieval times.

In New Testament times, the nation of Israel was occupied by the

Roman government. This fact is most relevant because it shaped the way the Jews at that point in history understood their own identity, their own spirituality, and the government of God. The understanding of "kingdom," therefore, and of a king and what a king does, largely came from their understanding of the Roman government.

The Roman government was powerful, forceful, and covered a great expanse of territory. Its central "king" was an emperor, an individual who was believed to be in office not just by human interest, but by divine choice. The term "Son of God" comes from such a ruling tradition, as it indicated one was the physical embodiment of a god here on earth. As a result, the emperors were seen as literal gods, given authority and ultimate power. The result of such power was a desire for even more power, and to maintain their positions of power and the expansion and maintenance of the empire, citizens were heavily taxed. Israel's forced occupation only added to matters, whereas the Jews considered themselves oppressed and in need of political freedom.

The first century impression of what the Messiah should be, therefore, contrasted with the oppression of the Roman government. The Jews believed the Messiah would come in as larger than life to crush the Roman Empire. The result would be establishment of a Jewish political state that would dominate and control all its enemies. The Messiah was to come in as a king and establish a kingdom that looked a lot like the ones they had already seen and was going to use the same methods to topple their enemies.

That's not what they got, nor is it the Kingdom promised them. Instead, they got a King Who promised a Kingdom that couldn't be easily seen…at least right now. The work of Jesus as Messiah related to salvation and our interactions and conduct as we prepare to receive the Kingdom, in full, throughout our lives. It had nothing to do with overthrowing the Roman government or anything having to do with anybody else. Jesus desired that His followers, His people would clean themselves up so they would be able to withstand spiritual judgment, have better direction from God, and obey God through love. The people of Jesus' day cared about what everyone else was doing, while Jesus wanted them to care about their own actions.

For everyone has sinned; we all fall short of God's glorious standard. (Romans 3:23)

Many people have an idea of Jesus as a personal Savior, which expresses the Lordship that Jesus has over one's life. This is a fine idea and absolutely relates to how we understand His rule on a personal level, but it's obvious it wasn't one that people had of the Messiah in the first century. It wasn't how they saw Him, but such a concept wasn't new to the first century, either. If we study the Old Testament carefully, the Israelites always wanted God to fix or change their perceived enemies, when God wanted to do a work within them. They wanted to be rescued out of their every trial, but God wanted to rescue them from sin and restore them to a place where the "Kingdom of God" was within them (and among and around, as the Greek word indicates such a presence). This, and only this, would result in a permanent change within people.

One day the Pharisees asked Jesus, "When will the Kingdom of God come?"

Jesus replied, "The Kingdom of God can't be detected by visible signs. You won't be able to say, 'Here it is!' or 'It's over there!' For the Kingdom of God is already among you." (Luke 17:20-21)

Understanding these historical facts makes Jesus' words about the Kingdom of God within (and also among and around) more profound and purposeful than we might have ever thought when reading the Bible. Speaking of the Kingdom of God within us is an expression of the fullness God desires to do within us. It is His will that we are transformed from the inside out. God wants us to be a part of His Kingdom, where He is our Lord and we are His people, and He is the One Who guides and directs us. By walking with Him, we are to discover He is within us, and we are within Him.

CITIZENS OF HEAVEN

Sometimes we can get confused reading the Scriptures. Don't feel bad if you don't have the Bible all figured out. None of us have it all figured out, even if you are following the leadership of a seasoned minister who has been studying and devoting themselves to the work of the Kingdom for many, many years. As of the writing of this book, I've been in the ministry for over 20 years, and I am still learning and figuring things out. There are passages of Scripture I must read, and re-read, and then go study the Hebrew and Greek to understand. I read the Scriptures daily and still get something new out of them, time and time again. It's perfectly normal and all right to admit that parts of the Scriptures aren't as clear as others, and it's even all right to think that parts of the Bible don't always make sense. One of the areas where many of us trip up is when it comes to our "citizenship." The Bible says we are citizens of heaven, but it also tells us to abide by and follow the laws where we live. It tells us to follow the laws and the rules but also encourages us to abide by God's laws. Where is the line, and what does this all mean?

The truth is that if we look over history, there is no one thing that being a "citizen of heaven" has clearly meant. There have been all sorts of historical attempts to try and mix the Kingdom of God with secular kingdoms, often with disastrous results. How we can best live our faith in societies that are often in conflict with what we believe to be spiritual beings is not always clearly understood. When people have studied the Bible, there have often been peasant revolts, advocacy of justice, civil rights, and governmental overthrows. This hardly sounds like a group of people who are submitting themselves to higher authorities and watching the world change in the process.

On their arrival in Capernaum, the collectors of the Temple tax came to Peter and asked him, "Doesn't your Teacher pay the Temple tax?"

"Yes, He does," Peter replied. Then he went into the house.

But before he had a chance to speak, Jesus asked him, "What do you think, Peter? Do kings tax their own people or the people they have conquered?"

"They tax the people they have conquered," Peter replied.

"Well, then," Jesus said, "the citizens are free! However, we don't want to offend them, so go down to the lake and throw in a line. Open the mouth of the first fish you catch, and you will find a large silver coin. Take it and pay the tax for both of us." (Matthew 17:24-27)

Later the leaders sent some Pharisees and supporters of Herod to trap Jesus into saying something for which He could be arrested. "Teacher," they said, "we know how honest You are. You are impartial and don't play favorites. You teach the way of God truthfully. Now tell us—is it right to pay taxes to Caesar or not? Should we pay them, or shouldn't we?"

Jesus saw through their hypocrisy and said, "Why are you trying to trap Me? Show me a Roman coin, and I'll tell you." When they handed it to Him, He asked, "Whose picture and title are stamped on it?"

"Caesar's," they replied.

"Well, then," Jesus said, "give to Caesar what belongs to Caesar, and give to God what belongs to God."

His reply completely amazed them. (Mark 12:13-17)

But Paul replied, "They have publicly beaten us without a trial and put us in prison—and we are Roman citizens. So now they want us to leave secretly? Certainly not! Let them come themselves to release us!" (Acts 16:37)

So the commander went over and asked Paul, "Tell me, are you a Roman citizen?" "Yes, I certainly am," Paul replied.

"I am, too," the commander muttered, "and it cost me plenty!" Paul answered, "But I am a citizen by birth!" (Acts 22:27-28)

So now you Gentiles are no longer strangers and foreigners. You are citizens along with all of God's holy people. You are members of God's family. (Ephesians 2:19)

Above all, you must live as citizens of heaven, conducting yourselves in a manner worthy of the Good News about Christ. Then, whether I come and see you again or only hear about you, I will know that you are standing together with one spirit and one purpose, fighting together for the faith, which is the Good News. (Philippians 1:27)

But we are citizens of heaven, where the Lord Jesus Christ lives. And we are eagerly waiting for him to return as our Savior. (Philippians 3:20)

If there's one thing the New Testament tells us, it's that Christians are in process. We don't have all the answers, and we deal with societal questions and conflicts as we go along. It might seem like those who follow politics, advocating one way or another, have what is "Biblical" all figured out, but really, it's not that simple. Our faith is a process and discovering just how we can best walk out this walk is something we discover in large part as we go along.

Being a "citizen of heaven" means that even though we live down here, we recognize we are a part of the Kingdom of God. That Kingdom is our primary source for order and authority, and what we are supposed to do is to fall within that spiritual guidance. Our earthly citizenship takes second place. Now this doesn't mean we are supposed to take on the entire secular government and try and turn it into something else. No, what we are called to do is, above and beyond, live our faith.

This sounds easy, right? "Oh, just live your faith!" Spoken like living one's faith is nothing, whatsoever. You can go to churches or online and do a search on the topic of living one's faith, and you will find a myriad of different statements, lists of conduct, and things you should do exteriorly to appear to be a Christian. Most of these lists probably don't agree with one another. They might adhere to some very old codes and while parts of them might be similar, most of the bottom-line of matters are very different. Even Christians don't always agree on how to best live their faith, and there is a very good reason for this. Outside of general guidelines on how to live and how to express what we believe, how we live our faith varies based on what we are called to do and how we do it.

For example: Many years ago, I had a friend in Pakistan who would pray five hours every single day. He told me if I wanted to see any spiritual results in my life, I had to do the same thing. I wanted to see changes at that time in my life, so I tried to pray that many hours of the day. It didn't take long before even praying a third or half that amount of time became completely impossible. It interfered with something else I knew God had anointed me to do – write books and curriculum. It also impeded my ability to counsel others and spend time in pastoral care ministry, which was the majority of what I did in those days.

I don't believe my friend had a bad motive for telling me to pray so many hours of the day. He was passing on to me what he felt brought power to his own ministry and spiritual walk. The problem is that his call to pray for so many hours a day was a personal call of faith for him, unique to what he did and how he was to do it. It didn't make the leap to my own life and call. Prayer is, no doubt important, but so are the other things I did in my ministry. They weren't more or less important, but they were equal enough to say that I needed to spend my time on my assignment rather than trying to fit into someone else's version of what my work should look, feel, or sound like.

I give this example to make the point that while he and I might have shared in the essentials of our faith and even agreed on other points of doctrine (we were from the same denomination), the way we walked out our faith day in and day out was different. Neither of us was in a state of spiritual misunderstanding or lack; we were both ministers of the Gospel! Our callings, however, and our positioning in church administration were quite different, which meant my day had to allow for different tasks and duties than his, and vice versa. We were living our faith; we were obedient to God, and we had great spiritual understanding – but we were both still different.

And, simply put, there was nothing wrong with being different.

There are variations on the specifics of how we might walk as believers while we adhere to and maintain the purpose of faith and practice that our ancestors also believed down through the ages. We believe God is one, we believe in the supremacy of our Lord Jesus Christ, we believe in the work of the Holy Spirit, and we understand that living according to those things means we do certain things, and we do not do others. Beyond this, we are all unique, with our own purpose and calling in this world. Walking with God and standing in Christ means we figure out just how we are supposed to do that. Once we've gotten past the "dos and don'ts" (which we will talk more about later), it is a matter of discerning the voice of God in one's life and learning to follow the leading of the Spirit to the place that is revealing and purposeful for you in Christ.

Perhaps the major thing being a citizen of heaven means is that when you are walking in your faith right, you probably won't fit in very well where you used to fit perfectly. Sometimes you may feel like you don't fit well anywhere. (This is different from being difficult or contrary, or just behaving in a manner that makes it difficult for others to be around you.) Being a part of God's Kingdom means a time will come in your life where your purpose, identity, and viewpoints of matters will not align with many of those you might have known at one time or those who might be around you. Being a Christian – doing this Kingdom thing right – means a huge and incredible change, a transforming of your mind that happens as God works within you. It's awe-inspiring, incredible, and a little intimidating at times. This is why it is so important we have support and fellowship on our journey. We need to find that place of connection with other people who are processing or have processed through a similar journey to find encouragement as we go along. For this reason, we find our spiritual settle in church, which literally means "called out ones." God has called out those who have heard His cry to us for repentance and change from their former ways, to now assemble together as they work to participate in this great and wonderful Kingdom God has created.

No, the people we encounter as citizens of heaven aren't perfect. You may even meet a few people along the way who claim to be a part of God's Kingdom, but they are not. Never let the imperfections of other people take you away from the Kingdom you know is true. Your citizenship is in heaven, and that challenges the things of this world. It is a counter, and a threat, to the authority that is here. Sometimes being a citizen of heaven will be hard but remember: you have this Kingdom inside of you, and that means you have something better than the world can offer. Never be ashamed of it and never fear embracing it to the fullest. God has something wonderful in store for you, so celebrate your citizenship! You are a citizen of heaven!

The promise of Kingdom connection

Earlier in this chapter we discussed the literal dynamics of Kingdom and the way that Kingdoms function on earth. There is one major principle that worldly kingdoms lack, and that is direct connection to a king or monarch. In earthly kingdoms, seldom if ever do citizens or subjects get a direct experience or audience with their leader. Seeing a monarch, having a monarch wave in one's direction or shake one's hand is still a huge deal, because it isn't an everyday occurrence. There's a reason citizens of a kingdom are often called subjects, and that is because they subject themselves to the king. Their status as subjects indicates subordination to the governance and will of that leader, and most of the time, the king or monarch of a kingdom has never met the majority (if any) of his subjects. The subjects of a nation are not entitled to spend time with their leader, nor do they expect to receive personal attention from that leader. They aimlessly follow their leader's guidelines out of required obedience to do so.

As Christians, we don't have to blindly follow God in the way that people followed monarchs of this earth. Sometimes people talk about "blind faith," but that's not really a Biblical concept or what God requires us to have. God calls us to know Him in relationship: knowing our King, His will, and following Him out of loving obedience. We follow God and embrace God because we love Him and recognize all He has done for us. Being a believer is a choice we make, because God desires we come to Him out of choice and will rather than force. As we come to know God, we have a better sense of His will for our lives and the way the Spirit of God directs us in our daily living.

Being a part of God's Kingdom is not always a "trip to the altar," as I say. There are going to be times when you feel God's presence so profoundly, it has a powerful impact on you in that moment. You will speak in other tongues or fall on the floor with a "Holy Ghost zap" or experience gifts of healing, miracles, teaching, or utterance. There are incredible things that will happen as you follow God and work with Him in your spiritual life. This doesn't happen all day, every day, however. There are plenty of times when you are going to have to do daily, ordinary things: take out the garbage, maintain your physical health and well-being, go to work, sit in a traffic jam, stand in line at the post office or grocery store, deal with difficult family members or neighbors, or have a day where you just don't feel right and everything makes you upset. Even though it might not feel like it, you are just as much a part of God's Kingdom on these other days as you are when you feel God move in or through you mightily.

Connecting to God in a profound way is not just about the signs and wonders you experience in your walk with God. It's not that signs and wonders are a bad thing; it is that they are not the only thing. There are going to be plenty of times where you must rest on your faith to recognize that God is with you just as much at that moment as He is when you see powerful and mighty spiritual outpourings. Learning to recognize God's quiet voice as much as His powerful showdowns is a part of spiritual maturity, and it is essential to success in the Christian life. We cannot ever find ourselves in a deep relationship with God – one that changes us from the inside out, and everything in between – if we are not willing to take the quiet time to know God for ourselves.

Be still, and know that I am God! I will be honored by every nation.
I will be honored throughout the world. (Psalm 46:10)

But how do we connect to God outside of our incredible spiritual outpourings? We learn to discover God in spiritual experiences beyond these encounters. We are still and we let go of every distraction and thing in this life that hinders our relationship with God and get to know this Being that loves and cares for us beyond anything we can ever imagine.

There are those who treat their relationship with God as if it is a burden. The cares of life overtake them, and they miss their key time with God, something they should take every day. Sometimes they fail to have regular prayer, only praying when things are difficult or in crisis. While understandable on a human level, it is not understandable on a spiritual level. In practical terminology, we make time for the things that are important to us. If knowing God is important to us, we will make the time to be still and know Him. We won't skip out on it or treat it as if it's the last thing in the world we want to do.

How do we make that time? There are many different ways people work to maintain their spiritual devotional time with God. There isn't one method that is superior to others; it is a matter of trying different things to come to a better understanding of your calling. A combination of these things is best for figuring your way:

- **Scriptural study:** We will talk about the importance of Bible study in a later section. There, we will examine the specifics on how to study the Bible, so it makes better sense in one's life and is applicable to whatever you are going through. Studying the Scriptures is a must for every believer, but the way you might study may vary based on your own walk and experience with God. It might take some time to figure out what way is best for you.

- **Devotional focus:** Many people enjoy daily devotional readings because they explain or provide example for Scriptural application or divine experience in a short form. It can be a great way to start or end your day. Others practice devotional periods through meditating (focusing on one thing over and over) on the Scriptures or thinking about nothing but God for a while with quiet music playing. Devotional focus is an act of worship, something that recenters us from the distractions in our lives so we can fully maintain God as our primary focus throughout our lives. It's not so much the activity we choose as to why we do it, thus leaving room for variation in one's life.

- **Prayer:** You can pray at any time of day, but many believers find it most profitable to set aside time for prayer during their devotional times. You don't need to adopt a specific posture, but you just need to talk to God. Share your thoughts, feelings, and petitions with Him. Pray prayers of praise and thanks and delve into deepest periods of worship. Petitions for your family, your leader, the ministry you are part of, your relationship with God, world events, and anything else that comes together in your periods of prayer.

- **Ordinary tasks:** One of the biggest challenges believers face today is ordinary life. Our world surrounds us with people who seem to, through reality TV shows and internet fame, exist in an extraordinary realm where one makes millions just for…existing. They have servants, housekeeping, and staff. The more outrageous they behave, the more money and fame they seem to generate. Ordinary tasks seem beneath such people. They don't handle their own chores and have so many assistants, they do not have to take the time to remember anything. There is a certain level of discipline and freedom that we find in doing ordinary tasks and work. It humbles us and brings us to a place where we are in touch with the consequences of sin that relate to hard work. At the same time, we find satisfaction in working hard and completing tasks. Through this process, we cry out to God and find meaningful connection between the labor of human existence and our need to connect with the divine.

- **Interacting with others:** No person is an island, even when we are Christian and don't fit in the world like we might think we should. Doing good for others, talking to others, being there for someone else, and caring about others all helps us to find God in our human existence. Through such connection, we find a point of love that we can't discover if we are consistently on our own.

CHANGING FROM GLORY TO GLORY

Change. Now there's a scary word, isn't it? It's one of those words we throw around and we say we want, right up and until God drops change right on our front step. That's because we want our circumstances to change for us in a form that will make life easier, but we don't want to have to change us. It's easy to sit back and think it's everyone else who is the problem, and if they just go away or become different, our lives would be easier. It's a lot harder to confront the real problem: our greatest problem in this life is each one of us, individually, ourselves. We might overshadow that battle and try to cast shade here or there, but in the end, the only one we can control is ourselves and the only one we can change is ourselves. Who we choose to be in a relationship with, engage with, and entertain are choices we make, and that means we reach a point where we either accept people as they are, or we don't. We can't keep making the excuse that someone doesn't treat us right or do the right things, and that's ruining who we are. We either need to confront why we have them around and deal with it, or we need to accept things the way they are.

But whenever someone turns to the Lord, the veil is taken away. For the Lord is the Spirit, and wherever the Spirit of the Lord is, there is freedom. So all of us who have had that veil removed can see and reflect the glory of the Lord. And the Lord—Who is the Spirit—makes us more and more like him as we are changed into His glorious image. (2 Corinthians 3:16-18)

It might seem like this is an odd topic of conversation for Kingdom living, but the reality is that living in God means we change. Our entire walk with God is about change; changing from a worldly way of being to a godly way of being and learning all about our call and specifics of that walk as we go along. We often pray prayers and "believe God" to change everything around us, but what God really wants to change is us, ourselves. When this process starts, count on being uncomfortable for a while!

We are uncomfortable in change because it reminds us of our base experiences of conviction to turn around and change directions. "Conviction" is a word that many Christian preachers throw around without ever defining it. When someone feels conviction, it means they know they are doing something that needs to be changed. When we feel conviction, it doesn't always mean we know just how to change it, but it does mean we know a change is necessary. When we discuss conviction is it often in the context of sin, because the Holy Spirit moves within us when we know we are doing something that goes against God. Conviction is not just about sin, however. We can experience the call to conviction about any change that's needed or whenever we feel the need to take a stand because something isn't right. Conviction motivates us to do something different; to stand up and say, it's time to do something different. This ushers in an entire wave of change in one's life.

In those days there appeared John the Baptist, preaching in the Wilderness (Desert) of Judea

And saying, Repent (think differently; change your mind, regretting your sins and changing your conduct), for the kingdom of heaven is at hand.

This is he who was mentioned by the prophet Isaiah when he said, The voice of one crying in the wilderness (shouting in the desert), Prepare the road for the Lord, make His highways straight (level, direct). (Matthew 3:1-3, AMPC)

Then John went from place to place on both sides of the Jordan River, preaching that people should be baptized to show that they had repented of their sins and turned to God to be forgiven. Isaiah had spoken of John when he said,

"He is a voice shouting in the wilderness,
'Prepare the way for the Lord's coming!
   Clear the road for Him!
The valleys will be filled,
   and the mountains and hills made level.
The curves will be straightened,
   and the rough places made smooth.

*And then all people will see
   the salvation sent from God.'"* (Luke 3:3-6)

Most of us have heard about the work of John the Baptist at some point in time. John was a spiritual walk on the wild side, with a message of change and challenge to those who would hear and receive what he had to say. In those days, John's purpose was to prepare the people for the spiritual reception of Christ into this world and into their lives. He was coming, and John knew Who He was as well as the advance of His powerful presence. The people, who were comfortably looking for a totally different type of savior, needed to be prepared! They needed to get ready! They needed to repent!

Wait, what?

The word "repent" literally means to change direction. It is about a change in thought, a change in action, and ultimately, a change in life. The people of Israel wanted a change, but they didn't want to change. It was fine to focus on the realities of the Roman government and everything that was done to Israel, but the people of Israel didn't want to deal with the things they were doing wrong. Even in the best of situations where the sins were minor, there were still changes, convictions, directions, and actions that needed to be different than they were. They needed to turn, to start again, to be different, to do different, to become something other than where they started.

This is what repentance is; it is change. It is change for the better, a change in a greater way toward God and away from the things that keep us from Him. Yes, we understand the concept of repentance from sin and turning away from those things that displease God, but there is also the reality that many times in our lives, our turning away from one thing to something else isn't always about sin. Sometimes we need a change of direction to avoid sin in the future or just to find a better way in our lives. Throughout our Christian lives, we will experience the call to change, and change, and change again. Whenever we feel that conviction and hear that call, it is time to change!

The Kingdom of God represents a powerful change in this world to a place where order sets aright and God stands mighty over all things. Our changes, our little transformations, are smaller types of that larger victory to come. Every one of us talks about changing the world, but none of us like the idea of having to change ourselves. That's where this all starts, however; it starts with you. The Kingdom of God works and changes and transforms within first. If you want to be different, if you want to make a difference, if you want things to be different, you must first start by allowing God to usher in that powerful transformation within you – that turns your thoughts, heart, and mind toward the wonderful things that God has for you.

- CHAPTER TWO -
THE KINGDOM OF GOD IS AROUND YOU!

THE concept of the Kingdom of God within us is amazing enough to fathom, all on its own. The idea that God comes to dwell with us through the Holy Spirit is incredible and unfathomable. It becomes even more incredible when we realize the Kingdom of God is not just within, but also around and among us. The Kingdom of God is such an incredible thing, it can't just stay to itself. It is something that we want to experience and share with others. Our total joy of Kingdom living is something we desire and hope to see all throughout the world!

As we develop a greater sense of the Kingdom of God within, we start to venture and see more of it outside of us, too. It starts to become about more than just "us and God." This calls us to start examining the dynamics of the Kingdom of God to see just how we fit within it and how we can best experience it. In this chapter, we are going to examine these different dynamics that help us live and interact properly within God's Kingdom. Here we will focus on our dynamics of identity: the things that make us unique, set us apart, and open the door to interact with others who are both in the Kingdom and those who do not realize yet the fullness of what they have as part of its awesome benefit.

A Chosen People, A Royal Priesthood

All throughout the Bible we see a specific pattern that we mentioned in brief in the last chapter: God called people living their lives, they answered (or sometimes did not answer that call), and He created a new nation from those individuals, unique for His own. The people who answered God's call became a special people who were set apart to stand as God's own, His representatives in this world. This was a special position and a special honor before God. It wasn't something designed to be burdensome or unfair, but something that honored God's special people with that special relationship.

Human nature has a way of being…well…all-too-human at times. Over time, this project, started with enthusiasm, waned into a state of complaints and whining. The Kingdom of Israel found themselves disgruntled when they didn't get to have the things that everyone else got to have. When other nations got to indulge in crazy, wild religious ceremonies, the Israelites desired to follow suit. When it was expected the Israelites obeyed God's commandments and behaved honorably with each other, they often failed. They would steal and cheat from each other and fall into the practices of their neighbors. The Israelites wanted the benefits of being a part of God's Kingdom, but they didn't want to do what it took to maintain their status as such.

It's easy for us to sit back and judge Israel for their failings. We sit back and say, "How could Israel act like that?" "They had such a special connection to God!" "Why would they want the things of everyone around them when they had God?"

Then we go out and do the same things. Yes, we want to be saved, but the world and its enticements call to us…and we often answer. That money calls, that alcohol calls, those drugs call, our ex-boyfriend, girlfriend, or partner calls, that opportunity to be mean presents itself in full array and splendor, overeating calls, those old feelings call, those old behaviors and ways call, and the temptation to do and be something that one is no longer supposed to be calls, loudly…and we answer. Time and time again, I meet people who sing the loudest at church on Sunday and are the first ones to criticize everyone else who are also the first ones to jump into their old lives and old ways the second they come calling.

This is the parallel between us today and the people of Israel, back then. Israel wanted God, but it wanted everything else, too. It wanted the benefits of being in God but still wanted to fit in and be the same as all their neighbors. When we want everything, we wind up with nothing. That is why as Kingdom people we must identify who we are and embrace that.

Throughout much of Christian history, it's been hard to tell the world from the church. The church's history is one of overlaps in power, gaps between the rich and the very poor, cultural influences, and behaviors that weren't always the best of alignment with Christian belief. This is in part because a lack of education and teaching made sure Christians didn't have proper knowledge of their beliefs and unique identity in God's Kingdom.

Down the line to modern times, we now see an intense battle between those who feel the secular world should conform to Christian belief, coupled with a pervasive attitude that for believers to maintain their faith, our governments must be Christian. This is in total opposition to the call that believers have had throughout history. From the very beginning, God's people have been called to be different, stand different, work different, and exemplify God's precepts in atmospheres and areas that are completely hostile to their existence.

No matter what someone's secularized concept of being a Christian may be or how someone feels about being a Christian in any special or national situation, being a Christian is something that should define us in our identities. We need to know who we are to know what we are supposed to do and who we are ultimately supposed to be. Whether we live in a nation that is hostile to our faith or not, we should always be distinguishable as a people. People should notice there is something different about us and even though they might not always know what it is, there should be something that separates us from everyone around us. Even though we are a part of society, we are a part of the world in which we live, and we function in many of the same ways as others do, we have been set apart to make a difference in this world.

1 Peter 2:4-12 gives us some great insight into just what it means to be a Kingdom people living in the world today, and of our position therein:

You are coming to Christ, Who is the living cornerstone of God's temple. He was rejected by people, but He was chosen by God for great honor.

And you are living stones that God is building into His spiritual temple. What's more, you are His holy priests. Through the mediation of Jesus Christ, you offer spiritual sacrifices that please God. As the Scriptures say,

"I am placing a cornerstone in Jerusalem,
  chosen for great honor,

*and anyone who trusts in Him
   will never be disgraced."*

Yes, you who trust Him recognize the honor God has given Him. But for those who reject Him,

*"The stone that the builders rejected
   has now become the cornerstone."*

And,

*"He is the stone that makes people stumble,
   the rock that makes them fall."*

They stumble because they do not obey God's word, and so they meet the fate that was planned for them.

But you are not like that, for you are a chosen people. You are royal priests, a holy nation, God's very own possession. As a result, you can show others the goodness of God, for He called you out of the darkness into His wonderful light.

*"Once you had no identity as a people;
   now you are God's people.
Once you received no mercy;
   now you have received God's mercy."*

Dear friends, I warn you as "temporary residents and foreigners" to keep away from worldly desires that wage war against your very souls. Be careful to live properly among your unbelieving neighbors. Then even if they accuse you of doing wrong, they will see your honorable behavior, and they will give honor to God when He judges the world.

As Christians, it is imperative we understand our spiritual identity. Whenever we go chasing our identity in things that define us in this world, we find ourselves led astray. This is true even when we let the world tell us what it means to be a Christian or how we should be one. There were many believers throughout history and even now who, although very sincere, never knew or know who they are, because the wrong things have defined them. What is the answer to such? Well, we find it in the passage above. In it, we see many insights about our spiritual identity. If we don't understand who we are, we won't understand how to live and what it means to be a Christian beyond just a statement of thought. We must embrace who we are and what God has for us to be, and here, we learn just what that is.

- **We come to Christ:** In coming to Christ, this means we recognize Who He is and the fullness of what He can do for us. Christ can do for us what no one can do for themselves. He has saved us, and He stands as a living cornerstone – a foundational block, the sturdiest and largest stone – in the edifice of the church. Even though we see He was rejected, we know He has this prime honor in our faith, now.

- **We are living stones, built into His spiritual temple:** The church of God is not about a specific physical building, but a spiritual edifice. All of us – every single one of us who are believers – make up that physical building. We bring the gifts and abilities God has given to us to complete this incredible spiritual creation, known as the church. We are not dead, but we are living; lively and connected to new life.

- **We are chosen people:** In our modern society, we place a lot of emphasis on being the person who is "chosen" to do something. It signifies a favoritism or a specialness, something that is perceived to make us better than someone else. This isn't exactly what it means in Biblical understanding. Being a "chosen people" doesn't mean that Christians are better than anyone else, or that they are superior in some sense. What it means is that God has called us to follow Him, to live by His precepts, and we have answered. We are, therefore, special to God, and are called to live by His example to this world.

- **We are His royal priesthood:** In Old Testament times, it was the priests who worked as leaders in the temple. The priests were set apart for the responsibility of temple work. They offered regular sacrifices on behalf of the people for the redemption of sins. So, what does it mean to say that we are all priests now? Does it mean we are all leaders? It doesn't mean we are all called to be leaders, but it does mean that we have the responsibility of standing set apart and holy as representatives of the sacrifice made for us through Christ. To be a Christian, we make the sacrifice of ourselves: of our flesh, the things we might want or the impulses we have, to pursue and show a better way. We are to be distinct and different as an entire "nation," or Kingdom group, showing the way for the redemption of sins through Christ to the rest of the world.

- **A holy nation:** In Old Testament times, God literally had a "nation" with political borders and boundaries. His Kingdom was a literal "kingdom" in the sense of the term we are most familiar. Over time, however, Israel made it clear they were missing the point of being God's nation, and when the fullness of the time had come, God sent Christ to make a better way for us to fully belong to God, without any questions asked. We are now God's holy "nation," even though God's nation transcends borders and political limits. We are a part of God's governance and have accepted God's rule and way in our lives. No matter what happens down here on earth, we answer to and accept a higher rule, and a higher authority.

- **God's very own possession:** We belong to God, valued and precious to Him. We are His own, which makes us unique from others. By being His own, we reflect His nature. Others can see we have a special relationship with God, and that will make some of them desire to have it, too.

These essential aspects of our faith make up our Kingdom identity. This is who we are, and what it looks like, feels like, and is like to be a part of God's Kingdom. We have privileges, duties, responsibilities, obligations, and benefits. It is a whole package, just like living with and experiencing the benefits of any Kingdom entity. When we walk in this identity, it helps us have a better spiritual experience, a deeper relationship with God, a more motivated perspective to participate in spiritual things, and a better sense of ourselves. When we know who we are in Christ, it makes living for Him much easier and much more exciting. We can rise to the challenge, because we know who we are!

Kingdom Law

People have questioned the reason why horrible events, such as war, rape, incest, adultery, power and control struggles, and other issues are found in the Old Testament of the Bible. They can't figure out why God would relate such awful stories as part of the record for His people. There was a law (that we read today) that seems relatively easy to absorb and understand and would be the "mark" of His people's identity. So why did God publish the failures of His people more often than their successes? Why is the Old Testament full of the wickedness of humanity, the things they did incorrectly, and the places where they just did not measure up to God's standards?

There are two reasons why these failures are included along with the successes of the people in the Old Testament (and why there are far more failures than successes). The first reason is because failure is a part of life, and not everyone gets things right all the time. It's safe to say that if we look back on our lives, we have probably failed far more times than we have succeeded, especially when it comes to our spiritual lives. We mean to do better; we intend to try harder; we will walk away from everything bad or negative tomorrow…but despite our best efforts, we don't do it. Seeing that others have also failed is a reality, not to be ignored or glossed over. To doctor Biblical history to make it only mention good things, rather than everything, would be dishonest. History is supposed to include the good and the bad, and we are supposed to be learning from both. The second reason is to prove that no matter how much the Israelites thought their problem was everyone else: their neighbors, surrounding idolaters, nations occupying or attacking them, and influencing them – their neighbors were not their problem. Israel was its own problem, with each Israelite dealing with the various temptations, lusts, desires, selfishness, and personal interests. The problems Israel faced were within them, and it was God's desire that, through the written law, they would realize this about themselves.

That is the ultimate purpose in the law of the Old Testament, also called the written law. It serves to make us aware of what was deemed right and wrong and is to bring us to a place where we realize we can't do it all ourselves. The more Israel tried to follow the law, the more they failed. The same is true for us. The more we try to adhere to different rules and laws and try to add on to the more complicated points of the law with our own ideas, the more we set ourselves up to fail. This is why the law can bring about a revelation, but in and of itself, it has no power to save anyone. We can see this point in Romans 7:7-25:

Well then, am I suggesting that the law of God is sinful? Of course not! In fact, it was the law that showed me my sin. I would never have known that coveting is wrong if the law had not said, "You must not covet." But sin used this command to arouse all kinds of covetous desires within me! If there were no law, sin would not have that power. At one time I lived without understanding the law. But when I learned the command not to covet, for instance, the power of sin came to life, and I died. So I discovered that the law's commands, which were supposed to bring life, brought spiritual death instead. Sin took advantage of those commands and deceived me; it used the commands to kill me. But still, the law itself is holy, and its commands are holy and right and good.

But how can that be? Did the law, which is good, cause my death? Of course not! Sin used what was good to bring about my condemnation to death. So we can see how terrible sin really is. It uses God's good commands for its own evil purposes.

So the trouble is not with the law, for it is spiritual and good. The trouble is with me, for I am all too human, a slave to sin. I don't really understand myself, for I want to do what is right, but I don't do it. Instead, I do what I hate. But if I know that what I am doing is wrong, this shows that I agree that the law is good. So I am not the one doing wrong; it is sin living in me that does it.

And I know that nothing good lives in me, that is, in my sinful nature. I want to do what is right, but I can't. I want to do what is good, but I don't. I don't want to do what is wrong, but I do it anyway. But if I do what I don't want to do, I am not really the one doing wrong; it is sin living in me that does it.

I have discovered this principle of life—that when I want to do what is right, I inevitably do what is wrong. I love God's law with all my heart. But there is another power within me that is at war with my mind. This power makes me a slave to the sin that is still within me. Oh, what a miserable person I am! Who will free me from this life that is dominated by sin and death? Thank God! The answer is in Jesus Christ our Lord. So you see how it is: In my mind I really want to obey God's law, but because of my sinful nature I am a slave to sin.

This passage of Scripture might seem complicated, but it's not as involved as it seems. The Apostle Paul is pointing out two important things for us. The first is that there is nothing wrong with the law, in and of itself. The law is a spiritual thing, and it brings about its purpose, time and time again. The law served its purpose: to make people aware of their own sins and failings. The problem with the law is when it is used as a means to save someone, or when we rest on the law and adherence to it for our own self-righteousness. No matter what those who try to reimpose the law might say, the reason they seek to do it is to make themselves feel better about their own faith. They aren't relying on the work of Christ for their salvation, but trying to give themselves a boost up, a sense of self-importance, something to point to that makes them seem better than someone else.

This was the opposite of what the law was about, which brings us to the second point the Apostle Paul sought to make. The purpose of the law was to make us realize we needed the ability to live. Trying to follow the law could never lead us to life, but it can stand as a signal to us that we need to change. The law was never meant to be kept, but it did serve a purpose – to convict of sin. Its purpose was to stand as a reflection of our human limitations, not to make us self-righteous when we got some part of it right. It made us aware there was more out there, we need more, we are to find more. No matter how hard we try, no matter how we perceive ourselves, and no matter what we hope to find within the good of humanity, we won't find it. We need to look to God and to the promise of His Savior to save us and maintain our faith therein. The result will be the change that He seeks to make in us.

The law of the Old Testament stands in history as the literal "Kingdom law" of God's nation. If we are now God's holy people, priesthood, and chosen nation, where does that leave us? If the law was never meant to be kept, how do we govern ourselves rightly? How do we structure ourselves for success and operation?

WRITTEN ON OUR HEARTS

The word "covenant" is an old word for an agreement between parties. In covenant, both parties agree to abide by certain terms and arrangements to make their partnership work. In the context of salvation history, scholars estimate there are anywhere from one to 12 different covenants present in the Bible between God and different individuals or God and His people. There are two major covenants we often speak of: the old covenant and the new covenant. The old covenant is what is better known as the "Mosaic Law" or the Old Testament law. It is what we always speak of when we talk about "the law" and the written code that made people aware of sin. It can feel like understanding that law is almost impossible and burdensome, and like we are always failing God if it's all we see through to recognize. If we don't understand the proper light of the law through the new covenant, it can make us totally misunderstand Who God is and what He offers us in eternal life.

The answer to avoid this is to recognize just what the Apostle Paul said in the passage we previously studied: the law was never meant to be kept, but to make us aware of sin. This law, however, is not the end of the story – not by a long shot! Even in the days of the Old Testament, God promised a time would come when He would do a "new" thing. It probably sounded weird at the time, but now that we have come into a place where we can experience it, it makes more sense. God promised He would give us a better covenant, something that would replace the old one. This became the new covenant, the one by which we operate, today. Instead of coming to death through the law, we are able to come to life through the Spirit.

But now Jesus, our High Priest, has been given a ministry that is far superior to the old priesthood, for He is the One Who mediates for us a far better covenant with God, based on better promises.

If the first covenant had been faultless, there would have been no need for a second covenant to replace it. But when God found fault with the people, He said:

"The day is coming, says the LORD,
 when I will make a new covenant
 with the people of Israel and Judah.
This covenant will not be like the one
 I made with their ancestors
when I took them by the hand
 and led them out of the land of Egypt.
They did not remain faithful to My covenant,
 so I turned my back on them, says the LORD.
But this is the new covenant I will make
 with the people of Israel on that day, says the LORD:
I will put my laws in their minds,
 and I will write them on their hearts.
I will be their God,
 and they will be My people.
And they will not need to teach their neighbors,
 nor will they need to teach their relatives,
 saying, 'You should know the LORD.'
For everyone, from the least to the greatest,
 will know Me already.
And I will forgive their wickedness,
 and I will never again remember their sins."

When God speaks of a "new" covenant, it means He has made the first one obsolete. It is now out of date and will soon disappear. (Hebrews 8:6-13)

It is not that the old law was bad or that the old law's purpose is totally nonexistent (as the passage says it will soon disappear). We can still draw on the teachings of the old covenant to help teach us about sin and show why we need the work of a Savior in our lives. The promise we have here, however, is that God has done something new to instill life and hope in His people. Instead of feeling the weight and heaviness of the law, we are no longer under a covenant that is all about imposing death for sin. We now have something new, where God brings His precepts to His people, and we know what is right because the Spirit leads us to such knowledge. Instead of having to memorize a bunch of laws we can't keep anyway, we live under a covenant that leads us into all truth, into what is right because of the work of the Spirit. It may not be what we deserve to have (as we are still sinners), but it is something God gives to us, because it makes the way for us to share in eternal life with Him.

This concept is what we call "grace." It's not something easy for us to define, because grace is about the recipient as much as about the One Who gives it. God's grace is sometimes described as "unmerited favor," but grace is more than just getting something we don't deserve. Grace is a gift, something that gives us the ability to live in spiritual victory and see the workings of God in our lives, even when we miss the mark or don't seem to have things all together. God allows His grace to work in and through us as part of this new covenant, which gives us the ability to walk in our faith and follow Him for as long as it takes us to get it right (and in our case, that will be as long as we live on this earth or until Jesus comes back). This new covenant marks a different way of interacting and understanding God, and of having that special relationship with God, because Christ's death on the cross made the way for us to have it. This is a better way and a better day for us, and it is all thanks to God's love and work in our salvation.

For the sin of this one man, Adam, caused death to rule over many. But even greater is God's wonderful grace and His gift of righteousness, for all who receive it will live in triumph over sin and death through this One Man, Jesus Christ. (Romans 5:17)

Well then, should we keep on sinning so that God can show us more and more of His wonderful grace? Of course not! Since we have died to sin, how can we continue to live in it? Or have you forgotten that when we were joined with Christ Jesus in baptism, we joined Him in his death? For we died and were buried with Christ by baptism. And just as Christ was raised from the dead by the glorious power of the Father, now we also may live new lives. (Romans 6:1-4)

God saved you by His grace when you believed. And you can't take credit for this; it is a gift from God. Salvation is not a reward for the good things we have done, so none of us can boast about it. (Ephesians 2:8-9)

Grace doesn't mean we deliberately seek out to sin or to do wrong, but that our faith in Jesus Christ is what leads us to God's grace that saves us. The more we walk in our faith, the more we experience God's grace in our lives. We see it come to life, to animate our experience with Him and to bring God into our focus. We can see Him move on our behalf, work out things for our benefit, and encourage us in our darkest times. The grace of God brings us to a profound place in this new agreement that He has with humanity. If we are willing to have faith in Him, He will give us every opportunity to walk with Him through this life.

What about rules and regulations? Surely if we are still in a Kingdom, there must be some sort of way that we can control human behavior. What happens if someone isn't living like a Christian, does grace still cover them? Under this new covenant, there are still regulations; there are just not that many. Now we shall look at what Kingdom people do and how Kingdom people live in two commandments.

THE GREATEST COMMANDMENT

A commandment is a divine rule or required guideline, which means it's a rule with some weight added to it. It's different from the guidelines and regulations organizations set up in order to keep running properly and functioning well. In Old Testament times, the people believed the commandments of God all had equal weight, as they all came from God Himself. It's a misnomer to say the "Ten Commandments" people often talk about were more important than the others, because all 613 (I know, right? Wow!) were to be observed if one was to follow the law in full. We know it wasn't possible for anyone to do this, so what gives?

The commandments of old express a few important things for us about God and about being the people of God. The first thing they show us is that God cares about every aspect of our lives. Sometimes we are tempted to think God cares only about the things we do in public or the things that everyone else knows about. God knows all about us, and He cares about every aspect of our lives, even the ones we like to cleverly hide from other people. God cares about whether we have a right relationship with Him, whether we take proper care of ourselves, how we run our business, how we treat others, and how we are with those closest and most intimate with us. The second thing they show us is that God does care how we interact with other people. It's not as simple as saying we can treat people however we want and we will get the same results with God. We can't be mean and nasty and act however we please, anywhere we go. We must reflect a spiritual transformation, something that turns us away from behaving any which way and sets a different course, a different example for life.

The most important thing the commandments of old taught us was that God needs to be first in our lives in every sense. We can talk about grace, about our identity, about what Jesus did for us, and all the wonderful things God can do for those who are His own all day long, but if we don't talk about the positioning of God in our lives, we are going to miss the entirety of the point. If God is not guiding us in every area we choose to walk, we don't have a relationship with Him that has the power to transform.

I meet many people who are sincere in their faith and love God to a certain extent, but refrain from putting God first in their lives. They are very busy: they may be very involved with church, very preoccupied with their spouses, very into their families, very busy on their jobs, and very familiar with the standard church lingo that lets everyone know with whom they associate themselves. When it comes down to it, though, God is not a part of much of what they do. Even though they might look and sound like God is everything, when they make their decisions, spend their money, align their day, and set their priorities, God is not a part of the process.

If we want to experience this Kingdom thing for real, we must make sure we are following the commandments of our Kingdom. There are only two that we hold, because we know if we follow these two, the rest will fall in place.

One of the teachers of religious law was standing there listening to the debate. He realized that Jesus had answered well, so he asked, "Of all the commandments, which is the most important?" (Mark 12:28)

As we discussed earlier, the commandments of old were all considered equivalent. Yet even in Bible times, people wondered if certain commandments had more weight than others. We can see this thinking clearly present in the teacher of the law who came to trap Jesus with that question. It wasn't so much about sincerely understanding the law as it was about trying to see if Jesus could be tricked into answering the question in a way that could be proven theologically wrong. For example, if the teacher asked Jesus about which commandment was most important and Jesus answered that it was "You shouldn't murder," the ruler could come back and say, "Why is murder superior to stealing?" The never-ending back-and-forth would have resulted in a stalemate where the teacher could prove all the commandments were equal, and Jesus was somehow in error.

Jesus wasn't in error, however. As the Son of God, Jesus didn't just understand the law; He fulfilled it. He never sinned and was able to walk in the law with enough saving power to break its weight from our lives. This means Jesus knew the law in a way the teacher of the law did not. While the teacher of the law was busy trying to burden people with its conditions, Jesus was there to set us free from its confines. He was living it in a literal sense rather than compounding it with abstract subheadings.

Jesus replied, "The most important commandment is this: 'Listen, O Israel! The LORD our God is the one and only LORD. And you must love the LORD your God with all your heart, all your soul, all your mind, and all your strength.' (Mark 12:29-30)

Jesus clarifies for us the entire foundation for all our theology: we are to listen and hear that God is one, and God is the only Lord. If we understand this properly, it means we turn away from idols and turn fully toward God, without looking behind or looking away. If we recognize God as the supreme and only God, we must love Him with all of our being: our heart, our soul, our mind, and our strength. All of us must cry forth to God and believe in Him fully, in every way in our lives.

Why is this commandment the most important one? If we want to do and be right with God, we must love God. We can't aspire to desire to do the things of God and be used by God if we do not make that effort to get to know Him. When we truly love someone, it is our blessing and our pleasure to spend time with them, to learn what they like and do not like, how to live with that individual, and to engage with them in a productive and effective way. God desires us to draw to Him in this way so we can know Him and have relationship with Him. If we don't love God with everything in us, we won't make the effort to have this relationship, and we will lack direction and guidance for the right way to go.

This kind of relationship takes time to develop, so don't be discouraged if you aren't finding yourself exactly where you want to be with God just yet. Most people don't isolate themselves in the wilderness or in a life where they can devote all their time to God without any distractions. The rest of us must learn as we go along, sometimes by trial and error, often through a lot of study and learning to recognize the conviction of the Spirit and the voice of God in our lives. What this means is that we might not see progress immediately, but we should see, and embrace change, over time. As we grow with God and our spiritual seasons change, we will come to recognize how much closer we are to God and how much victory we have gained.

Loving God is not the only commandment we have as Christians. There is another one, one that is often just as difficult for believers. Difficult or not, it is part of our command, and a part of living and believing in God fully, in this Christian life.

Love your neighbor as yourself

The second is equally important: 'Love your neighbor as yourself.' No other commandment is greater than these."

The teacher of religious law replied, "Well said, Teacher. You have spoken the truth by saying that there is only one God and no other. And I know it is important to love Him with all my heart and all my understanding and all my strength, and to love my neighbor as myself. This is more important than to offer all of the burnt offerings and sacrifices required in the law."

Realizing how much the man understood, Jesus said to him, "You are not far from the Kingdom of God." And after that, no one dared to ask Him any more questions. (Mark 12:31-34)

I am going to confess a secret that will probably get me in trouble: Christians don't like talking about love. That's why they stick to "safe love" topics: husbands and wives, parents and children, and families. Seldom do you ever hear a message on love outside this immediate context. Even in this limited scope, we still often don't get love right. It's something most Christians admit is a part of Christian identity, but are tempted to fill in the blanks with a lot of "buts:" "Yes, I know we are supposed to love others, but…" That "but," whatever follows it, keeps them from seeing God at work in their lives and from the most powerful witness they can have with others.

I have often been asked what makes Christianity different from other religious groups. There are two answers to this question. The first answer is that Christianity espouses a different doctrine than many other religions. In Christianity, we celebrate the only religious figure in history Who rose from the dead. The second answer relates to the first: we are the only religion in history in which God has reached out to humanity to accomplish what we could not do for ourselves. While other groups might acknowledge deities that require sacrifices and offerings to them, their gods do not do anything for humanity out of nothing but love. God has done for us out of love, because God is Himself love. God did not just tell us He loved us or pretended to love us but showed us just how much He loved us through the sacrifice of Christ. Now, because we have received that love, we are able to spread it to others. While other religions might encourage charity or good works, not having that foundation of love means they give out of obligation rather than a witness to what they've received.

This is why we are commanded to love our neighbor as ourselves. It's a no-gimmick, pulling no punches, adding no words command that is the ultimate challenge for us in this world. There are no exceptions, no additions, and no implications. Every time we add a "but" we take away that opportunity to draw closer to the Father while drawing someone to Him. It's a command and an obedience that will be life-long, intense, and expect more of us than we would like to give.

I once met a man who was part of a very traditional Christian background (one to which I once also belonged). We had a mutual friend that I mentioned and in passing, I said something I thought he already knew about her. (I wasn't aware it wasn't public knowledge.) It wasn't a big secret, and I am not sure how he didn't realize it about her, but he didn't, and he flew into a furious rage. His response to me was that he "loves everyone, but…" I interrupted him and told him that the "but" in the sentence was the problem. He claimed to love everyone, but whatever comes after that "but" means he doesn't love everyone.

We are conditioned through human nature to love "who we love:" those who look like us, talk like us, are most like us, and don't challenge us to grow or change into anything else. We gravitate toward all things that make us feel comfortable, and we say we "love" them. It's the people who make us look at ourselves, who make our perceived comforts disappear or who impact our ease of access in this life that make us "dis-love" them. We want to be number one, look out for ourselves, and forget about everyone else.

The passage Jesus quotes from in Mark 12:31 is a rather obscure command in the Old Testament, smashed between a bunch of other passages that one probably wouldn't think much about if they were reading the Bible in passing. Because it wasn't a passage that jumped out in lights, most of the Israelites probably didn't think a lot of it. It was just another regulation, and it certainly didn't rate being on par with loving God in totality, did it?

Yes, it did. Yes, it does.

The Israelites found themselves repeatedly tripped up in the area of personal superiority complexes. Being the nation chosen by God as His unique people turned into a superiority complex where they felt they were superior in race and belief to those around them. At the same time, they were so driven and intrigued by everyone around them, they kept falling into the same traps of envy all over again. This crazy cycle meant Israel was not the witness they needed to be to stand as God's people to the world. They couldn't follow their own regulations, and they still wanted to be like everyone else. They did not love their neighbors, but instead, both envied and felt superior to them.

Jesus' command to love our neighbor as ourselves wasn't just about the people who might live next door to us or the ones we might see every day in our neighborhoods. The concept of "neighbors" in Biblical times was about nations and differing religious groups and those seen as "inferior, yet sometimes enviable" by the people Jesus taught. It is no different for us today. Every one of us deals with the temptation to see someone else as "less than us" and even find some of those "enviable" because we've decided we are more worthy of whatever it is they have than they are. Neighbors are about those who are decidedly different, not like us in every way except when they live in a different house. Jesus called us to rise to the challenge and love every single person who was not us or like us on this planet, fully well knowing such would be uncomfortable. That's the point: we need to be uncomfortable. We need to crawl out of ourselves and into Him and overcome the biases that keep us from reaching out to the rest of the world. Yes, we believe in truth, yes, we uphold what we believe, but loving someone else means we want for them exactly what we would want for ourselves: the best, nothing more, and nothing else.

This changes how we view the world. We can see a world full of hostile enemies, or we can see a world full of unmet friends. We can judge the world as inferior, or we can see the world as an open door to share the equality of the Gospel. We can view the world through transformed eyes, or we can insist on upholding the ways and wiles of the flesh, which prevent us from interacting well and in hope and kindness with others. We can be part of the problem, or part of the solution. This is why we can do a million good things with no love attached to it and make no change in this world. Tons of great programs exist that in theory should have transformed the world ten times over and yet haven't even made a dent in our issues with one another. We have to change how we see others if we want to have an impact, and that starts with God's love to us.

The teacher who came to Jesus acknowledged the truth in what He said. Israel could have offered billions of burnt sacrifices but would never have come close to what God required of them. Shouldn't we even more see the relevance in it? One step at a time, we reach out to others and change the way we see the world. Start by learning, growing, and embracing others…especially those most different. Then learn what you can do for them to help their lives aspire to everything you desire to see in your own.

What does loving your neighbor look like? We can answer that by looking at some of the finer points of Old Testament precept and realizing if we love our neighbor, we won't do those things.

- If you love your neighbor, you won't set out to defraud them for your own gain.

- If you love your neighbor, you won't seek to harm them, abuse them, mistreat them, or kill them.

- If you love your neighbor, you won't steal from them.

- If you love your neighbor, you won't think what they have should be yours.

- If you love your neighbor, you won't disregard their family life, status, or social situation.

- If you love your neighbor, you won't wish a curse (bad things) on them.

- If you love your neighbor, you won't commit adultery with their spouse.

- If you love your neighbor, you won't disrespect your parents or elders.

- If you love your neighbor, you won't slant the laws in your favor and to their disadvantage.

- If you love your neighbor, you won't seek to take your portion out of their share.

In other words: If you love your neighbor, you will deal honestly with them, and you won't deliberately seek to wrong them in the pursuit of having what you perceive to be your best opportunity. It is no longer about you versus them, but the awareness that in God's economy, there is enough for everyone.

GOD DOESN'T PLAY FAVORITES…AND NEITHER SHOULD WE

When you were growing up, did your parents have a favorite child? Did your teachers have favorite students? Were you the favored one, or were you on the other end of it? If you were the favorite, they didn't do you a lot of favors in this world, even though it might have felt like that. It might have felt good at the time, but there was someone, somewhere in time, who did not agree with their view of you, and the favoritism bubble burst. If you have never been someone's favorite, you know what it feels like to be on the other end of that experience. You feel like nothing you do is good enough or measures up enough. You watch someone else get something that you might like to have, and you do without it because it won't be given to you. You are aware this is the way it is, and it stings of a deep unfairness that cuts at something you can do nothing about.

Favoritism isn't just seen in interpersonal relationships. It is seen on a wide scale through racism, sexism, cultural biases, discrimination of all kinds, and battles between the rich and the poor. Whether we call it prejudice, bias, partiality, bigotry, a phobia, or an "-ism," favoritism cuts at the very core of what the Kingdom of God is about. The whole point of the Kingdom is not exclusion or elevating certain people above others, but that through Christ, we can stand equal before God. No longer will we be judged for what someone else did, but we can stand before God for ourselves, covered by the grace of God and strong in our faith in Christ.

In Christianity, favoritism is a dirty little sin that many people don't want to talk about. People don't want to admit there are entire ministries that offer priority seating for their biggest paying customers…uh…I mean donors, special privileges and private audiences for their biggest contributors, and some who even go as far as to only offer services for a certain race or group of individuals. We still know racism is alive and well in much of Christianity and was a motivating factor for many mission organizations in the 1700s and 1800s. Governments desired to colonize African nations, India, and other countries and missionaries became a perfect way to infiltrate their nations with European culture and attitudes. These darker aspects of Christian history aren't a reflection of God's attitudes, but those of people, of individuals who tried to use the faith for a more sinister motive. Even now, attitudes about favoritism and partiality are the core foundation of some organizations and philosophies, and they are frequently marketed in a package of "authentic" or "orthodox" Christianity.

If we look at the first church, we can note it was full of people who, for one reason or another, were considered "undesirable." Jesus' earliest followers were poor people, women, slaves, young people, and foreigners. This is not to say there were no people who were rich or powerful interested in Jesus, but they were not the majority. What we might have seen are a few rich and mighty interested in His work, but the majority didn't stick around very long. They were either given a message that cut at their societal privileges, or they didn't find themselves drawn to the message because it was too contrary to the social structure in which they lived. All of a sudden, Jesus came along and proclaimed a Gospel that promoted a sense of equality, one that gave the same benefits and rights to the poor or those considered most base in society, and the Kingdom belonged to them as much as it could belong to anyone else. Those in society who were never given a fighting chance to get into a traditional kingdom culture now had the full opportunity – and right – to be a part of God's Kingdom.

This doesn't mean everyone liked this idea, however. Even in the earliest decades of Christianity, we see this very issue addressed in more than one place. Sometimes God dealt with the first leaders directly, and other times, as in the passage we are about to study, sometimes God dealt with the specific issues present in the church at large through the leaders.

I solemnly command you in the presence of God and Christ Jesus and the highest angels to obey these instructions without taking sides or showing favoritism to anyone. (1 Timothy 5:21)

My brethren, pay no servile regard to people [show no prejudice, no partiality]. Do not [attempt to] hold and practice the faith of our Lord Jesus Christ [the Lord] of glory [together with snobbery]!

For if a person comes into your congregation whose hands are adorned with gold rings and who is wearing splendid apparel, and also a poor [man] in shabby clothes comes in,

And you pay special attention to the one who wears the splendid clothes and say to him, Sit here in this preferable seat! while you tell the poor [man], Stand there! or, Sit there on the floor at my feet!

Are you not discriminating among your own and becoming critics and judges with wrong motives?

Listen, my beloved brethren: Has not God chosen those who are poor in the eyes of the world to be rich in faith and in their position as believers and to inherit the kingdom which He has promised to those who love Him?

But you [in contrast] have insulted (humiliated, dishonored, and shown your contempt for) the poor. Is it not the rich who domineer over you? Is it not they who drag you into the law courts?

Is it not they who slander and blaspheme that precious name by which you are distinguished and called [the name of Christ invoked in baptism]?

If indeed you [really] fulfill the royal Law in accordance with the Scripture, You shall love your neighbor as [you love] yourself, you do well.

But if you show servile regard (prejudice, favoritism) for people, you commit sin and are rebuked and convicted by the Law as violators and offenders. (James 2:1-9, AMPC)

Paralleling what we spoke of earlier, if loving our neighbor is a central tenant of Christian belief, introducing inequalities to our Kingdom breaks that command. Inequality is based on this world, on injustices and prejudices that do not reflect a transformed life as a new creature. Anyone who becomes a Christian is supposed to reflect a different attitude about these matters than those who follow the ways of the world.

Not just this, pay careful attention to the terminology that is used in this passage…the Apostle James clarifies for us that to engage in partiality or favoritism is a sin…heavy! It's not just a cultural slip or a little mistake, it is something that displeases God and separates us from Him. If we love our neighbor as we love ourselves, we fulfill God's commands to us and we are not penalized by the law. Yet if we don't love our neighbor as we love ourselves, we are to be convicted by the very law that it comes from.

Loving our neighbor as ourselves is not taught to be an impractical command. As we read through the Scriptures, we learn more of the common sense it involves: interpersonal consideration. None of us are an island, and just like none of us sin by ourselves, none of us come into the Kingdom alone, either. Once we are a part of God's Kingdom, we don't remain in it by ourselves. If we are going to do this faith thing right, we have to learn how to get along with others and show the love of God to them through our behavior.

Developing your identity

There are two main ways that we come to better understand who we are in Christ. The first way is through our lives and applying God's precepts to them. Our walk with God is, in many ways, a "crash course," of sorts. Everything we have discussed in this chapter has been about discovering our identity and experiencing that identity in our lives. We find it as we live, move, and have our being in God. Through our lives, we will have many moments when we realize God is speaking to us, teaching us, or reaching out to us through situations, victories, difficulties, teachings, connections, and life's encounters. This is an ongoing experience, one that inspires us sometimes, makes us mad at others, and convicts us as we need it.

The second way we come to a better understanding of who we are in Christ comes through the discipline of Bible study. I know that it is an area of the Christian life that is most intimidating to many. It doesn't help that there are tons of books out there about the "right" way to do it and none of them seem to agree with each other. It's also true that down the line there are many, many different perspectives and opinions as to what one passage might mean, how it is studied, or how many Bible words are defined from their original languages. As intimidating as it might be, it is still something that every believer should take on as their own and rise to the challenge to understand more of themselves and more of what God has for them.

The Bible itself tells us why studying the Scriptures is so important:

But as for you, continue to hold to the things that you have learned and of which you are convinced, knowing from whom you learned [them],

And how from your childhood you have had a knowledge of and been acquainted with the sacred Writings, which are able to instruct you and give you the understanding for salvation which comes through faith in Christ Jesus [through the leaning of the entire human personality on God in Christ Jesus in absolute trust and confidence in His power, wisdom, and goodness].

Every Scripture is God-breathed (given by His inspiration) and profitable for instruction, for reproof and conviction of sin, for correction of error and discipline in obedience, [and] for training in righteousness (in holy living, in conformity to God's will in thought, purpose, and action),

So that the man of God may be complete and proficient, well fitted and thoroughly equipped for every good work. (2 Timothy 3:14-17, AMPC)

By studying the Bible, we are able to learn about salvation, find purpose in instruction, correction, conviction of sin, discipline, obedience, and training in right living. This must mean part of being a Christian is being a modern-day Bible person, one who has a relationship with God and lives out that faith, one step at a time. To better understand that experience, we must discipline ourselves to Bible study. This introduces us to God in a different way and to our ancestors in the faith, whose experiences with God help us find truth and lead us to hope.

How can we make Bible study a little less intimidating? Let's start by clearing up a few things that will make the Bible a little more understandable, and a little less scary.

- The Bible is also called "the Word" or "written Word," the "Word of God," "the Book," "the Holy Bible," "Holy Writ," "the Scriptures" or the "Holy Scriptures."

- The Bible is thought of as being a "book," but it is actually a group of several books authored over thousands of years. In some instances, we know who authored the books, and in some, we do not. The point of inspiration is not that the Bible was ushered down from heaven on a cloud or that it is absolutely infallible, but that God has a hand in preserving, promising, and sending all of us a message through it. The Bible contains many different types of writings, all of which express different thoughts, feelings, and understandings of one's relationship with God. Some are easier to understand than others. The Bible consists of stories, poetry, songs, wise sayings, eyewitness accounts, genealogies, letters, detailed visions, insights that foretell the future, sermons, and dialogues.

- Different Christian groups acknowledge different books as "authoritative," or "canonized" in the Bible. Some Bibles contain 66, some 72, and some even more than that. Most books present in the Bible are agreed upon by all groups, but there are some exceptions.

- The Bible itself is a record of God's interactions with those He called to stand as His people throughout what we call "salvation history." It is not a record of every person who was ever called by God, nor is it a record of every interaction people ever had with God throughout history. It is also not a record of everything God ever did throughout history. It shows His hand in creation, in working in and through the hearts of people, their successes and failings, and the establishment of a group for which His Son could come into this world. After His coming, He was crucified, died, and rose again to overcome sin. We then find the record of the first believers in Him, who went on to establish this Kingdom established before the foundations of the world as present in His church. It ends with pictures of what is to come, although we don't understand just what all those details mean right now.

- The purpose of the Bible was not to be the final answer of everything under the sun, nor was its purpose to create so many conflicts for people about things such as science, medicine, or history. The purpose of the Bible was to inspire and guide on faith and show all the ways human life overlaps with spiritual realties.

- The Bible's contents are inspired, which means they are "God-breathed." This means while God used human beings to author the books of the Bible, He was behind their desire to write those words and influence future generations. Thus, The Bible has authority to guide us by our faith in our lives.

- The original writings of the Bible (those in the oldest portions of the Old Testament) consisted of what we know as "oral tradition." This means before they were written down, they were stories that recounted incredible things God did for people as passed down from generation to generation. Because people could not read or write, oral tradition made sure people could know and remember what God had one for people of the past. In some instances, some Bible stories were not written down until several thousand years after they first happened.

- It is not possible to take every single passage of the Bible literally, all at the same time. To do such would not make much sense and does not consider the fact that the Bible itself was not written all at one time. The Bible reflects culture, faith, social mores, and changing times, and all of this serves an important part in inspiration. It's not about a literal understanding but coming to see from this record what God has to say to us, right now, as we draw on the amazing history and inspiration found in His Word. The Bible speaks of Scripture being "fulfilled," which means it is something meant to be lived, not understood with static.

- The Bible itself was not written in English, but in a mixture of ancient Hebrew, Aramaic (a Hebrew dialect language) and koine Greek (or common Greek). The earliest translations of the Bible were in Syriac and Latin, not English. This means every time we use a translation of the Bible in a modern language, it is just that – a translation, not a literal rendering of its original wording. There are passages of the Bible that it is just not possible to translate into our modern languages with the same meaning, and a few other passages that we don't know for certain what they meant, at all.

- Bible times were not like modern times. The Bible reflects a different type of culture, different traditions, different governing and ideas about governing, and different customs than we see in society. The social and ethical mores of Biblical times are quite different than those we find in modern society today. Some passages may seem extreme or hard to understand given modern standards. This doesn't mean we can't learn from it; it means we have to learn more to understand its contents, precepts, and words that much more.

- The King James Version of the Bible is not superior to other translations in any way, shape, or form. While many people prefer the King James Version as they feel it is more traditional, this doesn't make it a better translation. The King James Version was written for the same reason as any other modern-day translation: to ensure people of the day could read and understand the Bible. It's important to have a Bible translation you can understand in a language usage familiar to you, to maximize your best chances of having a great relationship with the Scriptures. Never feel bad about finding a translation that you feel comfortable using.

- It might seem like some passages of the Bible contradict one another. What it more likely might be is different passages refer to different times and circumstances, and those sometimes require different actions. The Bible proves that faith, ethics, and life are not in a vacuum, and figuring out what to do or what God is leading in any given situation may vary at times. It doesn't mean that one's belief system is subjective, but that it is objective, as one discerns just what God has to say in every situation.

Keeping these things in mind will make Bible study a lot easier as you start to study more about the Bible and its contents. This also helps when you start to hear more about the Bible from other sources. Sure, it can feel confusing sometimes, but there is no reason to run or hide from the Bible. As a believer, you need to know more about what the Bible has to say to you and how you can understand what it is saying, in and out of season.

Where do you start? The first thing to do is set aside some time and get familiar with the Bible. Many people confuse Bible reading versus Bible study, but they are quite different. There is nothing wrong with reading the Bible or setting time aside to read it every day. If you are new to the Bible in your experience, I'd say daily Bible reading is probably a great place for you to start. Reading the Bible familiarizes you with its contents, with where different books of the Bible are located, and with what translations you find most useful for your purposes. It is perfectly possible for God to speak to you through Bible reading, and to encourage you through it.

Bible reading, however, isn't enough for a serious Christian. The Bible isn't a novel, something we read cover-to-cover and then leave for someone else at a garage sale. As Christians, we should desire to dive into the Scriptures and understand the people, places, culture, language, and life of those in Bible times. Learning about these things helps us to better understand what God has to say to us right now, dealing with and confronting the things we do, today. It helps us realize that even though times and cultures change, human nature does not so readily transform without divine intervention. It also helps us to see that God is with us and loves us, no matter what culture or situation we may find ourselves in.

There are a few different ways we can study the Bible. There isn't one way that is better to study the Bible than another. At some point in time, most believers will probably study the Bible in all these different ways. Doing so and incorporating a certain level of flexibility into one's Bible study will help to maximize your ability to take away much from your Scripture study.

- **Preaching and teaching:** The Scriptures speak of the importance on hearing the Word of God both preached and taught. When we hear a word that is preached or taught, we hear a message that is divinely inspired and opens the Scriptures to us in a new and practical way.

- **Verse-by-verse:** Some people prefer to study the Bible a verse at a time, examining every single verse in Scripture and building up to completing an entire passage.

- **Chapter summary:** Chapter summary study is when one chapter of the Bible is studied at a time, exploring its contents in full and thoroughly researching them before moving on to another chapter. This can lead to cross-reference study, as a topic in one chapter may be more fully developed somewhere else.

- **Book survey:** When someone studies an entire book of the Bible by itself, one is surveying and studying the contents of that book exclusively. When one engages in a book survey, they may read through it many times, explore the chapters in it, and study the background of the book, including history, context, dating, authorship, culture, and historical timing.

- **Thematic:** Thematic studies consist of selecting a general theme or idea present in Scripture and then studying all the verses and passages that pertain to it. In thematic study, the goal is to find certain patterns and ideas about large Bible topics, rather than ones that are more immediate and can be contained in a topical study. An example of a thematic Bible study might be prophecy.

- **Topical:** A topical Bible study is like a thematic one, only it is on Biblical topics (subjects and ideas that are more limited) instead of themes. In a topical study, one would pick a topic and research all passages in the Bible that are about that topic. An example of a topical Bible study would be baptism.

- **Word studies:** Many scholars study the original Hebrew, Aramaic, and Greek words present in the Bible to more accurately understand their context and literal understanding. This kind of study is not for everyone, but some people enjoy the linguistics of Bible language, even on a simple level. An interlinear Bible and good Bible dictionary can help to understand words and terms better, even if you aren't looking to become a great scholar in Bible linguistics.

Studying the Bible opens the Kingdom of God to us in a new way. It helps us to see God and how much He has always loved and cared for His people, and it helps us to embrace more of who we are and who God wants us to be. When it's confusing, ask questions, study different aspects of Scripture, and pray. Always be encouraged as you make efforts, because God is there for you, revealing Himself even when it is hard.

SUMMARY OF BIBLE BOOK CONTENTS

Your experience with the Bible will probably come in the form of the common Protestant canon, which contains 66 books. As we discussed earlier, there are other canons, but if you are starting out in your Bible experience, you will probably encounter the western Protestant canon. When exploring the Bible for yourself, it can help a great deal if you are able to have a general idea of what each book of the Bible contains. Here I will provide some general summaries of each of these books, so you are able to dive in and explore the Scriptures better for yourself.

- **Genesis:** The "book of beginnings." Genesis chronicles the creation of the world and all it contains (including human beings) as well as the earliest experiences of humanity. There's at least 2,300 years of human history covered in Genesis (probably more). Much of Genesis focuses on individuals and families that descended from them, and the complications of their cultures, choices, and actions. Major figures include God as Creator, Adam and Eve, Noah, Abraham, Sarah, Jacob, Rachel, and Joseph.

- **Exodus:** Details the enslavement of the Hebrew people and their divine departure ("exodus") from Egypt. After leaving Egypt, the Hebrews spent 40 years in the wilderness. In Exodus we meet Moses, who was the leader of the Hebrew people through their wilderness experience. We also see the introduction of the written law and the construction of the tabernacle. Major figures include Moses, Miriam, Aaron, Zipporah, Pharaoh's daughter, and Jethro.

- **Leviticus:** Another book that details the written law, specifically relating to the sacrifices offered in the tabernacle and the holy days of ancient Israel. The book also addresses general laws of living, diet, and hygiene. Major figures include Moses and Aaron.

- **Numbers:** So-called because the book opens a census of the Israelites, Numbers deals with the ordering of the Hebrews into those who are able-bodied for military service, divided into groups, and able to travel as an entire unit, divided for different services and purposes. This book contains the sacred record of the Hebrews' experiences as they moved from place to place in the wilderness. Major figures include Moses and Aaron.

- **Deuteronomy:** Literally meaning "second law," the book of Deuteronomy is a re-stated summary of the written law and the experiences of the Hebrew people in the wilderness. Deuteronomy ends with the death of Moses and the institution of Joshua as the next leader of Israel. Major figures include Moses and Joshua.

- **Joshua:** The book of Joshua details the 25-year experience of the Hebrew people under the leadership of its namesake, Joshua. It details the period covering the inspection of the Promised Land, the fall of Jericho, the seize of the Promised Land, and the conflicts the Hebrews started having with their neighbors. Major figures include Joshua, Rahab, and Caleb.

- **Judges:** A descriptive title that details a long period of Israeli history (somewhere between 350-410 years) in which the Israelites were governed by a diversity of judges, rather than a specific, central Hebrew leader. Major figures include Deborah, Jael, Samson, Jephthah, Gideon, Othinel, Ehud, Jair, Shamgar, Abdon, Abimelech, and Judah.

- **Ruth:** A short book that tells the story of Ruth and Naomi (daughter-in-law and mother-in-law); Ruth, a pagan, and Naomi, a Jew. After all the men in Ruth and Naomi's family died, Ruth makes the commitment to travel with Naomi to Bethlehem to care for her, even though such was uncustomary and not required according to ancient custom. Ruth's tender care for her mother-in-law leads her to Boaz, a man who can serve as a kinsman-redeemer (one who restores property rights) for the family. We aren't sure how many years Ruth covers, but it's estimated to be a few, from start to finish. Major figures include Ruth, Naomi, and Boaz.

- **1 Samuel:** A book detailing the history of Israel from the birth of the Prophet Samuel, one who began a lineage of prophetic voices to provide the voice of God to the people and the leaders, down through the ages. Samuel was a priest, prophet, and judge, who served to guide and lead Israel throughout his life. The book of 1 Samuel continues until the death of Saul, who was the first king over Israel. It covers a period of about 110 years. Major figures include Hannah, Samuel, Saul, David, and Jonathan.

- **2 Samuel:** 2 Samuel was originally part of 1 Samuel but was divided up into two parts due to its extreme length. 2 Samuel examines the history of David, the second king of Israel. It covers approximately 25 years. Major figures include David, Absalom, Joab, Ish-bosheth, Bathsheba, Ahitophel, Nathan, and Abner.

- **1 and 2 Kings:** Part of another long record of Israel's history, 1 and 2 Kings examines Israel's history after the death of King David until the early Babylonian exile; a period of well over 400 years. It opens with an extensive detailing of King Solomon's rule (King Solomon being the son of King David) and then discusses the divisions of Israel and how they formed: the northern kingdom being Israel and the southern kingdom being Judah. From these records, we are able to see why the two kingdoms formed, the leadership of both, and how both fell away from the will of God, despite God's warnings and prophets sent to guide them. 2 Kings was originally part of 1 Kings but was divided up into two parts due to its extreme length. 2 Kings begins after Ahab's death in the kingdom of Israel and the death of Jehoshaphat in the southern kingdom. By this time, the two kingdoms were very distinct, and we can see much of the same detailing as we did in 1 Kings: histories of kings, the falling away of the nations, and God's warnings sent through prophets. Major figures include Elijah, Elisha, Solomon, Ahab, Hezekiah, Jezebel, and Josiah.

- **1 and 2 Chronicles:** 1 and 2 Chronicles tell of an overlap of a period as 1 and 2 Samuel and 1 and 2 Kings, existing to provide additional details that were left out of those earlier records. Like those other books, 1 and 2 Chronicles was originally one book, divided due to the overwhelming length. They are considered an expansion of the detailing of Israel's history. Between the two books, they cover about 517 years' worth of history. Major figures include David, Solomon, Rehoboam, Asa, Jehoshaphat, Ahaz, Hezekiah, Zerubbabel, Nathan, Gad, and Samuel.

- **Ezra:** Originally combined with Nehemiah to form one book, Ezra details the work of the priest and scribe, Ezra, who led a group of Babylonian exiles back to their home city, Jerusalem. The book of Ezra has a strong theme of admonishing the Hebrews who returned with him to follow the law and avoid intermarriage with pagan peoples. The book itself covers about 80 years of history. Major figures include Ezra, Zerubbabel, and Nehemiah.

- **Nehemiah:** Originally combined with Ezra to form one book, Nehemiah is a continuation of Ezra. This portion of the book focuses on the rebuilding of Jerusalem now that the exiles have returned. It focuses on the Prophet Nehemiah's work to rebuild the wall around Jerusalem. The book covers approximately a 12-year period. Major figures include Nehemiah, Ezra, Zerubbabel, and Artaxerxes.

- **Esther:** A story named after its heroine, Esther, a young Jewish girl that becomes Queen of Persia, under the rule of King Xerxes. Focused on the rule of the Persian empire, we see the threatened extermination of the Jews through the entire Persian Empire because of the wickedness of a ruler in Xerxes' court, named Haman. Thanks to the information and influence of Esther's relative, Mordecai, Esther enters in the picture to rescue the Jewish people from extermination. The end of the book details the feast of Purim, celebrated in honor of the salvation of the Jewish people. The entire book covers a period of about ten years. Major figures include Esther, Moredcai, Vashti, Haman, and Xerxes.

- **Job:** Job reflects an ancient tradition of wisdom literature by which someone goes through a situation and gains divine insight as they examine the wonders of life and creation through their trial. Job was a blameless man, targeted by Satan because he believed Job would concede and curse God if he went through enough difficulty. Instead of cursing God, Job examines the wonders of thought, human experience, creation, and divine wisdom, coming out on the other side with greater insight. No one is exactly sure how many years the book of Job covers, with estimates anywhere from a few months to two years, to as many as 40 years! Major figures include Job, God, Satan, Job's wife, Job's three friends (Eliphaz, Bildad, and Zophar) and Elihu.

- **Psalms:** A collection of ancient songs that were set to music and used in the sacred services and worship of ancient Israel. The Psalms are a universally loved portion of Scripture, as they depict a variety of contents that express worship, praise, despair, joy, hopelessness, trust, and abiding confidence in God. The Psalms were written over a period of many years, with major writers including David, Asaph and his family, the Sons of Korah, Solomon, Moses, Heman, and Ethan the Ezrahite.

- **Proverbs:** A collection of wise ideas and sayings that cause thought and ponderance on one's position before God, self, and others. Proverbs is usually attributed to Solomon. Other contributors include Agur and King Lemuel.

- **Ecclesiastes:** As authored by an individual known as "the Philosopher," the book of Ecclesiastes explores the meaning of human existence. The ultimate conclusion is the importance of focusing on and learning through the journey, rather than obsessing on the destination. The major figure of Ecclesiastes is Qoheleth, which is Hebrew for "teacher" or "philosopher." Many associate this individual with Solomon.

- **Song of Solomon (Song of Songs):** A beautiful, royal wedding song that depicts passion, love, and desire between a couple. Often taught to be a comparison between God and His people. The major characters are the couple (the woman or beloved and man) and their friends.

- **Isaiah:** The book of Isaiah records an extensive prophecy given to the people of Israel by the prophet Isaiah. There are three main divisions in Isaiah: Chapters 1-39, which offer the direct words of Isaiah, and cover matters of both judgment and later restoration for Judah, the city of Jerusalem, and several other nations; Chapters 40-55, which covers Messianic history that shall one day overthrow the oppression of Babylon; and Chapters 56-66, which covers the promise of a time of restoration and peace that shall follow the overthrow of the Babylonian captors. The time (including prophecy) covered is approximately 200 years. Major figures include Isaiah, Uzziah, Jotham, Ahaz, Hezekiah, and the concept of the Messiah (spoken of as a "suffering servant.")

- **Jeremiah:** The book of Jeremiah chronicles the prophecies of the Prophet Jeremiah as he was sent to minister to the Israelites about the Babylonian Exile, which would last for seventy years. Through powerful imagery and prose, the Prophet Jeremiah addressed the need for a new covenant, one that would supersede the existing law and be written on the hearts of God's people. The book itself covers between 20 and 40 years. Major figures include Jeremiah, Baruch, Josiah, Jehoahaz, Jehoiakim, Jehoiachin, Zedekiah, Ebed-Melech, and Nebuchadnezzar.

- **Lamentations:** A collection of poems that display laments, or sorrow, about the destruction of Jerusalem. These poems are attributed to the Prophet Jeremiah. While not specifically stated, the Book of Lamentations covers approximately 50 years. The primary figure in Lamentations is the Lady Zion, a personification of Jerusalem.

- **Ezekiel:** A complex book, both in symbolism and prophecy, the book of Ezekiel details the prophetic work and symbolic actions of the Prophet Ezekiel. His prophetic work related to the coming destruction of Jerusalem, restoration to come for the land of Israel following the Babylonian captivity, and greater prophecies of a temple vision to come in a time after the coming of the Messiah. It covers a period of about 22 years. Major figures include Ezekiel, Jehoiachin, and Zedekiah.

- **Daniel:** The book of Daniel details the work of Daniel in the court of Babylon and the way God worked for him and his friends as well as powerful prophetic visions that relate to history down through to the end of the age. It covers about 70 years. Major figures in Daniel include Daniel, Shadrach, Meshach, Abednego, Nebuchadnezzar, Belshazzar, the Ancient of Days, and the Archangel Michael.

- **Hosea:** The book of Hosea details the personal and intimate way in which God asked the Prophet Hosea to illustrate the idolatry Israel kept falling into, time and time again. The Prophet Hosea was sent to marry a prostitute named Gomer and then raise up children with her, which displayed the unfaithfulness of Israel. Comparing the relationship between God and His people as an unfaithful marriage, Hosea and Gomer separate, only for God to send Hosea to Gomer again, to remarry her. The book also relates direct prophecies to the two kingdoms of Israel, the coming fall of both, and the promised restoration of the people of God. It covers a period of approximately 60 years. Major figures include Hosea, gomer, Jezreel, Lo-Ruhamah, Lo-Ammi, Uzziah, Jotham, Ahaz, Hezekiah, and Jerobam.

- **Joel:** The book of Joel details the call of Israel to examine themselves and their actions after a severe locust invasion. The locusts devoured everything, to the point where the people felt they had reached the "end" of everything. Joel encourages repentance, personal examination, and the remembrance of God's faithfulness unto blessing and promise. We don't know exactly when Joel happened, so we don't know exactly how long the time frame it covers. Major figures include Joel and the locust plague.

- **Amos:** The book of Amos details a powerful prophecy given by the Prophet Amos to the northern kingdom of Israel during a difficult and dark period in Israel's history. His words exposed corruption and expounded upon a need for social justice and coming divine judgment upon Israel's people. His ultimate promise was the restoration of the house of David, signifying a coming day of Messianic leadership. It covers approximately 15 years. Major figures include Amos, Jeroboam II, Uzziah, and Amaziah.

- **Obadiah:** The shortest prophecy found in the Bible, the book of Obadiah is a prophetic vision detailing the fall of Edom, a nation that was founded by the Biblical figure, Esau. The nation was destroyed due to its arrogance and violence against Israel. It covers approximately 100 years in time. Major figures include Obadiah and the relationship between the descendants of Esau (Edom) and Jacob (Judah).

- **Jonah:** Different from the other prophetic books, the book of Jonah details more about an experience of the Prophet Jonah versus his actual prophecy. God called Jonah to prophesy to the citizens of Nineveh in the land of Assyria, giving them a message of oncoming destruction for wickedness. Instead of going to Nineveh, Jonah went in the opposite direction and began a journey with God that challenged everything he thought he knew about Him. In the end, Jonah went and preached to Nineveh, the people repented and God did not destroy them. Jonah, however, was still angry and continued to battle with God in this powerful story of repentance and God's mercy. No one is certain how long the events of Jonah took to occur. Major figures include Jonah, God, and the people of Nineveh.

- **Micah:** The book of Micah records the prophecies of the Prophet Micah. It combines realities of doom for injustices (especially social injustices and class distinctions) and the promise of hope throughout its contents. It covers approximately 20-25 years. Major figures include Micah, Jotham, Ahaz, and Hezekiah.

- **Nahum:** The book of Nahum details the Prophet Nahum's vision of the coming final fall of Nineveh, thus symbolizing the fall of the Assyrian Empire. We don't know the exact time frame the prophecy covers, but some believe Nahum prophesied for about 50 years. Its major figure is its author, Nahum.

- **Habakkuk:** The book of Habakkuk details a dialogue between the Prophet Habakkuk and God. In it, Habakkuk cries out to God over the injustices he sees around him. God tells him the Chaldeans will be sent as judgment over Israel for their sins, and then the Chaldeans will also be judged by God. The book ends with a song. The book doesn't chronicle a specific period of time, but it was likely within the first few years of Jehoiakim's reign (609-598 BC). Major figures include Habakkuk and God.

- **Zephaniah:** The book of Zephaniah details the Prophet Zephaniah's words to the southern kingdom of Judah. Though they had been faithful at one time, they too refused to obey their covenant with God, even though it wasn't all that long ago their people had lived in exile. The people are urged to obey God, because a day of judgment was coming, once again. It covers approximately ten years. Major figures include Zephaniah, Cushi, Gedaliah, Amariah, Hezekiah, Josiah, and Nebuchadnezzar.

- **Haggai:** The book of Haggai details the Prophet Haggai's words to Israel, commanding the people to stop putting themselves first and rebuild the temple. They'd waited too long to start the building project since they'd returned from captivity. The book lauds Zerubbabel, a governor, as God's chosen leader, and there will be national downfalls to come. It covers approximately four months in time. Major figures include Haggai, Zerubbabel, and Joshua.

- **Zechariah:** The book of Zechariah details the visions, prophecies, and words of the Prophet Zechariah during the reign of Darius the Great. Much like the Prophet Haggai, the Prophet Zechariah takes interest in rebuilding the temple, because doing such would strengthen the leadership of Israel and bless the Jewish people. The book contains warnings for the people, visions that symbolized the history of Israel, and the coming leadership of the Messiah. It covers about 50 years. Major figures include Zechariah, Joshua, and Zerubbabel.

- **Malachi:** The book of Malachi recounts the Prophet Malachi's word to wayward temple leaders who were comfortable breaking the laws as pertained to proper sacrifices and offerings. They were comfortable taking the best part for themselves and ignoring God's precepts of legal adherence. In the process, they misled the people, married pagans, improperly taught the Scriptures, and served as bad examples. They were commanded to repent, before the time when God would shut them down, all together. The conclusion of the book assures the day of judgment will come, and a forerunner of the Messiah shall herald this coming day. It covers a period of about 40 years. Major figures include Malachi, the priests, the people of Israel, and the messianic forerunner.

- **Matthew:** The first book of the New Testament, Matthew is a Gospel account written to prove Jesus is the Messiah. Its fashion was designed to reach Jewish people with the good news about Christ. It details Christ's genealogy and some details of His divine birth, followed by many chapters that expound upon His ministry and teachings. The book concludes with the details of His crucifixion and resurrection. Major figures include Jesus, the twelve disciples (who became among the first apostles), Mary (mother of Jesus), Joseph, John the Baptist, Mary Magdalene, Pontius Pilate, and the Pharisees and Sadducees.

- **Mark:** Mark is a simple Gospel account designed to recount the ministry, death, and resurrection of Jesus Christ in an easy-to-read format. It unfolds much like ancient dramas, highlighting the miracles of Christ, the call of His disciples, His final days and crucifixion, and His resurrection, moving along rapidly between events. It is not as focused on the details as the Gospels of Matthew and Luke, driving home at the important points of the story. Major figures include Jesus, the twelve disciples (who became among the first apostles), Mary (mother of Jesus), Joseph, John the Baptist, Mary Magdalene, Pontius Pilate, and the Pharisees and Sadducees.

- **Luke:** The Gospel of Luke was written for Gentile believers, focusing on Jesus Christ as the Savior of all humankind. It pays heavy attention to details, including those surrounding Christ's conception and birth, His encounter with John the Baptist, much of His earthly ministry, and His crucifixion, death, and resurrection. Through the attention to detail and the centrality of Christ, Luke gives us great insight into the powerful saving nature of Jesus, all throughout His life on earth, and now that He is living as the resurrected Lord. Major figures include Jesus, the twelve disciples (who became among the first apostles), Mary (mother of Jesus), Theophilus, Anna, Simeon, Elizabeth, Zechariah, the Archangel Gabriel, John the Baptist, Mary Magdalene, Pontius Pilate, and the Pharisees and Sadducees.

- **John:** The Gospels of Matthew, Mark, and Luke are known as synoptic Gospels. This means the information contained in them is very similar; they recount the same stories (sometimes with different details), often in like fashion. The Gospel of John is different, appearing to reach out to all prominent audiences of the early church: converts from Judaism, Greek culture, and Roman culture, inclusively. His style of writing was prevalent in Greco-Roman biographical writing and establishes Christ's authority and origin prior to His incarnation in this world. We are then brought directly into His ministry, focusing heavily on the teaching of Christ, the spirituality of Christ's message, the miracles of Christ that are not always contained in other Gospels, the universality of His message to cross cultures, and ultimately, His death and resurrection. Jesus, the twelve disciples (who became among the first apostles), Mary (mother of Jesus), John the Baptist, Mary Magdalene, Mary sister of Lazarus, Martha, Lazarus, Pontius Pilate, and the Pharisees and Sadducees.

- **Acts of the Apostles:** Authored by the Gospel writer, Luke, the Acts of the Apostles (Also called Acts) recounts approximately 30 years of experiences in the early church, beginning with the Ascension of Christ into heaven, followed by Pentecost, and the empowered preaching of the early leaders and members of the church, transforming the world as they formed with power and fire. The first part of Acts focuses much attention on the work of the Apostle Peter, and the second part of Acts focuses much attention on the work of the Apostle Paul. Major figures include Peter, Paul, Barnabas, Stephen, Philip, and Ananias and Sapphira.

- **Romans:** The book of Romans was a letter from the Apostle Paul to Christians in Rome. From what we know, the recipients appear to have been Christian converts from Judaism with many questions about the nature of salvation and who can come into the church to receive such. With salvation as a major theme, the Apostle Paul clarifies for his readers that salvation comes through Jesus Christ, not through the law or one's adherence to such works.

- **1 Corinthians:** 1 Corinthians is the first of two letters we have written by the Apostle Paul to the church at Corinth. The church at Corinth was heavily invested in the Greek culture of the city and, as a result, many of the believers present there were converts from paganism. They hadn't always abandoned all their ways, however, and that meant there were issues of division, immorality, social difficulties, and questions about the resurrection. 1 Corinthians addresses matters of structural importance: unity, social morality, order in worship, interpersonal relationships, and spiritual insights, all presenting the lines of where following social custom interferes with faith – and figuring out what to do in such instances.

- **2 Corinthians:** 2 Corinthians is a follow-up of 1 Corinthians, and largely addresses questions the Corinthian church had sent to him. Much of 2 Corinthians defends the Apostle Paul's call to apostleship, and the different ways he has worked on behalf of the Corinthian church for the betterment of their faith. He also provides detailed information for taking collections.

- **Galatians:** Galatians was written by the Apostle Paul to the Christian church at Galatia. Largely composed of Jewish converts to Christianity, it addresses the questions they had about whether a Gentile could become a Christian by faith in Christ, without having to become a Jew first. The answer was no, one does not have to become a Jew or uphold the Mosaic Law to become a Christian. The believers were, instead, to consider the relevance of righteousness by faith and live peaceably with others.

- **Ephesians:** The book of Ephesians was written by the Apostle Paul to the Christian church at Ephesus. It shows the purpose of the church prophetically, as the promise of the Gospel message dates to the earliest of human experiences. As a result, the book examines the purpose of the church, the leadership of the church (with special emphasis on the call and purpose of the apostle), the mystery of the church present in interpersonal relationships, and the call of believers to stand prepared for the eternal battle between good and evil.

- **Philippians:** A short book with a powerful message, the letter of the Philippians was addressed to the church at Philippi by the Apostle Paul. It is an overall message of optimism, acknowledging the apostle's state as a prisoner and how such a circumstance is spreading the Gospel. He is grateful to those who have supported him and warns the Philippians about those who try to reimpose the Mosaic law through rules of circumcision. The letter concludes as the Apostle Paul attempts to resolve conflicts that exist in their church.

- **Colossians:** The letter to the Colossians was written by the Apostle Paul for the Christians at Colossae. The book affirms and instructs on the supremacy of Christ and the results of salvation therein. Christ is our hope! As a result, we should not uphold extreme practices or revert to the Mosaic Law, because our faith does not lie in such things.

- **1 Thessalonians:** 1 Thessalonians was written by the Apostle Paul to the church at Thessalonica. It is largely personal in nature, discussing the Apostle Paul's relationship with the church and specific issues he saw therein, including relationships with one another and ways Christians should behave.

- **2 Thessalonians:** 2 Thessalonians was a second letter written by the Apostle Paul to the church at Thessalonica. It stands to praise the church for enduring through persecution and teaches extensively on the world before and around the Second Coming of Christ. The believers are encouraged to hold fast, despite the times that are to come prior to Christ's return.

- **1 Timothy:** 1 Timothy is a letter written to Timothy by the Apostle Paul. It consists of discussions about church organization and responsibilities for different leaders all while encouraging the faithfulness of the truth. This letter displays the relationship the two had, with the Apostle Paul serving as a spiritual leader and mentor to Timothy, a young apostle.

- **2 Timothy:** 2 Timothy is another letter written to Timothy by the Apostle Paul. It is of a markedly different tone than 1 Timothy, reflecting many ideas and thoughts the Apostle Paul had toward the end of his life. He encourages the Timothy to remain consistent in faith and to be patient through difficulties, all the while upholding the dignity and responsibility of his work as a church leader.

- **Titus:** The epistle to Titus was written to Titus, a bishop in the early church, by the Apostle Paul. Its contents are extensive requirements for elders, deacons, and bishops, desiring to set the churches and their needs in proper order.

- **Philemon:** The letter of Philemon is a short letter written to Philemon by the Apostle Paul on behalf of Onesimus. Onesimus was a slave who had run away from Philemon, his master. Onesimus was to return to Philemon, and Philemon was encouraged to receive him as a beloved brother rather than wayward property. It is a letter encouraging oneness in Christ and love among the brethren, despite social status.

- **Hebrews:** Hebrews is a complex book written to Hebrew Christians (Jewish converts to Christianity) in Jerusalem from an unnamed author. Its contents focus on the centrality of Christ in our faith, written in a style that would have been familiar to Jews of the first century. The issues present in Hebrews provide a powerful lead-in to understanding and seeing faith in Christ as saving, proving such was promised and predicated in the Mosaic Law. By looking at the promises of the Old Testament, we are able to see how we arrived where we are today, and where we will be as we await the time when Christ will take His full power as King over the entire world.

- **James:** The book of James was authored by the Apostle James, to believers scattered throughout the world. His simple letter is easy to understand and echoes basics of the disciplines of church life: how believers should interact, avoid sins, avoid favoritism, and live in simple ways, always remembering the importance of prayer.

- **1 Peter:** 1 Peter was written by the Apostle Peter himself, from "Babylon" (probably Rome) and addressed to the churches of Asia Minor. Its major themes include identification of God's people and their important position as such, as well as encouragement for remaining faithful in persecution and trial, enduring through social discrimination, and being steadfast in the faith.

- **2 Peter:** 2 Peter was written by the Apostle Peter, although its contents are very different from 1 Peter. It was written prior to his death, and encourages believers to remain faithful in Christian living, condemns false teachers, and addresses matters related to the Second Coming.

- **1 John:** Written by the Apostle John (same author as the Gospel of John), 1 John was written in a simple form, using a Hebrew poetic style to reemphasize common themes in different ways. Its main theme is love of God and fellowship with Him, and that the Spirit moves through His people unto righteousness. This is in contrast with false teachers, who do not display or exemplify the love of God with one another.

- **2 and 3 John:** 2 John and 3 John are both authored by the Apostle John, to churches: 2 John is to the "elect lady" (either a reference to a female church leader or the church herself) and 3 John to Gaius, a church leader. Both contain similar themes, discouraging false teachers (antichrists) who deceive Christians), encouraging love, and lauding hospitality.

- **Jude:** Traditionally ascribed to the Apostle Jude, the brother of Jesus, Jude is a short, controversial letter in the New Testament that examines the doctrine of Christ and uses a brief rendition of salvation history to examine that God was not hesitant to handle unbelievers, or those who fell away from the faith. The book contains apocryphal references, namely, those of the Book of Enoch and the Ascension of Moses.

- **Revelation:** Probably best known for its apocalyptic contents, the Revelation (also called the Apocalypse) of John was authored by John the Apostle toward the end of his life, while a prisoner in exile on the Island of Patmos. The Book of Revelation consists of intense visions and mystical experiences had by the Apostle John, revealing the history of the church and its importance, from the earliest of its existence, to the time after Jesus returns. This book concludes with a look at creation after Christ returns, unto His eternal reign, and beyond.

These summaries of Bible books are not meant to be complete, by any stretch of the imagination, but are here to serve as starting points for your study and examination into the Scriptures. By having an overview, you have a launching place to gain a general idea of each book's contents, and study more deeply into the specifics contained therein.

How can a young person stay pure?
   By obeying Your word.
I have tried hard to find You—
   don't let me wander from Your commands.
I have hidden Your word in my heart,
   that I might not sin against You.
I praise you, O LORD;
   teach me Your decrees.

I have recited aloud
  all the regulations You have given us.
I have rejoiced in Your laws
  as much as in riches.
I will study Your commandments
  and reflect on Your ways.
I will delight in Your decrees
  and not forget Your word. (Psalm 119:9-16)

You will probably find yourself more interested in some books than others. This is to be expected, as we all hear God speak to us and reveal powerfully in different ways. All God's Word is a message for us, and we start by receiving from what we understand and experience best as we go along. Start where you understand; start with what you find easiest to receive; and move out from there. When you come across challenging passages, spend more time studying them and learning about their contents. As long as you are willing to take the time, God will continue to speak – and reveal to you – through all the Scriptures. As time goes on, you will probably review and study things again, and get even more out of them than before. This, too, is to be expected. Be encouraged, and continue on in your study!

BIBLE STUDY TOOLS

If you want to study the Bible right, it only makes sense you will need some tools. There are many things people tell us we need for study and service in modern times, but many of them are unnecessary. For solid study, I recommend the following:

- **A Bible:** I acknowledge the importance of Bible apps in our world today. I think it's great we can have the Bible at our fingertips, especially in any time of need. At the same time, we cannot underestimate the value of a printed, bound Bible in tangible book form. Every serious and sincere Bible student needs to be able to use the Bible in book form, without a digital screen or chargeable device. If you desire to use electronic forms of a Bible in addition to your main book-form Bible that's fine, but you need at least one or two Bibles in printed book form for comprehensive reading and study.

  As a secondary point, if you're looking for Bible apps for additional usage, sites such as biblegateway.com and blueletterbible.org have fantastic apps full of research tools. These include concordances, search options, encyclopedias, historical references and tools, and other options that are great for studying the Bible with your fingertips.

- **Notebook or journal and pen:** As a studying student, you should always be prepared to take notes from lessons, sermons, personal studies, and personal revelations received while in study. If you are more into digital notetaking, using a digital writing tablet, notes app on your phone, or other manner of notetaking is essential. However you can best remember and store your notes is the best way to take notes to study the Scriptures.

- **Reference works:** The number of reference works you need varies depending on your aspirations in the faith. Obviously, as a minister with over 20 years of experience, I have a huge library of reference works, books, encyclopedias, and commentaries on different aspects of faith. Someone who is just starting out or doesn't examine and handle Bible discussion and commentary for a living doesn't need to have as much. Still, it is advisable that all serious Bible students should have a few basic tools at their disposal to use for questions and exploration as you go along. I recommend every Bible student have a Bible concordance (a book that lists every word in the Bible and where they can be found), a Bible dictionary, and a Bible atlas (shows different Bible lands and their locations).

- **Devotional works:** Not everyone is into devotional reading. If you are just starting out, it can be very helpful in learning more of the Scriptures. Devotional books take small portions of Scripture and give everyday life stories and applications to help teach lessons from the selected passages. There are many available and there is something for every believer if you are looking for short inspirational words for every day in your life.

SELECTING A BIBLE

So, the last question of Bible study is this: What Bible should I get? This is a valid question, as there are dozens of Bibles and translations available. Walking into a bookstore or a quick glance on the internet can make the process of Bible selection seem overwhelming and intimidating, almost as much as approaching Bible study!

Different Bibles and Bible translations serve different purposes. Much like study materials or devotional books, there is a wide variety of choices to make sure there is room and consideration for everyone. Most people have a preferred translation of the Bible and then a specific Bible that is their favorite, in that same translation. There are many reasons why someone may select a favorite translation and Bible: they love the beauty and eloquence of the language used, they are able to understand it well, it is a translation or Bible that has been used in their family for a long time, they like the way it simplifies Bible ideas and concepts, or they use a Bible that holds significance for them in their lives (such a minister's Bible or a recovery Bible).

The difference between Bibles is not just one of translation, but also one of the nature of commentary or special footnote material therein. Devotional Bibles focus on daily insights around a special theme. Minister's Bibles focus on leadership and ministry issues and may contain additional elements for performing ceremonies, such as weddings or funerals. Some Bibles are designed for recovering addicts, believers who want to study Hebrew better, who speak many languages, want to pray, are in a certain profession, are getting married, or are children. For as many different kinds of people there are, there are Bibles designed to speak to individuals, wherever they may be.

I recommend every Bible student have one of the following:

- A classic translation (Such as the King James Version)
- A modern translation (Such as the New International Version, Amplified Bible, or New Living Translation)
- A paraphrase translation (such as the Message Bible or The Living Bible)
- A translation of the Bible in a language other than your native tongue (a copy in the original Hebrew/Greek, Spanish, French, German, Korean, Japanese, etc.)

In addition to a favorite translation, it is good to have at least a few different ones in order to help compare passages and understand them better. Although it is not possible to expound upon every single translation possible, here is some information on a few common ones to help you understand what is often available.

- **The King James Version (KJV; also called the Authorized**

Version; AV): Either a revision of or the literal 1611 issue of a Bible translation commissioned by King James I of England and brought about by a committee of scholars devoted to promoting the Bible in the English language. Its reading is considered archaic today, but it had a profound impact on language and literature. It is considered a "public domain" work (meaning it is not protected by copyright) and is still popular in many churches. Modern versions of this translation attempt to correct the archaic language and some of the inaccuracies in the text. These include the New King James Version (NKJV), the Modern English Version (MEV), and the Modern King James Bible (MKJV).

- **New International Version (NIV):** The New International Version was commissioned in the mid-1960s by an independent, cross-denominational Christian panel of scholars known as the Committee on Bible Translation who desired to undertake an entirely new translation of the Bible. The project took over ten years and has undergone a few revisions, most notably the 1984 version. It was revised again in 2011 (although some users prefer the 1984 version). Variations of the NIV include Today's New International Version (TNIV), which merged with the New International Version text to create the 2011 revision. The New International Version is lauded for its ability to capture the concepts behind Scriptural passages and for being a readable, relatable translation. It is available in English, Spanish, and Portuguese.

- **New Revised Standard Version (NRSV):** The New Revised Standard Version is an update of the Revised Standard Version (RSV), which was a revision of the American Standard Version (ASV) of 1901. Its goal was to present a readable, scholarly accurate translation of the Bible. Even though it is not popular within the non-denominational Christian sector, the New Revised Standard Version is the authoritative translation in many high Protestant and Catholic circles. It is unique in that it has received approval from Protestant, Catholic, and Orthodox clergy. It seeks literal understanding of the text and was completed in 1989. A recent revision is the NRSVue, which includes 12,000 edits and 20,000 changes. It includes inclusive language choices and a number of scholarly and ecumenical incorporations.

- **The New Living Translation (NLT):** The New Living Translation was inspired by the Living Bible, a popular Bible paraphrase in the 1970s and 1980s. Its translation was completed in 1996, and it has been revised twice since: in 2004 and 2015. Rather than just stand as a paraphrase, the New Living Translation seeks to incorporate the readability of the Living Bible with an actual translation. Instead of striving for literal understanding, the New Living Translation aims to interpret Biblical thoughts and ideas into understandable English. Its simple language makes it appealing to many and has caused it to be one of the best-selling English Bible translations for that reason.

- **Amplified Bible (AMP or AMPC):** The Amplified Bible is technically a revision of the American Standard Version of 1901, but it does so in a unique way. The Amplified Bible can be considered both a translation and a paraphrase, as it offers "amplification" of the text, expounding upon word definition, usage, and thoughts through additional words inserted into passages. It was first published in 1965, although the project itself was revised and expanded over a 30-year period, as it was primarily handled by a singular woman named Frances Siewert. The Amplified Bible has undergone a few revisions over the years, most notably in 2015. Previous versions are now known as the "Amplified Bible Classic Edition."

- **The Message Bible (MSG):** *The Message: The Bible in Contemporary Language* is a paraphrase (meaning it does not seek literal accuracy but rather thoughts, ideas, and interpretation of the text) by Eugene H. Peterson. Eugene Peterson was a Presbyterian minister who sought to make the Bible understandable and relatable in everyday modern English. His project took about nine years to complete, and the entire Bible was released in 2002. Many like the Message Bible because find it easy to understand its essence.

- **The Living Bible (TLB):** The Living Bible was a paraphrase completed by Kenneth Taylor in 1971. Another version that relied on the American Standard Version of 1901, Kenneth Taylor sought to convey thought and idea found in the Bible in common, everyday English. The Living Bible is now only available in limited printings but was a common feature for youth ministry in the

1970s and 1980s. It was the inspiration for the modern-day New Living Translation.

- **International Children's Bible (ICB):** The International Children's Bible is a Bible translation designed to be simple and readable for children. It was translated by scholars who had participated in other modern-day translations and seeks to expound upon the Bible in a way that any child can understand. It was first completed in 1986 and underwent revisions in 1988, 1999, and 2015.

Concerns of Personal Progress

The more you study your Bible and learn about Kingdom people of old, the more you may find yourself tempted to compare yourself to them. We read about Moses and go, "Wow! What faith he had!" It's incredible to think Moses went before Pharaoh, led the Israelites through divine miracle after divine miracle, and stood as their leader through their time in the wilderness. We might look at other Bible figures, such as David or Ruth, or Mary or Peter and Paul in total and complete awe, wishing we had half the faith they did.

It might also be tempting to look around at other believers you know and compare yourself to them. Sister so-and-so is great at volunteering, or Pastor so-and-so is a great preacher, or Brother so-and-so is so profound in his faith, he gets great results from his prayer life. Sometimes our discouragement doesn't even come from looking at others; it comes from within ourselves. If we know we can do better or think we should be somewhere different than where we are, it's tempting to feel down, to feel discouraged and intimidated by this walk of faith. We can wonder if we are even welcome citizens in God's Kingdom anymore.

The first thing we need to step back and realize is that we aren't all the people we are comparing ourselves to…and neither are they! Every Bible character who seems great and laudable had some point in Scripture where they didn't measure up. Moses got frustrated and temperamental with the Israelites. David had an affair with Bathsheba while Bathsheba was married to someone else. I'm sure Ruth had periods where she was frustrated and tired, as she had to labor in difficult conditions for survival. Mary sought to show off Jesus' abilities at the wedding at Cana. Peter and Paul both had intense tempers and liked to exert authority, whether it was always appropriate to do so. For every reality we see that's great and faithful, there is another side to those people.

Does this mean they were all failures? No, it means they were human beings, just like we are. Their failures exist to inspire us through ours. No matter how many times we trip and fall, we are given God's grace to get up again. Instead of looking at Bible characters and feeling hopeless, we should feel encouraged to know that if God stuck with them, He will also stick with us.

The same is true for those you look around and see in faith today. You don't know what happens behind closed doors, when no one is around, or what problems they might have in their personal lives. Not everything is the way it looks on a Sunday morning or in a social media photo. No one finds themselves consistently happy or enthralled with things all the time. We all face discouragement, difficulties, and periods where we question our faith. That is why we are encouraged to be honest about such things, even if other people aren't. Comparing ourselves to what we think exists is like trying to do something you have never done before and expecting it to come out perfect. You don't know the struggles or difficulties of those who handle their own issues, so how can you ever assume you are handling it in an inferior way?

God knows who we are and what He is getting when we surrender ourselves to Him. He knows we aren't perfect, and He knows we are going to mess up. That is what grace is for; those times when we just don't feel like we've done the best we can do. God does desire, however, that we stop focusing on our failures. The concepts of conviction and repentance are there to let us know when it's time to turn around, to change, and to do something different. If we learn to listen to that rather than our own feelings of insecurity or inferiority, we will go a long way in our spiritual progress. Our advancement in the Kingdom might not look like someone else's or feel like someone else's, but if we learn to rely on God's direction and have trusted people we can talk to and lean upon through difficult times, we can believe we will wind up where we are, when we are supposed to be there.

Don't grumble about each other, brothers and sisters, or you will be judged. For look—the Judge is standing at the door!

For examples of patience in suffering, dear brothers and sisters, look at the prophets who spoke in the Name of the Lord. We give great honor to those who endure under suffering. For instance, you know about Job, a man of great endurance. You can see how the Lord was kind to him at the end, for the Lord is full of tenderness and mercy.

But most of all, my brothers and sisters, never take an oath, by heaven or earth or anything else. Just say a simple yes or no, so that you will not sin and be condemned.

Are any of you suffering hardships? You should pray. Are any of you happy? You should sing praises. Are any of you sick? You should call for the elders of the church to come and pray over you, anointing you with oil in the Name of the Lord. Such a prayer offered in faith will heal the sick, and the Lord will make you well. And if you have committed any sins, you will be forgiven.

Confess your sins to each other and pray for each other so that you may be healed. The earnest prayer of a righteous person has great power and produces wonderful results. (James 5:9-16)

It is God's ultimate desire that we come to a point where we are willing and able to work together for the good of each other and the edification of His Kingdom. When we fail, we should be able to confess our failings to one another and pray for one another. We should reach a place of maturity where we stop talking about one another behind our backs and stop complaining about each other. When one of us is suffering, we should be there to support each other and encourage one another in the faith. By studying the Scriptures, we are especially encouraged to examine the situation of Job. Job had to endure through terrible times and people who told him to abandon his faith and His God. He had a long discussion with God and those around him about creation, wisdom, suffering, and why we face difficulties in life. Yet through it all, we never once see Job abandon his faith. While others around him seemed to live in wealth and promise, Job had to endure through a time of difficult suffering and the temptation to believe his trial was because of the unfairness of God. Job persevered through, proving to all of us that difficult times never last, and we can always come into a good place if we remain faithful to God's promises in His Kingdom.

There is no question there will be times when you will feel like Job and face situations that don't seem to have an answer. These times can become discouraging. In such times, reflect on your faith, and how far you have come. Don't look at everyone else or compare yourself to others; instead, be encouraged. See the humanity of all God's people and know you will be able to get through this. Rely on Kingdom friends, embracing the community He's sent into your life to encourage and edify you in difficult times. Above all, embrace the presence of God Himself. The

Kingdom of God will take you a far distance in your life if you are able and willing to remain a part of it!

~ CHAPTER THREE ~
THE KINGDOM OF GOD IS AMONG YOU!

So far, we have studied two main headings of the Kingdom of God and its positioning in our lives. This will be the third main heading we will use for that purpose, even though Kingdom and Kingdom life will be a continuous theme throughout this book. Here we are going to look at the ways the Kingdom of God works among us, as a dynamic between others and ourselves in our lives.

As we've already discussed, none of us are an island. We have interactions with other people, we engage with them, we experience life through them, and we have the opportunity to see God work through them and God work through us on their behalf. Here we are going to take a long look at these different dynamics, how they work, and how we can best participate in this Kingdom of God working within, around, and among us.

<u>THE KINGDOM OF HEAVEN HERE ON EARTH</u>

I've been asked many times, what is the difference between the Kingdom of God and the Kingdom of heaven? The simplest answer is nothing, save location. The Kingdom of God is the Kingdom of heaven here on earth and in heaven, because it all belongs to God. The Kingdom of heaven represents the location of God's throne, the seat of His authority. This means the Kingdom of God is the Kingdom of heaven come to earth; the "meeting place," if you will, of those who love and follow Him and accept His authority. It is the place where the veil between our current realities and time meets eternity and touches it, bringing us into a realm that is beyond what we can see with the naked eye.

It is this profound spiritual meeting that makes us realize God's power and the transformation we undergo now as "citizens of heaven." No matter where we are, God transforms our time and space. We have the power to know He is with us, and we are with Him. Not only is He with us, but He is also among us, because we are a part of eternity with Him.

I decree that everyone throughout my kingdom should tremble with
fear before the God of Daniel.
For He is the living God,
and He will endure forever.
His kingdom will never be destroyed,
and His rule will never end.
He rescues and saves His people;
He performs miraculous signs and wonders
in the heavens and on earth.
He has rescued Daniel
from the power of the lions. (Daniel 6:26-27)

He prayed, "O Lord, God of our ancestors, You alone are the God Who is in heaven. You are ruler of all the kingdoms of the earth. You are powerful and mighty; no one can stand against You! (2 Chronicles 20:6)

"Repent of your sins and turn to God, for the Kingdom of Heaven is near." (Matthew 3:2)

From then on Jesus began to preach, "Repent of your sins and turn to God, for the Kingdom of Heaven is near." (Matthew 4:17)

So if you ignore the least commandment and teach others to do the same, you will be called the least in the Kingdom of Heaven. But anyone who obeys God's laws and teaches them will be called great in the Kingdom of Heaven. (Matthew 5:19)

Seek the Kingdom of God above all else, and live righteously, and He will give you everything you need. (Matthew 6:33)

Whenever we talk about the Kingdom of God, we are talking about a powerful unity in existence. It relates to God's authority as our Creator and as the single entity that is God in any realm. It acknowledges the special relationship we have with God. No matter what might be going on in the world, we answer to heavenly authority. This is why the Kingdom of heaven is spoken of being "at hand." That literally means it is so close, we can reach out and touch it. It is God's Kingdom, it is within, around, and among us, and there is no reason we need to ever question, or doubt God is with us. Sure, we all have periods in our lives where God feels silent, but silent does not mean absent. It just means God desires to sit and rest with us awhile, to relax our over-troubled minds and anxieties in His loving silence. He is the Ruler of all, He is powerful and mighty, and has entrusted us as guardians of His glory and His Kingdom here on this earth.

This realization should cause us to stand back in a certain level of awe and amazement at the wonders of God. The honor we have as individuals in His Kingdom is overwhelming! We are a part of something bigger and stronger than this world. To reap its full benefits, we are called to conduct ourselves on this earth as we would if heaven was right here (because in the Kingdom, we understand that it is). How we behave matters because it reflects the power of our King, the One Who rules our Kingdom. He's not far off or distant, like some earthly kings. We don't have to go miles away to find Him. Through the Spirit, God guides us through each and every situation that is hard and guides us to the right thing, no matter how impossible it may seem.

This means it is possible for us to walk the Christian walk as God desires us to do so. We won't do everything right all the time, but we can always make that effort, pick ourselves up, and follow the leading of the Spirit next time. If we see ourselves as walking in the bigger picture of eternity, it gives everything we do that much more meaning and purpose. What we do isn't just about now or even tomorrow but about connecting with and being part of the life of God, something that will last forever.

The Kingdom is shared

It's a nice idea to think the Kingdom of God is just your own personal entity and nothing you do, or anyone does, has any impact on anyone or anything else. It's wrong to assume that no matter what we do, God will look the other way or that we can do the wrong thing and not have any consequences. This attitude is a frustration of grace, one that is all-too common among many people. God's grace doesn't erase our wrongdoing; it makes the way for it to find a place of redemption. God still expects us to consider the way our actions impact on our relationship with Him and on other people.

Whether someone else is already a believer and part of the Kingdom or someone has not yet become fully aware of all there is to experience in Kingdom life, one of our primary responsibilities as believers is to live this Kingdom experience. That means how we live is important to God, and important to all of us who are in the Kingdom. What one does reflects on the Kingdom as a whole, and that means it all matters.

The Kingdom of God is about God and His interactions with all of us. This means the Kingdom of God is special, because it's not just about us as individuals. It's about you, me, and every other believer throughout this world. It's about just how much we believe in God, and just how much God has transformed us through this Kingdom living. Because we now live as part of this Kingdom, it has transformed us from the inside out. We are now different, and it's a difference that is to be celebrated.

And so, dear brothers and sisters, I plead with you to give your bodies to God because of all He has done for you. Let them be a living and holy sacrifice—the kind He will find acceptable. This is truly the way to worship Him. Don't copy the behavior and customs of this world, but let God transform you into a new person by changing the way you think. Then you will learn to know God's will for you, which is good and pleasing and perfect.

Because of the privilege and authority God has given me, I give each of you this warning: Don't think you are better than you really are. Be honest in your evaluation of yourselves, measuring yourselves by the faith God has given us. Just as our bodies have many parts and each part has a special function, so it is with Christ's body. We are many parts of one body, and we all belong to each other. (Romans 12:1-5)

There are many Bible passages that people question, debate, and study with a powerful curiosity because their contents aren't always what they might seem on the surface. This isn't one of those passages, although some backstory information helps us understand it more. In Biblical times, people didn't just practice magic with herbs and wild potions; they also practiced magic with their bodies. They believed by offering up their very literal selves (often in sexual rites) it would unite them with their gods and would bring about pleasing results in their lives. The Apostle Paul contrasted living for God with living according to these different ways, those that united with demons and thus led to living in ways completely contrary to the Kingdom of God. We are urged by the Apostle Paul to make sure that we live right in every possible way, that we treat our very being as a reflection of God and a temple of the Holy Spirit, a place where God's Kingdom can reside and work within us. Instead of offering endless sacrifices, God asks us to offer ourselves to Him. Instead of being like everyone else, God wants us to come to know His will for us, and reside in that promise that is good, pleasing, and perfect.

The Apostle Paul also warns us against thinking more of ourselves than we ought. In the Kingdom of God, we all start again when we are born again. It doesn't matter what successes we have in this world; we all start again and come to a true place of equality in our walk. As great and grand as the world may view us, we should always esteem ourselves properly. We must recognize who we are and that the advancements we've made in our faith are all thanks to God's work within us, not our own powers or our own desires to be better people.

The Apostle Paul also clarifies that in this Kingdom, we all have a purpose. Recognizing our purpose in God's Kingdom helps us to know what we have to offer and identify where we best "fit" in the Body. Because we are a part of many parts, we need to know just how we can operate (what we can offer) to make sense of Kingdom participation. When we know this, we are better able to interact in the Kingdom with others and to offer the proper honor, respect, and yes, even submission where it is due in the Kingdom.

Want to know more about this? Keep reading!

Discerning Kingdom Purpose

Answering the questions, "Why am I here? What am I supposed to do?" are among the most difficult tasks we face in this life. From the time we are very young, we are often asked, "What do you want to be when you grow up?" by well-meaning adults (some of whom probably didn't have answers to these questions for themselves, either). As we grew, we figured out certain answers to that question were more desirable than others. We got far more praise from others if we said we wanted to be a police officer or doctor than we did if we said we wanted to be a garbage collector or a store clerk. It was obvious we were encouraged to pursue certain interests more than we pursued others.

If we look back over our lives, it's probably safe to say we had many influences that shaped what we desired to do and who we desired to become. When we've become Christians and are overlooking Kingdom life, one of two things often happens: either we have many influences, or we don't have many. The longer we are believers, the more it is often expected we will be able to sort some of these things out on our own. It's assumed that as we study the Bible more, attend more classes, services, and are around Christian influences, the more we will figure out where we best belong in the Kingdom on our own.

Sometimes it's easy to figure out our purpose in God's Kingdom; sometimes it's more difficult. We usually reach a place where we can see the overall vision, but figuring out the details is often what trips us up. We might know what God wants us to do but taking each and every step to get to the overall vision may be much more difficult to discern.

What is God calling you to do? Who is God calling you to be? How do you best fit in the bigger picture of His Kingdom? Let's look at these questions, one at a time.

For we are God's [own] handiwork (His workmanship), recreated in Christ Jesus, [born anew] that we may do those good works which God predestined (planned beforehand) for us [taking paths which He prepared ahead of time], that we should walk in them [living the good life which He prearranged and made ready for us to live]. (Ephesians 2:10, AMPC)

Ephesians 2:10 gives us true security to know that since God is our Creator, He knows us in a way that is for our great benefit as we come to know ourselves. What better way to know ourselves than to know the One Who made us? He can give us insights into what is best for us, where our talents and gifts can best be utilized, what will work with our temperaments, and what to do when we encounter situations that bring us into new levels of spiritual growth and understanding. He has prepared us to have a good life, one that connects us to Him. What exactly it means for the life to be "good" does vary, and it's not just about money or prestige. It's about quality and following the paths and promises He has for us through that good end.

Our ultimate purpose with God is to know Him, love Him, and come to a place in our lives where we are willing to serve Him in His Kingdom. This means whatever we are called to do will bring us closer to Him. God isn't going to call you to do something that will take you away from Him in this life, so it's safe to say whatever He calls you to do should enhance your practical life as well as your spiritual life. Communion with God is not just something for ministers, but something for everyone in Christ. No matter what you are called to do, do it with joy and with all your heart. There is no position that is lower than another in the Kingdom. It is just as important if you are called to operate an auto parts store or work as a store clerk than it is if you are called to be a banker, lawyer, or full-time minister. We need a diversity of people called to do different things so we can trust those who operate in their professions. The Kingdom's purpose is to expand, spread, and influence people in every dimension, and that doesn't just mean such influence is restricted to preachers. Every one of us is called to stand solid in what we do, properly representing our faith at work, behaving in a manner that is both relatable and likable to other people, doing honest work, and behaving with ethics everywhere we go. No matter what you are called to do, you can always live your faith while you do it.

God often speaks to us about our calling through the things we do best and find most interesting. If you have a real knack for something or find something real interesting, there's a good chance that you have a skill that will relate to the development of something that can serve as a calling for you. What speaks to you in life? What interests you? What inspires you? Whatever it is, seek out God in prayer about it. Talk to a trusted friend or leader about it. Learn how you can pursue it more in your life and see where such leads you.

In asking who God is calling you to be, the answer is three-fold. The first is He is asking you to become the best version of yourself that He has created you to be. This involves rising to the challenge as God starts to work within you. As we start to change our behavior, we can see our negative, fleshly behavior often masks the true nature God has placed within us. As our actions change, we can see parts of ourselves, our personalities, and our being come to light.

This means what you feel drawn to in this life may change, but that's not necessarily a bad thing. It's great to want to expand your life and your interests. The more we expand out, the more things we will find that lead us to God and help us to love Him, even more. This is the second part of who God is calling you to be: He is calling you to be His child, His believer, His warrior, all in a different way than you have done before. This will challenge you to take greater strides in your faith and move toward deeper things.

The third aspect to who God is calling you to be has to do with how you engage with and treat other people. If you are really working with God, you should reach a point where you aren't comfortable mistreating other people. There is no reason, nor excuse, to be rude, abusive, arrogant, or hateful in your conduct, speech, or actions. Just as the Holy Spirit moves in us by grace and power, so we should move in the same way. We should be people who reflect the purpose, or fruit of the Spirit's work, within us.

The next question is related to the first two: How do you best fit in the bigger picture of His Kingdom? No matter what the answer is to that, there is a place for you in God's Kingdom. It may not always feel like it and sometimes it takes you awhile to find your right fit, but there is somewhere in God's Kingdom for you. It may change over time as you come to a better sense of your purpose and calling, but the fact that you fit into this Kingdom is a huge definite. As people growing in God, we need to hear great teaching that brings out the work of the Spirit within us, that educates us and encourages us. We need the fellowship of other trusted Christians to bless us. We also need to have great leaders we can talk to and sort out whatever we are experiencing as we go through our spiritual transformations and growth.

I can't answer for you how you best fit in the bigger picture of God's Kingdom, because as a reader, I don't know you personally. I haven't seen your walk with God, and I don't know what your spiritual gifts are or where your strengths lie. I can tell you, however, that the answer to where you best fit in lies in the areas I just mentioned. Prayer and recognizing God's leading in your life is essential! This is why it's so important to develop a great relationship with other Kingdom believers and with a leader who can help you sort out and answer all these questions. If you have people in your life who know you in a profound way.

Know that no matter where you are in your discernment process, it is all right to be where you are. You don't have to have everything figured out right now. It's all right if you don't have the job of your dreams, or to have days where you trip up and don't act as right as you know you should. We are all figuring this thing out, and working things out, one at a time, is how we get to the victory in Christ. Whatever happens, don't give up. God is not going to give up on you, even when you don't get it right. That's what grace is for: when we do our best, but still slip up, God reminds us that He is still there for us and we still need Him in our lives.

The Product of the Spirit

No matter how long you've been a Christian, you have probably heard of "the fruit of the Spirit" at some time. It's a curious topic to many because while it is mentioned from time to time, there isn't a lot of devotion to it as a topic. As an overall thematic topic, the fruit of the Spirit is involved. It's not a complicated subject matter, but it is intense and hits home at everything that's part of the believer's life. The fruit of our Christian life – of the work of the Spirit within us – is not found in spiritual gifts or speaking in tongues, even though these things are important evidence of the Spirit's presence in our lives. While spiritual gifts reveal the Spirit is present somewhere, the fruit of the Spirit does something different within us. The fruit of the Spirit is different in that it is a product of a long-term cooperative effort as you work with the Spirit and the Spirit works to transform your personal nature into something different from where you started. Where you used to chase after things that were not of God and did not lead to life, you now have the reflection of a spiritual nature at work within you.

So I say, let the Holy Spirit guide your lives. Then you won't be doing what your sinful nature craves. The sinful nature wants to do evil, which is just the opposite of what the Spirit wants. And the Spirit gives us desires that are the opposite of what the sinful nature desires. These two forces are constantly fighting each other, so you are not free to carry out your good intentions. But when you are directed by the Spirit, you are not under obligation to the law of Moses.

When you follow the desires of your sinful nature, the results are very clear: sexual immorality, impurity, lustful pleasures, idolatry, sorcery, hostility, quarreling, jealousy, outbursts of anger, selfish ambition, dissension, division, envy, drunkenness, wild parties, and other sins like these. Let me tell you again, as I have before, that anyone living that sort of life will not inherit the Kingdom of God. (Galatians 5:16-21)

When the Spirit doesn't guide our lives, we chase after things that our own nature, the creation of ourselves in this world, craves. We want to do things that are self-centered, controlling, pleasure-seeking, keep God from being first in our lives, angry, quarrelsome, difficult, jealous, dividing, envious, given to the abuse of substances, and wildly seeking after partying lifestyles. If we look at the list provided, many of the behaviors that deter us from others are found on that list. No one wants to be around someone who is controlling or enchanted by all the wrong things. We don't like the company of people who are self-centered, angry, argumentative, difficult, or jealous and envious. It's impossible to maintain friendships with people who are always causing division, and after a while, sexual impulsiveness, partying lifestyles and addicts are difficult to keep around as friends or family members. They are behaviors that repel, that keep from solid connections and make it so others don't want to be around them.

It only stands reasonable that things which repel us would be unattractive to others in us, as well. It also only stands to reason that if it is God's desire to draw people to Him, the Spirit would not work within us in a manner this repelling to others. We can't maintain a bunch of behaviors that think only of ourselves and nothing of others and call ourselves "Christians." No matter how much we might experience incredible spiritual outpourings and how much we might see the signs and wonders of God, we cannot rightly draw people to the Father through

our witness if we act unseemly (in the flesh) at other times in our lives.
This is where the fruit of the Spirit comes in.

But the Holy Spirit produces this kind of fruit in our lives: love, joy, peace, patience, kindness, goodness, faithfulness, gentleness, and self-control. There is no law against these things!

Those who belong to Christ Jesus have nailed the passions and desires of their sinful nature to His cross and crucified them there. Since we are living by the Spirit, let us follow the Spirit's leading in every part of our lives. Let us not become conceited, or provoke one another, or be jealous of one another. (Galatians 5:22-26)

What is most notable to me about this passage is the statement made by the Apostle Paul after the list of attributes present in the fruit of the Spirit (we will discuss those momentarily). The Apostle Paul makes the statement that there is "no law against these things!" When speaking of the things relating to the flesh's nature, we find a long list of things that are "regulated" by various legalities all over the world. There are many, many sinful behaviors that have their origins in the laundry list of fleshly issues listed earlier in Galatians 5. All sorts of governments have rules about immoral sexual behavior, drug and alcohol abuse, trying to take something over that isn't yours, practicing magic, or behaving in wrong ways. Yet if we look in contrast with life in the Spirit, there is no law against experiencing the product of spiritual fruit in one's life. It is a powerful thing to let the Holy Spirit change our nature, and by doing so, we are led into a place of life where we seek no harm and cause no offense to anyone.

The fruit of the Spirit, as a product, is identified as a singular "fruit," not "fruits." This is because when we walk in the Spirit, we find the product of those things to come from the one Spirit of God. Those are listed as love, joy, peace, patience, kindness, goodness, faithfulness, gentleness, and self-control. What do these things look like, and what do they mean?

- **Love:** When the Bible speaks of "love" and loving others, it's not in a romantic context. It is in a practical context that we seek whatever we might desire for ourselves for others, in the highest hope and possible good. We are called to love others with this hope and love, because we recognize love comes from God. If we truly love God and we find ourselves motivated by Him, we should have the ability to see others through this love lens. It is not flouncy or dependent on the way we feel about people, but a true spiritual expression that runs through everything in our lives.

- **Joy:** Joy is a consistent outlook on life that recognizes what we have in God and sees our spiritual realities as a source of delight and hope. We can recognize the desires of our heart through the Lord and that state of hope, of desiring greater spiritual things, manifests in the way we see our lives. Even in difficult times, we can trust God has our well-being at hand and that spirituality is our true measure of success.

- **Peace:** Biblical peace is more than understanding it as the absence of difficulty and strife. In Bible languages, peace represents a state of wholeness or completion, one that reflects a state of satisfaction and contentment. To find exterior peace, we must first find this true state of peace in our spiritual foundations. When we are at peace with God, we are at peace with ourselves and are better able to exercise a place of peace with others. It keeps us from seeking out the hostile route with others in our lives and causes us to hate strife and love contentment.

- **Patience:** Patience is more than being able to wait for things or to wait for things well. Patience is the ability to remain consistent and work constantly for the end goal while waiting. It determines our faithfulness to a thing or a situation, even when we aren't sure how long an outcome might be.

- **Kindness:** As a rule, many who claim to be Christian are highly defensive of their belief systems and their faith. They feel others are automatically against them and reflect a sense of hostility and anger in their general interactions, whether such is intended. Kindness breaks through that barrier, with the ability to turn enemies into friends and strangers into family. Kindness is the quality of being kind, of being sincerely interested in the welfare of others and presenting that interest in a genuine fashion. It isn't about "making nice" or pretending to be something that one is not but about taking a genuine interest in others and offering what someone has to better another.

- **Goodness:** Goodness is exactly what it sounds like – the manifestation of good, of the attributes of God that have the power to transform any situation into something spiritual. It is not fake goodness or goodness there to please others, but remembering that no one is good, except for God, that God works within us to bring about good things in this world. We can do good within ourselves and good for others because God lives within us.

- **Faithfulness:** Faithfulness is the quality of being able to stand faithful or remain with something long-term because we trust or have a standing faith in it. This is most poignant when it comes to our faith, but also relates in other areas of our lives, as well. If we are people of faith, we should be those that can be trusted, relied upon, and can see something through from start to finish. If we are faithful, we should show commitment to our beliefs, to our relationships, to our jobs and responsibilities, and to the Kingdom of God, in all situations, no matter what comes along in our lives.

- **Gentleness:** Sometimes translated as "humility," gentleness relates to the state or condition by which we handle ourselves and situations in this world. When we are gentle, we recognize our power comes from the Holy Spirit, and not by exerting might or force. This means we will operate as the Spirit would desire – with peace and respect, not seeking to provoke others to anger or embitterment. In gentleness, we carry ourselves with spiritual insight, and seek solutions, rather than force, in every situation we face.

- **Self-control:** Nobody likes the idea of coming to a place of self-mastery in this world. We like the idea of blaming others for our problems or bad behaviors. Entire industries now exist where people spend lots of hard-earned money to be convinced their own issues came from somewhere else. There's no question it's great to understand more of the conditioning into who we are, but when it comes to understanding Scripture, we cannot deny we are supposed to be people who can control their impulses, actions, and desires. If we can't, we will face numerous problems that hurt us in the long run and will keep us from the spiritual advancement we desire. As human beings, we must learn the principles of self-discipline, sacrifice, and maturity. Those things only come about as we can control ourselves.

The fruit of the Spirit is a spiritual development, which means it can take a while to see all these nine aspects manifest in our lives. Founded on love and held together by self-control, seeing this work of the Spirit within you is most exciting and profound. The more ground you gain, the more you can recognize the Spirit's presence in your life, working through you and revealing more to you as you become more spiritually aware and perceptive.

Do unto others

When I was a child in a local public school, we had what we called the "Golden Rule." We were encouraged to always "do unto others as we would have them do unto you." I didn't realize it at the time, but it was from a passage of Scripture found in Luke 6:27-36:

"But to you who are willing to listen, I say, love your enemies! Do good to those who hate you. Bless those who curse you. Pray for those who hurt you. If someone slaps you on one cheek, offer the other cheek also. If someone demands your coat, offer your shirt also. Give to anyone who asks; and when things are taken away from you, don't try to get them back. Do to others as you would like them to do to you.

"If you love only those who love you, why should you get credit for that? Even sinners love those who love them! And if you do good only to those who do good to you, why should you get credit? Even sinners do that much! And if you lend money only to those who can repay you, why should you get credit? Even sinners will lend to other sinners for a full return.

"Love your enemies! Do good to them. Lend to them without expecting to be repaid. Then your reward from heaven will be very great, and you will truly be acting as children of the Most High, for He is kind to those who are unthankful and wicked. You must be compassionate, just as your Father is compassionate."

This plain, simple, and uncomplicated Biblical advice should make us realize much of what we try to do in this Christian thing isn't as hard as we often make it out to be. Whenever we must start asking the question, "what should I do?" or "how do I love my neighbor?" the answer is often much simpler than we would expect. We can debate and break things down into tons of specific examples, but there is no greater merit than to say if we want to show the world we love them and we have been transformed by the work of the Spirit, we treat them with the same intent and regard as we would want to be treated.

Think about it: How do you want to be treated? I would expect that whether you are someone's friend or not, you would still want to be treated as well as possible. You wouldn't want them to wait on you in a restaurant and spit in your food, or damage your clothes at the dry cleaners', or refuse you service somewhere all because they don't like you. You would still want to be treated like any other customer, given the same consideration as anyone else.

The Bible teaches us that loving our neighbor relates in many ways to how we treat our neighbor. It's not all about who we like best or cozying up to those most beneficial but about making sure we avoid partiality and instead treat other people right. This fact can be true regardless of how we might internally feel about someone, as hard as that might be to believe. I have met people who have the best of intentions with others, but because they don't make the effort to try and reach out and treat others well, their care for others remains nothing more than a musing.

This passage in Luke 6 speaks to me very loudly because Jesus' examples of doing to others as you would have them do to you are not about anyone with which the disciples would have been friends. Jesus never gave the example, "If you love your friends, it'll look like this." Nope! Jesus challenged them with examples of loving enemies: Roman soldiers, government officials, people who felt they were entitled to other's goods because of their social position, and those who are greedy or borrow without repay. All these people were those who were easily to dislike, and for good reason. Yet Jesus doesn't tell us we have to like all of them, but we must look out over the bigger situation and still witness and extend the love of God to them through our actions. Instead of returning their wickedness, we should treat them in the way we would desire to be treated.

We make the Kingdom of God manifest on this earth, reasonable and real to others, when we interact with others in a manner that edifies and encourages them. It's always good to take a step back and ask ourselves, would I be offended by such behavior done toward me? Would I be bothered if what I was saying was about me? Would it upset me if someone was doing to me what I am doing to them?

If the answer is yes, then it's time to realize you aren't loving others as you love yourself, and deal with that in your life.

Responsibility

There are some who teach that once you become a Christian,

responsibility is now fair game. We leave it up to God to "fight all our battles" and we blame everything on God or the devil. If something isn't going right in our lives, we blame the devil and complain of intense spiritual warfare. Sometimes it is true that we go through things that reflect spiritual battles, and we must rise to deal with those situations. It is also true that much of the time, things come up that we don't want to address and could be avoided or handled if we step up and accept responsibility in our lives.

Being a Christian doesn't mean we suddenly get to avoid responsibility for life. Our faith does not exist to help us ignore or sidestep life and its downfalls. On the contrary, it is there to help us get through them. Being a Christian, as we can see from our study on the fruit of the Spirit, should enhance our ability to do better and be better. Our faith recognizes that while we cannot do this alone, we can do it with God. That means we step up and are willing to do what needs to be done and be who we are called to be. Such shows spiritual maturity and that God can trust us with many more things, no matter how difficult they may seem. We can get through it, because God encourages us to responsibility.

Do the same if you find your neighbor's donkey, clothing, or anything else your neighbor loses. Don't ignore your responsibility. (Deuteronomy 22:3)

Take a lesson from the ants, you lazybones.
  Learn from their ways and become wise!
Though they have no prince
  or governor or ruler to make them work,
they labor hard all summer,
  gathering food for the winter. (Proverbs 6:6-8)

Work willingly at whatever you do, as though you were working for the Lord rather than for people. (Colossians 3:23)

But those who won't care for their relatives, especially those in their own household, have denied the true faith. Such people are worse than unbelievers. (1 Timothy 5:8)

What do these passages tell us about being responsible? A lot, actually. They remind us that it is important to be productive, diligent people. We should never be people who try to take the easy way out of things or who avoid doing a great job. On our jobs, we should aim to do the best possible job we can. In our lives, we should aim to be good friends, partners, and spouses. We should do what we see that needs doing instead of taking the lazy route. This is not saying we should become taskmasters and never rest, but it is also saying we need to find the balance between responsibly doing what needs to be done and finding time for rest in our lives. We can summarize our call to responsibility like this:

- If you make an agreement, you need to keep it.
- If you make a promise, you need to keep it.
- If you agree or promise to do something, you need to do it.
- If you've given your word, you need to keep it.
- If you have a job, you need to do it.
- If you have a family, you need to be responsible and take care of them.
- If you are part of a community, you need to participate in it.

When responsibilities arise, don't avoid them or try to get out of them.

SACRIFICE

Sacrifice is one of those terms that is almost treated like a cuss word in modern-day Christianity. We don't like the idea that sometimes we have to make choices and decisions between things and that we can't always have everything we want, all the time. Even as Christians, we must accept the fact that God does require us to make choices in our lives between things and sometimes it's nothing more than disciplining ourselves to choose the better or more disciplined option over another one.

Sometimes we must decide to do what is best for our spiritual growth and maturity rather than what might be the most fun, most entertaining, or most profitable. Sometimes we just must suck it up and accept our spiritual lives are for our good, not our amusement. If we are to be people of faith, we must do it all the way, not part of the way. Sometimes that means choices.

Once upon a time, I had a man on my Facebook page who deemed himself a relationship expert because he was divorced. The entirety of his posts was to prove he was ready for a new relationship, and he often gave out extensive marital advice. Whether or not he was qualified is a whole other issue all together, but he would pose questions online to create controversy and dissention in relationships. One day, he asked the question: If you are getting ready to go to church and your husband announces he doesn't want to go to church today, he wants to go to the beach instead of church, where do you go?

The question serves as nothing more than a trap to get people in trouble and cause trouble in marriages, and such was evident in the way people fought and argued with their answers. I was also shocked at the number of people who said they'd throw over church and just go to the beach, because their marriage was more important than attending a church service. There were no solutions offered to provide a compromise or some suggestions to find a middle road. The question simply posed trouble.

I say the question posed trouble because the implication behind the question is what was more important to you – your marriage or your relationship with God? The question pitted spouses against God and against support of that relationship with God. Everyone who said they would go to church were met with hostile comments and innuendos their marriages would fall apart. The fact that such was the outlook tells me one thing: we don't understand sacrifice, and that means we don't know the first thing about spiritual growth or how to make our interactions with others any better. This is all because we don't understand our relationship with God.

There were many different options that could have offered a compromise. The couple could have decided to go to the beach after church service was over. They could have decided to go to the beach on another day. They could have taken a vacation or scheduled a special trip to the beach. If they couldn't go to church and the beach on such short notice, they could have opted to do something else together that wouldn't seem like a tug of war between their relationship to God and their relationship with each other. There are many, many ways they could have come to an agreement that wouldn't threaten either relationship, but because many people didn't want to sacrifice their own interests or their own fun, they attacked those who sought to do what they felt was most important.

We've gotten the message over the past thirty or so years that the ultimate life goal is to "have it all." We expect we can have the great marriage, the great kids, the great job, the great income, the great relationship with God, and the great friendships and none of it come at a price. The truth is that life is just not like this. We can't "have it all," at least not at the same time. To have certain things and do those things well, we must have the needed focus and discipline to do them well. We can't do too many things at once and expect we will be able to handle everything in the way we might like to do so.

For example: If you are married, you must consider your career choices carefully. You can't spend all your time climbing the corporate ladder and neglecting the needs your spouse has. You can't have children and then not take proper care of them. You can't buy a new house and ignore its care and maintenance. Every time we choose to do one thing, we must consider the long-term repercussions for ourselves. We simply can't have it all, because God knows we can't handle it.

These choices are especially true when it comes to our relationship with God. I am not saying God is asking you to choose between Him and your spouse or others, because we already know God is supposed to be first in our lives. I also don't believe God puts us in the predicament of having to choose between spending time with Him and with others, as the man on Facebook did. I do believe, however, that at some times, we are confronted with the choice to do something that will enhance our spiritual lives, or not. It might seem like the choices pull at the very fabric of who we are: we have to choose between what we might like or want, versus what might be good for us.

Then He said to the crowd, "If any of you wants to be My follower, you must give up your own way, take up your cross daily, and follow Me. If you try to hang on to your life, you will lose it. But if you give up your life for My sake, you will save it. And what do you benefit if you gain the whole world but are yourself lost or destroyed?" (Luke 9:23-25)

Live a life filled with love, following the example of Christ. He loved us and offered Himself as a sacrifice for us, a pleasing aroma to God. (Ephesians 5:2)

And you are living stones that God is building into his spiritual temple. What's more, you are his holy priests. Through the mediation of Jesus Christ, you offer spiritual sacrifices that please God. (1 Peter 2:5)

No, God doesn't ask us to offer our own sacrifices for the sake of our sin and our redemption. There is a difference between the sacrifice for sin and the reality that sometimes we are forced to make choices between things for the good of our spiritual lives and to do what's right. That is what God desires us to see: we must be willing to offer up our own choices, one at a time, for the good of our own spiritual lives. We follow Christ's example in this.

Sacrifice doesn't seem fun when it comes up in our lives. It requires us to decide what is most important to us. Sometimes choices never seem like great options, and at other times, the choices we must make are hard or difficult. The most important thing to remember is that when we make these choices wisely, we come into a place of greater spiritual victory. It doesn't mean we won't face it again, but that as we learn the principle of sacrifice, we will find we gain something far more valuable when we walk away from whatever keeps us from God or better spiritual lives in the long run.

Humility

I was once on Facebook when someone came in my inbox, full of stories about himself. He was quick to state how great he was and all his accomplishments: he'd been on television and written many books. It was clear he was quite pleased with himself and felt his merits alone were enough to get my attention.

I, on the other hand, was not impressed. I even said so. I told him how much I disliked shameless self-promotion, and that humility was far more attractive than such obvious pride. It's probably not a big surprise to learn he didn't respond well to my lack of interest, but my experience with him drives home at a point we can all recognize. Every one of us has dealt with someone who was downright arrogant or "cocky," as we might put it in colloquial terms. Remember how awful it was to be around them? It was like no one – and nothing – mattered except for them.

What we experienced was a hard and uncomfortable lesson in the value of humility and why it's so important. Whenever we esteem ourselves in a way we shouldn't, avoiding one more reasonable or realistic, it is a deterrent to fellowship, friendship, and normal interaction. It turns people off to whatever we might validly have to offer, all because it came in a package that lacked appeal.

Humility is a view of oneself, one's importance, and one's abilities through the lens of who we are in Christ and our ability to stand before God. In humility, we recognize our failings as well as our successes, and we recognize that without God, we would have no successes. It reminds us that none of us is better than anyone else, because before God, we all stand equal. Our worldly accomplishments mean nothing in the sight of God. What matters to God is our faith, and our transformation through our faith.

In the same way, you who are younger must accept the authority of the elders. And all of you, dress yourselves in humility as you relate to one another, for

*"God opposes the proud
  but gives grace to the humble."*

So humble yourselves under the mighty power of God, and at the right time He will lift you up in honor. Give all your worries and cares to God, for He cares about you. (1 Peter 5:5-7)

Some people think humility is a bad thing. The world tells us we must as think of ourselves as much as possible to have a healthy view of human life, but the Bible doesn't support this. Others think humility is negative, living like a doormat and letting people mistreat you all the time. Humility is none of these things. The Bible tells us to stand up for what's right and in the face of wrong, which must mean that we don't have to just get walked all over through this life. Humility gives us the ability to esteem ourselves properly, never thinking more highly of ourselves than we ought. If whatever we have to offer is always about us, our focus is wrong. Humility changes our focus to the things of God, to recognizing we need God, and we can be comfortable with that understanding. It doesn't mean we never celebrate or feel good about the things we do; it just means we never forget our Source of good things.

If we are willing to humble ourselves, God will raise us up. It's impossible to be raised up if one has already exalted themselves, thus the reason why pride hurts us so much as people. God will give us the ability to speak rightly in the face of accusation, the wisdom to handle the wrong that comes against us, and to manage our reputations in the world in which we live. In humility, we honor all; we show proper respect; and we recognize that doing so takes nothing away from us. A humble person is one who is approachable, able to interact with others, and handles life with the grace of God, one step and moment at a time.

I Promise, It's Not a Dirty Word!

Submission. There's a word no one wants to hear, and definitely no one wants to follow. It sounds demoralizing. It sounds uncomfortable. It sounds like someone else has control over us. It sounds like…yuck.

Submission sounds like a dirty word because that's how we, as human beings, have been taught to approach it. In this world where we live, dominance and control are seen as the positions of power and authority. The more we control, the more we dominate, the better our position is. Willingly yielding to another, respecting authority, and respecting others is seen as something unpleasant, unfair, even unjust. No one could ever imagine we serve a God Who expects us not just to submit to Him, but to one another. Yet, as hard as it is to imagine, that is exactly the case.

And further, submit to one another out of reverence for Christ. (Ephesians 5:21)

There are many specific injunctions about submission throughout the Scriptures. We are commanded to submit to our governmental authorities, to our spiritual leaders, children to parents, workers to employers, and husbands and wives are commanded to submit in marriage. It sounds uncomfortable when we hear about it, but the thing we need to step back and realize is there is nothing wrong with submission. It is a principle of humility that teaches us to honor God first and because we honor Him, honor others as well.

Submission doesn't mean we let others walk all over us or that we allow ourselves to be mistreated. It doesn't mean someone is better than we are or superior to us, because we choose to honor them and the position they may have in this life. It's something that benefits us, because it both enhances our relationship with others and is a positive witness before God. What it does is allow God to work through us in our interactions with others.

So, what does submission look like?

- Submission does not consider oneself more highly than one should.

- Submission displays respect.

- Submission is considerate of the thoughts, feelings, and needs of others.

- Submission pays respect and honor where it is due.

- Submission knows the value of listening, just as much as speaking.

- Submission knows how to apologize when such is necessary.

- Submission recognizes that we are all equal in God's sight and recognizes differences in calling and purpose.

- Submission realizes our ultimate humility and homage belongs exclusively to God.

- Submission recognizes that treating others properly doesn't take anything away from oneself.

In specific examples, submission looks like:

- Being punctual and on time for work, church, assignments, etc.

- Being honest with our time and doing our job to the best of our ability.

- Refraining from gossip or slanderous talk about our spiritual leaders.

- Speaking to our spouse when something bothers us instead of talking to everyone else about it.

- Learning to "fight fair" in arguments.

- Apologizing when you know you were wrong in a given situation.

- Respecting the boundaries others establish for themselves in their lives.

- Preparing a favorite meal for a loved one.

- Helping out with a household chore, especially if you know your partner doesn't like doing it.

- Praying for those in leadership worldwide.

- Helping out at a church function.

If we are willing to walk into situations with this kind of attitude, we will go much further than demanding all the time the attention we feel we should get. When we humble ourselves, we find ourselves lifted and honored. Submission opens the door to allow God to work on our lives and on our behalf while giving that same space and allowance for God to work in and through others, as well. It acknowledges we can't change anyone but ourselves, and that we aren't responsible for what others do. When we step back and allow God to be God in our lives, submission allows for powerful things to happen.

TAME THAT TONGUE!

When we were kids, we used to recite the rhyme, "Sticks and stones can break my bones, but words can never hurt me." Another popular one was "I'm rubber and you're glue. Whatever bounces off of me, sticks to you." We usually said these things to try and prove we weren't offended or hurt by the things others said to us. It might have also followed up with a nasty comment or retort of our own! We learned how to be mean early on, and if you were good at being mean with your mouth, you often didn't have to do other things, such as fight with your fists, because you knew how to cut to the core with your words, all by themselves.

All of us have said something we shouldn't at some point in time. We've been the route where we are all too casual with our words and might have hurt someone else with what we said or damaged a relationship. We've also been on the other end of hurtful words, feeling the sting of a reality that we can't ever remove. We know and often focus on the fact that actions hurt people (and that is a fact), but our words can also hurt people. Even the improper words we say to other people can hurt us, too, in the long run.

Dear brothers and sisters, not many of you should become teachers in the church, for we who teach will be judged more strictly. Indeed, we all make many mistakes. For if we could control our tongues, we would be perfect and could also control ourselves in every other way.

We can make a large horse go wherever we want by means of a small bit in its mouth. And a small rudder makes a huge ship turn wherever the pilot chooses to go, even though the winds are strong. In the same way, the tongue is a small thing that makes grand speeches.

But a tiny spark can set a great forest on fire. And among all the parts of the body, the tongue is a flame of fire. It is a whole world of wickedness, corrupting your entire body. It can set your whole life on fire, for it is set on fire by hell itself.

People can tame all kinds of animals, birds, reptiles, and fish, but no one can tame the tongue. It is restless and evil, full of deadly poison. Sometimes it praises our Lord and Father, and sometimes it curses those who have been made in the image of God. And so blessing and cursing come pouring out of the same mouth. Surely, my brothers and sisters, this is not right! Does a spring of water bubble out with both fresh water and bitter water? Does a fig tree produce olives, or a grapevine produce figs? No, and you can't draw fresh water from a salty spring. (James 3:1-12)

James chapter 3 is directed toward individuals in the church who desire to become teachers, but the information presented is applicable to all of us when it comes to the things we say and the aspirations we have toward leadership. Most people think it's more desirable to be in charge, but when people are in charge, they have more responsibility. For teachers, it is that much more important to control what comes out of one's mouth and to control the things that they say. The principles about taming what we say, however, are important foundations for all believers.

The Apostle James was over one of the first churches in existence, which means he saw a lot of changes as he led the church of God through much of its literal infancy. He saw people come and go, he saw the problems that existed among church members, and he saw the way that individuals had the ability to influence each other. They had the ability to influence one another on to greater faith or away from God. This means that James had a great insight into how church worked and the role that speech played in people's instruction and faith. James knew people's words could enhance faith or lead them totally astray, and he wanted to make sure that those with authority were leading people in the right direction.

We can lead anyone in the right or wrong direction, whether we are leaders, or not. The first way we do this is through our actions, and the second way is through our words. Sometimes our words are people's first impressions of us, so what we say and how we handle ourselves is very important! Being able to control what we say is very difficult (and the apostle acknowledges that), but it is something we should aspire to handle. If we want to be a good witness to others, we need to speak right!

What does speaking right sound like?

- It avoids deliberately offending other people with our speech. We refrain from the use of any hurtful language that employs racist, sexist, bigoted, or offensive language to others.

- When speaking, we speak in a manner that is relatable, but correct, so our message can be understood by those who hear it.

- We should avoid using terminology that can be perceived as profane. There is no reason to be vulgar or rude in our speech with others.

- We should be quick to speak well of God and of what God has done in our lives through testimony.

- It's fine to have bad days and to admit when you are going through hard times, but it's not all right to start cursing God or other people in the process.

- We must be cautious about what we "wish" or hope happens to other people. We should never wish other people dead, harm, or "curse" other people. We should also maintain enough maturity to handle ourselves with courtesy in disagreements. It should be our position to seek to bless others, meaning we pray for and seek God's intervention in their lives, no matter how they need it.

In all things, we should seek to discipline ourselves and make sure our speech lines up with our lives, our beliefs, and with what we claim. We should aspire to say what we believe as much as we hope to live what we believe. If we do this, there will be no conflict between the two.

Yes, I know, we all have days where we slip up. Just keep going; don't let it stop you or hold you back. Keep your eyes on the goal, rather than on your failures. Acknowledge whatever needs to change and move forward. God's grace is there to help you keep moving forward.

Relationships

Relationships are the major area where all of us trip up in our Christian walk. After all, living with and dealing with other people is a very difficult part of any life, not just Christian life. People can be a frustrating mix of confusion and important to us, and the more we interact with others, the more we often come up short. What do we do about relationships, and how do we handle them?

So now I am giving you a new commandment: Love each other. Just as I have loved you, you should love each other. Your love for one another will prove to the world that you are My disciples. (John 13:34-35)

Always be humble and gentle. Be patient with each other, making allowance for each other's faults because of your love. Make every effort to keep yourselves united in the Spirit, binding yourselves together with peace. (Ephesians 4:2-3)

Let us hold tightly without wavering to the hope we affirm, for God can be trusted to keep His promise. Let us think of ways to motivate one another to acts of love and good works. (Hebrews 10:23-24)

The end of the world is coming soon. Therefore, be earnest and disciplined in your prayers. Most important of all, continue to show deep love for each other, for love covers a multitude of sins. Cheerfully share your home with those who need a meal or a place to stay. (1 Peter 4:7-9)

Let's define "relationships." When I am talking about relationships, I don't just mean marriage partners or family members, although they are part of relationships. Relationships are any interactions that we have with other people. We have relationships with our family members, our spouses, our friends, coworkers, neighbors, fellow churchgoers, all our leaders, people in our communities, and even those we meet on social media. Our relationships with others are the way we behave with them, they behave toward us, and that we maintain or dissolve connections with people.

The first thing we need to understand – and it is quite vital – is to see our interactions with others are a part of our relationship with God. It might be tempting and easy to say that how you treat others has nothing to do with your relationship with God, but that isn't true. How we interact with others displays just where we are at in our faith and where we need to improve. It's easy to be holy and spiritual by ourselves, but it takes true effort to make sure we live this life for real, in the real world, in a real context. We are here to grow spiritually against the opposition our situations present and to bless one another. We are also, of course, here to be a witness to the things God can do for us.

If we mistreat people, we cannot expect God will bless us. If we dishonor others, that shows God we aren't fully honoring Him in the way we should. This means to the best of our ability we show others our esteem for them as well as God's esteem for them when interacting with them.

It's important we set ourselves right to make sure our love for our family, friends, coworkers, leadership, neighbors, fellow church members, communities, and even those we encounter casually are visible. We shouldn't ever seek to be intolerant, abusive, mistreating, or inappropriate with our family members. Our behavior should maintain both respect for others and self-respect, and we should always pray for the ability to maintain godly interactions with others.

I don't have a big, long list of relationship "dos" and "don'ts." I think figuring out how to best love others relates to service, and people are all unique and different. It also takes some time to figure out how you best desire to be served in your own walk with others. Communication is key, and that is why relationships are so important. They force us to learn how to mutually submit with others, how to speak up about what we need or want, how to apologize when we are wrong, and how to encourage one another to better living. In our relationships, we learn, over time, to see one another as God sees us.

If we can't treat people well or find their behaviors too upsetting, disrespectful, or abusive to remain with them, we have every right to respect ourselves and respect God at work within us and walk away from those people. Family with God is far more than biology and He has the ability to put us in situations that are not so trying or frustrating for us. We can love other people from afar without somehow compromising our faith or compromising our ability to reflect God's transformation in us. Sometimes the best way we can love people is through boundaries and limits and recognize that it is better for all of us if there is some distance to allow God to work in their lives while He works in ours.

Allowing God to work and minister within you

If the Kingdom of God is working around us, it must work through us. Some people think the work of ministry is just for a minister, but this is untrue. A minister is recognized as such because they engage in their spiritual service as a primary position of leadership, but the word "ministry" means "service." Being of service, helping others, reaching out to others, and doing for other people. The essence of the Christian call is to reach out, transform, change, and make a difference. It might not be a difference that changes an entire nation, but an entire nation always changes with one interaction. As we reach out to people to serve them, we can bring a touch of God to a situation that might not have been there and without doing anything but caring for others, give them an encounter with the love of God.

"I am the true grapevine, and My Father is the gardener. He cuts off every branch of Mine that doesn't produce fruit, and He prunes the branches that do bear fruit so they will produce even more. You have already been pruned and purified by the message I have given you. Remain in Me, and I will remain in you. For a branch cannot produce fruit if it is severed from the vine, and you cannot be fruitful unless you remain in Me.

"Yes, I am the vine; you are the branches. Those who remain in Me, and I in them, will produce much fruit. For apart from Me you can do nothing. Anyone who does not remain in Me is thrown away like a useless branch and withers. Such branches are gathered into a pile to be burned. But if you remain in Me and My words remain in you, you may ask for anything you want, and it will be granted! When you produce much fruit, you are My true disciples. This brings great glory to My Father.

"I have loved you even as the Father has loved Me. Remain in My love. When you obey My commandments, you remain in My love, just as I obey My Father's commandments and remain in His love. I have told you these things so that you will be filled with my joy. Yes, your joy will overflow! This is My commandment: Love each other in the same way I have loved you. There is no greater love than to lay down one's life for one's friends. You are My friends if you do what I command. I no longer call you slaves, because a master doesn't confide in his slaves. Now you are My friends, since I have told you everything the Father told Me. You didn't choose me. I chose you. I appointed you to go and produce lasting fruit, so that the Father will give you whatever you ask for, using My Name. This is My command: Love each other. (John 15:1-17)

Some believers question why we are still in this world. It is true that if Jesus desired us to go to heaven or to take us all out, He did and does have the power to do so. He hasn't removed us, however, and that must mean there is a purpose. It is not to isolate ourselves from everyone, but to allow our faith to make a true difference on His behalf. This passage of Scripture tells us the very reason why we are still in this world: to experience the empowerment of the Spirit and to reveal His love.

We are still here because we are connected to Christ as branches to a vine. He is our main source, and because of Him, we can bear great fruit. This means we can bring about a great and purposeful product forth for Him, one that brings in more from it than just us. Because we are connected to Him, this world needs us, even though it doesn't realize it. We minister to the world every time we obey Jesus' commandments to us to love God and our neighbor as ourselves. We minister every time we walk in spiritual joy, showing the world some of what it is missing by not embracing the fullness of God within them. We also minister when we lay down our selves – our personal desires, wants, wills, and goals – for the sake of Kingdom discipline, as we lead others to the Lord. You may have a moment where you get a divine utterance, a healing gift, the ability to preach, or something else, but you will always be usable by God if you maintain a proper heart of service. Whatever God wants you to do will become clear as long as you focus on producing great fruit and great connection for God's Kingdom.

⸙ CHAPTER FOUR ⸙
THE ESSENTIALS OF OUR FAITH

WHENEVER we discuss faith, we inevitably come to the question of what we should believe. It's not a big secret that there are many different denominations in existence that all identify as "Christian." Within those different denominations there are differences: some are very minor, some are very major, and some have many commonalities that can make it difficult to tell them apart from each other. What do those differences mean? Do they qualify as being beliefs of a "different faith?" How concerned should we be about doctrinal differences? At the core of it all, what do we, as Christians, need to believe?

The answers to these questions are both basic and complicated at the same time. They can also be answered without a lot of judgment, but sometimes it means we must examine where we are at and tune into the leading of the Spirit for where we belong and what we need to do as part of belonging to our faith community. This chapter does not seek to be the ultimate answer for understanding everything relating to our faith, but a guide to make sure you are able to follow a right spiritual path that will help you gain all the needed spiritual insights to know God for yourself.

AN OVERVIEW OF EPHESIANS 4

In this chapter, we will examine the contents of Ephesians 4. Why that specific chapter, you ask? Because Ephesians 4 offers us a powerful summary of just what our "faith" essentials look like. The reason for this is simple: Ephesians 4 is about preserving unity in the church by looking at its unifying factors. Even in the first century, Christian communities had differences from one another. There were cultural influences, traditions, and practices that varied from each other and made each church experience a little unique. With the churches growing yet far apart and operating by a certain level of both independence and interdependence, how could the church maintain its unity?

Division in Christianity is not new. We talk about divisions among groups as if it's a new or modern thing, but it's not. If we are honest about the first century church, they were certainly not the fairy-tale setting we often try to weave when studying the Bible. The early church didn't have any special insight on overcoming human behavior that we don't have now. They were still people, overcoming the flesh, disagreeing with each other, believing in God, and empowered with the Spirit to try and figure this "faith thing" out. The temptations toward division, adopting the spiritual systems that were around them, and disrespecting one another (including their leaders) were all very real realities for the first century church. This is why the Apostle Paul, as a spiritual authority with the ability to intervene, sent the church at Ephesus this letter on what factors should stand to unify the church. What do we need to believe? What does our leadership look like? As Christians, what do we look like? We can find all these answers in Ephesians 4.

YOU HAVE BEEN CALLED BY GOD

Therefore I, a prisoner for serving the Lord, beg you to lead a life worthy of your calling, for you have been called by God. (Ephesians 4:1)

When we talk about "being called," we always think of our specific calling in this life. Yes, that does apply here, because we must operate our calling to find our greatest spiritual purpose in this life. It is through that calling where we will discover our greatest challenges, insights, and growth, because it is in that place where God reveals Himself to us. In a more general sense, however, we can recognize we are called by God to be believers. We have heard God's call to enter a powerful fellowship with Him as members of Christ's Body. Being here is not an accident, and being in this place, in this time, in God's plan, is all a part of His call to us.

The Apostle Paul urged us to live this worthy life because he was in prison for it. To spread the Gospel, build up these churches, teach people the faith, and lead them from a spiritual perspective, he had to pay a high price. His entire life was devoted to this, and now he was a prisoner on behalf of the Gospel cause that made a difference in the lives of these believers. If he had to be in prison, surely they should stand firm, and live worthy of their calling.

What does it mean to live "worthy of the call?" If we are to properly understand this, it means that we should not just live our calling, but live according to our calling. Our lives should reflect this incredible opportunity we've been given to start again. When called to change, we can do so with joy. We are on an adventure with God, and we have the honor of living worthy of that adventure.

But wait! If we are called by God to be in this place, what about non-believers? What about people who have never had the chance to hear the Gospel, are they not called? These are fair questions that deserve the time and attention to them for an answer. Often people brush off the world into the believing and non-believing, and don't take the time to answer such simple theological musings because they don't have the answer.

To answer the questions backwards, the truth is that we do not know what happens to non-believers who die and have not had the truth to hear about the Gospel in this lifetime. We don't know what happens to them because the Bible is not about them. The Scriptures are a record of those who believe, those who believe and do not do what they should, or those who refuse to believe. The focus of the Scriptures is not about non-believers, but there are a few things we can draw upon for those who have not had the chance to believe in their lifetimes from the Scriptures. The first is that God is merciful, and from what we can understand, non-believers appear to be judged according to their deeds. What exactly this means I don't know, because we do not see the mechanics of such matters in Scripture. What I believe this means is we entrust the souls of those who never had a chance to believe to God, and trust His love and mercy as extends toward them.

Does it mean that those who haven't heard are not called or loved by God? Of course not! It just means that person didn't cross paths with the Gospel in their lifetime. The human element in an equation tends to complicate things, and while in theory it should be easy for everyone to hear of Jesus Christ, it does happen that some do not. Government interference, lack of resources, language barriers, those who reject or avoid their call from God, or other obstacles can impede the ability to hear the Gospel. This doesn't mean that God doesn't desire to draw them to Him, however. Jesus died for everyone, and it is God's hope and equipping for the church that we can all come together and do this work as we are called so all can hear – and know – and decide for themselves about this wonderful work of salvation.

Being a disciple of Christ is about making the decision to accept salvation and follow that call for oneself. If one doesn't have the chance to make that decision, God must handle that matter in His own way, with that individual. It doesn't change, however, that God desires them to know, He desires them to be in relationship with Him, and He desires us to be a part of that process.

This is why it is so important for us to share our faith in a way that is relatable and understandable to others. We can all remember the person or people who first helped us to make that decision. Even if they are no longer in our lives, they are an important standing memory for us in the before and after of our decision-making process. Just as we have embraced our call, we must live worthy of it. We should be an example for others, a benefit to their lives, and someone who they can all declare that even though they may not agree with us, we help them to have a better sense of themselves because they know we love them.

Abiding in Forgiveness

Always be humble and gentle. Be patient with each other, making allowance for each other's faults because of your love. (Ephesians 4:2)

The second verse of Ephesians 4 is a little more involved than the first, because it reflects a principle of forgiveness that should exist between believers. Going along with forgiveness comes important discussions about personal conduct that come from the way our spiritual lives change our outward behavior. While forgiveness often sounds like a nice idea, it is more than just a nice idea. To be forgiving, we must take on God's nature within us. We must work at it, because forgiveness is not something that comes easy for most of us. The flesh likes to hold on to a grudge for survival purposes. If someone has wronged you, you want to remember it to make sure the incident doesn't happen again. This instinct kept our ancestors alive in dire circumstances, because it would keep them from being tricked by their enemies. When someone came at them wrong, they'd be sure not to forget it. Thus, grudges became something heavy-handed, a weapon to use to make sure no one was able to enter the camp or ambush someone else.

The problem with this survival instinct is it comes at a high price. The longer we hold onto the things that others do, the more we are often punished by them long after they have happened. While the offender goes on to do something else, we keep reliving whatever it was that happened. Yes, it's evident that some things are more difficult to overcome than others, especially when you must live in the same body, mind, and experiences as when it happened. But there is also truth that forgiveness is a part of the Christian life, not to excuse bad behavior or give people permission to mistreat others, but because living your life with one eye over your shoulder as you carry around the heaviness of hurt and pain is no way to live one's life.

Forgiveness is one of those principles that we love when it's applied to us, but not so much when we must apply it to others. Most of us have heard the term "toxic" applied in a relationship sense, and all of us have met someone we would classify as "toxic" in our lifetimes. Toxic people are those whose behaviors are offensive and problematic, and in some way, their behavior hurts, angers, or vexes us to a point where being around them is not good for us. It's true that there are some people who are just plain toxic all the time, but there is a much darker side to toxic behavior that we often overlook. Sin is a toxicity in this world, and every one of us has been "toxic" at some point in time to someone else. We might not have done it intentionally, but we have all exhibited behaviors that hurt someone else, caused someone else's pain, or caused someone else some sort of damage or offense.

This is not to say you should keep a toxic person in your life. It is just to point out that all of us have been toxic, which means all of us need forgiveness at some point in time. We also need to forgive to prevent the spread of sin to others and stop punishing ourselves for whatever was done to us, or we have done. That's where forgiveness comes in. In forgiveness, we open the door to find ourselves free from the holds of the past and open to do new things for the future.

Forgiveness doesn't make what other people did all right, and it certainly doesn't mean when we forgive someone, we never again have any repercussions from what they have done. The same is true for the things we do to other people. We all need to receive forgiveness, distance ourselves from the reactions, effects, and behaviors of sin, and start again, both with ourselves and with God.

If we hold to a humble and gentle attitude, we will have far less instances of sin in our lives. Patience goes a long way when dealing with the faults of others. This powerful combination of humility, gentleness, and patience recognizes people are human, we all mess up, and in that state of messing up, we remember just how much we need God to set us straight and do this work of faith right. This proves we all need God, and all of us need Him just as much as someone else does.

In this regard, forgiveness is also a powerful aspect of love and loving one another. There can be no love without forgiveness, and no forgiveness without love. It is part of learning how to live with us and others, bridging the gap that exists, not necessarily between our offenders and us, but others and us, breached by those who wronged us, and learning to come closer to God as we experience the love present in forgiveness for ourselves.

UNITY OF THE SPIRIT

Make every effort to keep yourselves united in the Spirit, binding yourselves together with peace. (Ephesians 4:3)

Unity is one of those topics that can always get people's attention, for one simple reason: It makes us feel like we are contributing to a problem's solution without having to do anything to make it better. It makes everyone feel warm and fuzzy and muse about how the church isn't united, but should be if we would just hear our condescending lecture telling us that unity is what the church needs. If we just will it hard enough, it'll be there.

The "ouch, amen" goes right there.

The problem with unity in the church is simple: we want it as an idea, but not a reality. It sounds great, warm, ideal, powerful, and beneficial, but when unity means we must make a sacrifice of ourselves, that maybe we don't get to be the top dog on the flyer, we don't get our way about something or we must wait our turn, unity somehow becomes far less appealing. We love unity when it involves us and our dictates, but the second unity becomes about something else…we back right off.

Let's refrain from idealizing the church of the past by thinking the struggle for unity is a new thing. As I said at the beginning of this chapter, the early churches also struggled with unity. The church throughout history has struggled with unity. Any church that tells you it is the mark of unity and has been from the beginning is boldly lying. History is full of the chronic divisions, complications, and human interventions in this thing we call church. The challenge of unity didn't just start in the year 2000, or in the 1960s, or the 1920s, or even at the Reformation. Unity is a fundamental issue, a challenge because of the realities of sin, and it is going to remain an issue until Jesus comes back. Those are the plain and simple facts of unity in the church.

Even though unity has its challenges, and those challenges will continue to exist until we see the Perfect appear, unity is still something we should seek as the Body of Christ. Unity is the opposite of the division created in life by sin, and is, therefore, something of great value and reason as we proclaim the Gospel to all the world. The reason we should seek it out is simple: working together in unity is something truly impossible this side of heaven with the complications we find as foundational to church identity. God calls all of us as very different people

– different languages, races, nations, cultures, genders, identities, ideologies, political influences, and educations – and expects us to come together and figure out Kingdom membership together. We do not hold barriers or discriminations in the Kingdom, which means all of us come into the Kingdom and willfully set aside social castes and societal ambitions to participate in the work of the Gospel together. It sounds totally unreasonable and impossible, but God has given us a secret to work out our differences and focus on the Kingdom.

The secret really isn't a secret; it is the work of the Holy Spirit within all of us. If the Spirit moves in, among, and through all of us, we should reflect the Spirit's change within, among, and through us! It's not complicated, but it is also not easy. If the Spirit works to produce fruit within us that leads us to greater love, joy, peace, patience, kindness, goodness, faithfulness, humility, and self-control, we should act in kind with each other. If we are all experiencing this great work, it should make it easier for us to step up and share, to walk in the gifts we've been given, and to behave accordingly with one another. As the Gospel is our cause, the Spirit empowers us and keeps us together for that purpose.

Because the Spirit moves and works in all of us a little differently, it takes time to identify these operations and recognize the ways the Spirit moves through all. This can mean there are inevitable conflicts as we learn the uniqueness of the Spirit in each of us and work to break down those barriers that keep us separated.

The Holy Spirit is the catalyst for unity in the church. We can't have unity in the church without His presence, and we certainly can't have peace without some semblance of wholeness and completeness, that being found in unity. It's not an accident that in churches where the Spirit is minimized or ignored, unity is frequently a more prevalent problem than in optimal circumstances. If we want unity to flow, we must let the Spirit flow too, having full reign and movement in all of us. That "us" starts with you, with me, with each one of us as we are willing to let the Spirit have His way within all of us.

The next time you hear a message about unity, you need to recognize it starts with you. Having a united church doesn't mean compromising on faith or doctrine, but it does mean we have to allow others to be themselves while they allow us to be ourselves. If you want to be a part of God's bigger, united picture, it involves flowing as He directs, following His voice, doing what He calls you to do, using the gifts He has given you, and allowing others to do the same. When we master this, we master working together in spiritual unity.

ONE BODY

For there is one body… (Ephesians 4:4)

Ephesians 4 lists seven different "ones" that mark the unity of our faith. Seven is the number of perfection as well as the "God" number (because God is perfection). These seven different "ones" help us to identify the essentials of our doctrinal foundations. Doctrine is frequently a big issue in Christian circles, something we debate, discuss, and examine, and that means there tends to be a great amount of confusion when it comes to just what Christians are supposed to believe. The Apostle Paul, however, makes it as basic and simple for us as possible, giving us seven different "ones" to look for as marks of relevancy in our faith.

Understanding why the Apostle Paul emphasizes the fact that there are "one" of these specific foundational things of faith is primary to seeing their relevance in our walk. In spiritual terms, the fact that God is one is of primary importance. God is one, which shows a wholeness and completeness within Him. He is not lacking, and He is our origin of such completion and unity. We cannot have "one" without God, because God is one. One represents our common spiritual source, Who is also one. To have our faith, a complete faith, we cannot do it without Him. Thus, we come together in unity to find our one, to find Him, in a more profound way.

The first "one" addressed is that of one body. In other words, the Apostle Paul was affirming the church is one. This doesn't make sense when we look at it from an earthly perspective, which is often why there is such confusion over the church. Its divisions are often held against it, not seeing such as the product of human realities.

Many years ago, someone asked me, "Which church is the true church?" He came from the perspective that only one of the many denominations in existence could be the true church, thus making the rest of them false. It's a good question, but I suppose we could say it is a human question. We assume unity and having "one body" will look a certain way to our own standards, and when that does not happen, we assume that only one can be right, and the rest must be wrong. My answer to this man was simple: I said they are all part of the church. Different denominations reveal different aspects of spiritual development and doctrine, and the world is full of believers who are at different stages of spiritual development. There are many good, sincere Christians around the world doing God's work that hold to the promise of sincere doctrine (as is found here in Ephesians 4). If a group adheres to the necessary understanding of one body, one Spirit, one hope, one Lord, one faith, one baptism, and one God and Father of all, they are doing the work of God in this world.

The one Body of Christ is the church universal, the Kingdom of God, present in this world and in heaven, representative of those living in this world and those living present in eternity. There are local communities that are a part of the church whole, rather than the other way around. The local churches are to represent the ideas and beliefs of the Kingdom at large, and that means each and every church member must attune themselves to that purpose and principle. There is no question that many denominations get lost in this process, listening to the voice of men rather than God, and for that reason, it is essential we all attune ourselves to the importance of unifying with others who also share Kingdom values.

We only have one body because we need to bring together all our abilities and gifts to make the church work and function. Armies that don't display unity do not go on to great victories, and the same is true with Kingdom mindset. If we don't find it within ourselves to serve our immediate functions, the Gospel cannot go into all the world. Our unity as one Body signifies the relationship between the Father, Son, and Spirit as one and the point that as many have come from God, we now stand for Him as one and shall return to Him as one.

ONE SPIRIT

...and one Spirit... (Ephesians 4:4)

In Bible times, most religions were what we would classify as either polytheistic or animistic. Both headings believe in the existence of many different spiritual beings that were guardians or bestowers of specific things within the universe. There was a god or a spirit for everything: rain, sun, war, peace, death, life, luck, fortune, lightning, trees, growth, animals, specific crops, and anything else you could imagine. When one had a need that related to a specific matter, they would make an offering of some sort to that specific spirit or deity. This effort was to appease the spirit or deity, and it was hoped that a favorable response would result.

The reason we have mention of "one Spirit" is because there are many gifts represented in the church. In a polytheistic or animistic understanding, all those gifts would come from a different source, rather than one common source. As much of the Apostle Paul's words were written to Gentile believers, they would have come from backgrounds that believed in many gods and/or many spirits. The world of monotheism was new to them, and with that came the need to understand the promise of one Spirit.

In the New Testament, we learn of one Spirit Who bestows many gifts on us for the purpose of the edification of the church. We are empowered by the Spirit so the Kingdom of God can multiply and go forth. The Spirit reveals Himself to us, comforts us, guides us, gives us great and wonderful spiritual gifts, leads us into all truth, and helps us maintain our unity and identity in the faith as we go through our spiritual walk in this world. This one job is handled by the one Spirit, which is the power and spirit of God living among us, today. It is not many separate gods or spirits, but one that empowers and loves us as God's own.

For this reason, it is essential that the church recognizes and edifies these gifts for its own spiritual edification. When the Spirit flows, the church moves, functions, and grows. When denominations or specific churches start working to shut the Spirit down or contain His necessary activity to the first century or another point in time, they are cutting themselves off from the spiritual flow that keeps the church alive, active, and relevant from age to age. The Spirit still moves, and as He moves, we must remain plugged in to recognize just where He is going and what is next to come.

ONE GLORIOUS HOPE

...just as you have been called to one glorious hope for the future. (Ephesians 4:4)

Christians differ on their interpretation of just what the "one glorious hope" referred to in Ephesians 4:4 is. Some believe it refers to heaven, some believe it refers to a doctrine known as the rapture of the church, and others believe it refers to the Second Coming of Christ. What we do specifically know is it speaks of this glorious hope, and the glorious hope is future, as in it is to come rather than something we receive right now. It is a hope, which means it is something we recognize and believe for by faith, which shall manifest at a future date.

Looking out over the survey of spiritual interpretations, I do agree it refers to the Second Coming of Christ, for one simple reason: the first-century church did believe the return of Christ was imminent in their lifetimes. It was the major hope, the one they felt would come and transform the entire world, and more specifically, their entire existence. The ultimate promise of the release of the ills of this lifetime were found in the Second Coming, the promise that Jesus was to return.

The study of "final things" is referred to as eschatology. It's probably not a big surprise to learn eschatology is a huge subject, and there are many nuances and differing opinions about the details of it. Much of the specifics on the return of Jesus Christ and even heaven and eternity aren't quite present or clear, and as a result, scholars attempt to fill in gaps and ideas with details that sometimes apply and sometimes do not. For us, today, I think the important point is recognizing that Jesus will come again, even though it has been so many years since the promise was made. It is a glorious hope to which we still hold fast, even though we don't understand all the details and sometimes find ourselves intimidated by them. We have no reason to fear sensational details or sensational preaching that is designed to create intimidation, because the Scriptures tell – and promise us – it is a glorious hope. It's not a minor hope, but one that reflects the glory and authority of God. No matter what happens this side of heaven, God is still God, and God's glory still has the power and influence to overtake every enemy.

It is very important Christians believe Jesus will return to us again. It's not just important for the theological implications, but for practical ones, as well. The Second Coming is the second installment of God's finished work within the bigger world picture, ushering us all from our initial present situation into that which is eternal. No longer will there be the distinction between where we are now and where we will be one day, but the two will become one, as the Kingdom transcends everything it touches. The promise of the Second Coming lets us know what we face in the immediate is not the end, and what we see now is not the end. As we walk in the Kingdom now, proclaiming its promises, one day all shall know and recognize the truth present in Jesus Christ as Lord.

As we talk about "marks" of true Christianity, it is essential to know how your church feels about the return of Christ. There are groups that profess Christian faith who do not believe Jesus is returning, or who believe it's already happened, yet everyone seems to have missed it. Some groups even go as far to say that Jesus Christ returned as their leader or some central figure in history. Don't fall for it, and don't believe it. We may not know every detail of Jesus' return, but we know enough to know it has not come to be yet. We still await, and trust with faith, in His glorious hope. Just as it took thousands of years for the Messiah to come for redemption the first time, we have no idea how long it will take for Him to return as the powerful King we recognize Him to be. The Bible tells us that none of us know the day or the hour, because we aren't on quite the same timetable as eternity, just yet. We do know it shall come to pass, however, and we do know with assurance such a promise is bound and ready to come at its fulfillment. In the meantime, we trust the promise of the Kingdom of God, which gives us that powerful vision and insight into all that is to come when that grand and glorious hope is fulfilled.

One Lord

There is one Lord… (Ephesians 4:5)

The word "Lord" was a common term in ancient times. It referred to a ruler or a governor over something or someone, or sometimes over both. The term was extended to individuals who were of specific social status that meant they were entitled to certain courtesy, most likely as wealthy individuals who controlled properties or extended governance in specific areas of society. This gives us a great picture of the concept of "lordship." Whenever we declare Jesus Christ to be Lord, we are affirming His rule, His governance, and His position over our lives. It is an affirmative statement and a negative statement at the same time. When we say, "Jesus is Lord," that means we are saying the governing authorities of this world are not. In Biblical times, it would be to say, "Caesar is not." In more modern times, we might understand it to say, "the president is not," or "the king is not," or "the governor is not." This is a huge and weighty statement, one that held very serious political realities with it in ancient times. To say "Jesus is Lord" was not just a statement of faith; it was a statement against the establishment of the day, as the governors and rulers were believed to be directly placed there by the gods, if not gods themselves. Accepting Jesus' Kingdom meant when it was a toss-up between accepting the idolatry and authority of the governor or accepting the honor and authority of Christ, the governing authority was going to lose.

In some parts of the world today, accepting Jesus as Lord is paramount to these same pressures, as it forms a political rebellion. Even in lands where Christianity is hallowed, recognizing the Lordship of Jesus can be socially radical. Having Jesus as Lord changes one's outlook on life and perspectives on what is or is not acceptable. It changes people's politics, ideas on relationships and interactions, and impacts the way we view social issues. This means recognizing Jesus is Lord can lead to conflicts, even now, and even in the best of circumstances.

We display our belief that Jesus is Lord as we accept the commands He has given us and live our lives in His true worship, adoration, and appreciation. We are sure to put God first and love our neighbor as ourselves. Now, in the Kingdom, we accept His governance and direction through the power of the Holy Spirit. We aren't ignorant to the fact that while we still live in this world, we are part of a greater and bigger Kingdom, one that leads us to the promises we know are real, because we have seen and experienced God's work in our lives. Jesus is our Lord, so we see His presence and His rule everywhere. He has transformed us by faith in a powerful and life-altering way.

It is for this reason that we are urged to respect those in secular governing positions. This may seem like a contradiction to what was said previously, but it is not. Jesus Christ advises us to pay our taxes and respect secular authorities that help establish order this side of heaven. When He said this, He said it to an occupied people, individuals who had no feasible reason to desire to respect their leadership. We are told to respect authorities because it is to our benefit. It benefits us to show honor where it is due, because it eliminates unnecessary conflict. The early believers dealt with enough violence and persecution due to their simple faith; they did not need to give the governing bodies good reason to come and infiltrate their lives. As we can recall from discussing the fruit of the Spirit, there is no law against displaying such fruit in our lives.

Thus, it's important for us to remember that Jesus is our Lord, and we should do all of what He has told us to do, even when it's difficult. This doesn't mean it's wrong to be a citizen or disagree with a civil leader, not by a long shot. We are all still people and entitled to our opinions about how things are handled while we are here. What it is telling us is to remember our consistent priorities. Long after any civil leader is dead and gone, Jesus will still be Lord. The Kingdom of God will still be a real, viable, and existing thing. Our one Lord governs the church and our lives, and reminds us that whenever we are discouraged, He is the One Who holds our answers. No civil authority can fix what is broken in human experience. Jesus is Lord is a statement of hope as much as it is a reminder to uphold the principles of the Kingdom, no matter what comes up in someone's life. No matter what government exists, on earth or in churches, Jesus is still Lord of it all.

ONE FAITH

...one faith... (Ephesians 4:5)

We live in a world where we are surrounded by an assortment of different belief systems, often described as "faiths." Even though there weren't as many to choose from (at least on the surface), the first believers still found themselves surrounded by a wide variety of beliefs that were in contrast or opposed to their own. Much like we do today, early Christians had a choice to make. They had to establish what was spiritually correct within themselves and recognize there is only one faith that leads to life, not many.

Most of us have probably heard the saying, "there are many paths to God" at some point in time. It's hallowed by television personalities, celebrities, and even some religious leaders. On the surface, it probably sounds reasonable. After all, God is a "big God," right? Surely Christianity couldn't be right for everyone, and there must be other ways that we can access God, right?

I believe we live in a world that tries to create God in an image that is completely contrary with the limits and religious impositions we found of Him in our childhoods. The truth is that God is certainly not what many of our rigorous denominations made Him out to be. That doesn't mean God stands for nothing or represents nothing. It also doesn't mean we have an absence of choice in spiritual our lives.

The sacrifice of Christ for sins gives us the opportunity to approach God, once again, in union and relationship with Him. His death and resurrection still stand as the only way to approach the Father, because it is the only way that was made to create life. Salvation is available to us, but we must still choose to accept that invitation. God doesn't force us to enter this awesome relationship with Him. That means as long as we live on this earth, it is a choice we will make. There are other options, and to find life, we must choose the way that leads to life. We must decide for ourselves that God is Who we desire.

Other religious systems might sometimes seem enticing or like they have better or stronger ideas than Christianity. It might even look like adherents of other belief systems are stronger in their faith or more devoted than Christians are to God. Sometimes, this is probably true. Closer inspection, however, reveals a much more realistic side to what we might see on the surface. All religious groups experience internal tumult, conflict, and people who just don't live up to their doctrines like they should. People are still people, are still people, and people have a way of ruining everything. If we put our confidence in people, thinking and hoping they will reflect what we hope to see, it won't matter what system we decide to follow. There will always be a point in our lives where someone, somewhere will fail us.

That's why God has made a better way for us, and why there is only one faith that leads us to salvation. Despite some of the peripheral differences in many churches, we still adhere to our one faith, which is in Jesus Christ. When we acknowledge Jesus as the only way, we are stepping up and admitting we are sinners, He has the only answer for our sins, and that there is no other possibility for our salvation anywhere else. We believe in this one faith, because it is through this one faith that we experience God's grace to live and love with Him. As the only faith in the world where our deity has reached out to us, Christianity offers us the possibility of eternal hope that we can't find anywhere else.

Saying we believe in "one faith" doesn't mean we seek to put down others who believe differently than we do. It's not saying all non-

Christians are bad. It doesn't give any Christian the right to look down on someone of another belief system or harass, mistreat, abuse, or belittle them. It is certainly not saying Christians are better than anyone else. It just acknowledges and affirms the work Christ has done and the promise of hope that He has given us. We are thankful, and grateful, and humbly recognizing Christ's Lordship in our faith. He has become Lord of everything, including what we believe about our faith matters.

ONE BAPTISM

...one baptism... (Ephesians 4:5)

Baptism by immersion was a common practice in New Testament times. It was often performed by students of Greek philosophy and symbolized initiation into their specific system of thought. When an individual was baptized, the ceremony would be done "in the name" of whoever their teacher was. For example, students of Platonian thought would be baptized into the name of Plato, and students of Aristotle would be baptized into the name of Aristotle. It showed a continuity in thinking and the idea that they were connected to their instructors now, bound by the way they think and teach others.

If we look at different places in the New Testament, we learn there was a great controversy in some churches over the proper name for use in baptismal ceremonies. We learn in Corinth that some people were being baptized in the name of the individual who introduced them to church, such as Apollos or Cephas, rather than in the Name of the Lord. Doing this created a situation where instead of adhering to a practice of one united baptism, the believers were all baptized into systems that followed people, rather than following Christ.

Some people use the principle of Ephesians 4:5 to argue that all baptismal formulas are acceptable, but I believe that's the opposite of what we are supposed to see present in this passage. The Apostle Paul was affirming that the church should have one baptismal method instead of many and was affirming that as part of the unity of the church, we are to be baptized into Christ, because that is how we are baptized into His death.

Our baptism in water unites us to Christ, raising us up as we die to ourselves to now live in Him. We should always be baptized by full immersion in water (unless such is unavailable in an emergency) and our baptism should follow Biblical formula, repeating the words both of Matthew 28:19 and Acts 2:38. This is the seal of our baptism, uniting us with Christ and solidifying the call for baptism throughout the church. It unites us together.

Sometimes people call speaking in tongues "the Baptism of the Holy Ghost" or "fire baptism." These terms exist to explain what happens when someone is full of the Holy Spirit, but it is not the same as water baptism, or the issue of baptism as is seen here in Ephesians 4. There is no conflict between the baptism in water and the baptism in the Spirit, because the Apostle Paul wasn't talking about the differences between the two. He was establishing water baptism as a uniting foundation in the church and avoiding the conflicts many created as they tried to do things that were their own way, versus God's way.

ONE GOD AND FATHER OF ALL

...one God and Father of all, Who is over all, in all, and living through all. (Ephesians 4:6)

Reaffirming there is only one God relates to the earlier mention of one Spirit. In a world that embraced many gods, it was important to recognize there is one God and one Father of all we see. It's a reminder we need to hear in a world today that often treats the enemy as powerful as God and are often afraid of new or different ideas from our own. We can still find ourselves intimidated by outside forces that do not come from God, and we need that affirmation we serve one God, Who is all-knowing, all-powerful, and all-capable. But why else is it so important for us to remember there is one God?

God, as our Creator, is the most powerful source for our own personal identity. How we see ourselves, who we are, what we are meant to do, and who we are to become are all rooted in our creation itself. God has given each of us something to do, and it starts as we come to see our purpose as part of His creation. This means God gives us a powerful identity in Him, not just with an identity as someone with a ministry call or gifts, but as a person, as well.

If we recognize God is our Father, that signifies none of us must embrace the lack in our lives caused by the negligence or absence of someone else in this world. In Biblical times, fatherlessness was a huge cause of financial disparity, orphans, widows, lost identity, lost inheritances, and other issues that could change a person's life and damage their self-perception as a result. Nowadays we know an absent father can cause these issues, but there are many other things in this life that are just as damaging and painful to our identities and circumstances as fatherlessness. Abusive parents, loss of a mother, addiction, mistreatment, pressures, confusion, and forced conformities to things that deny the essence of our being are all examples that will damage who we are and who we are to become. If we embrace God is our Father, that changes our perception of lack. It is God's belief and hope that in becoming one with Him and one in the family of God, we will find the completion and wholeness we seek. There is enough of God to go around and enough of God for all of us and all our needs. If we only will embrace Him and then embrace what He wants to do in each of us, we will find ourselves without the lack created by this world.

The balance to this principle is acknowledging the three subpoints mentioned in the verse: God is over all, in all, and living through all of us. We recognize the authority of God, the leadership of God, and that when it is all said and done, God is the One to Whom everyone will have to answer. The Kingdom of God is governed by God, as He has established and set in place all of us by His calling. Our positions may be different, but we are here by His purpose. We recognize God is in all, because we are created in His image. This mighty concept connects each of us back to Him and is something that helps us develop identity as we come to know God for ourselves. Even if someone isn't on that journey, however, we must respect the image of God present in that person. That respect may very well become the thing that shows them the greatness of God at another point in time. Lastly, God is living through all of us in the Kingdom, whether we want to acknowledge it, or not, through the work of the Holy Spirit. These balances help us remember not just who we are as individuals, but who everyone else is.

There is great importance in respecting the lives of others and their individuality, all for the purpose of edifying one another and working together for the building of the Kingdom. When there is no lack, there is focus and power to do the Gospel work at hand.

The Ascension Gifts

However, He has given each one of us a special gift through the generosity of Christ. That is why the Scriptures say,

"When He ascended to the heights,
 He led a crowd of captives
 and gave gifts to His people."

Notice that it says "He ascended." This clearly means that Christ also descended to our lowly world. And the same One Who descended is the one Who ascended higher than all the heavens, so that He might fill the entire universe with Himself.

Now these are the gifts Christ gave to the church: the apostles, the prophets, the evangelists, and the pastors and teachers. Their responsibility is to equip God's people to do His work and build up the church, the body of Christ. This will continue until we all come to such unity in our faith and knowledge of God's Son that we will be mature in the Lord, measuring up to the full and complete standard of Christ.

Then we will no longer be immature like children. We won't be tossed and blown about by every wind of new teaching. We will not be influenced when people try to trick us with lies so clever they sound like the truth. Instead, we will speak the truth in love, growing in every way more and more like Christ, Who is the head of His body, the church. He makes the whole body fit together perfectly. As each part does its own special work, it helps the other parts grow, so that the whole body is healthy and growing and full of love. (Ephesians 4:7-16)

The next focus of church operation and unity moves to that of leadership. I am going to speak about church leadership offices and appointments a little more in chapter 6, so we won't focus a whole lot on the specifics of what all these different offices do here in this chapter. What we will do is look at leadership as a gift, and why leadership is so vital and important to our church structure and Kingdom movement.

Sometimes called the "five-fold ministry," the "ascension gifts," the "*didomi* gifts," or the "Ephesians 4:11 model," the ministry leadership positions of apostle, prophet, evangelist, pastor, and teacher are spoken of as a gift. What does it mean to have a gift? Gifts are bestowed by a giver to a receiver. The gift given often speaks just as much to the one who gives it as the one who receives it. How do you feel when you are given just the right gift at the right time? How amazing is it when the one who gives you that gift plugs right into who you are and gives you that perfect gift, that's just right for you? On the reverse, how does it feel when someone just gives you whatever they have laying around with no consideration for who you are as a person or whether you might want to have it.

With God, we never have to worry the gifts He gives are disconnected from who we are or irrelevant to us. They always tune in, recognizing our personalities and the challenges and changes we must meet therein as we go forward in our journey with Him. Without repentance, the gifts can't be taken back. God knows what He is doing when He gives them to us, and for that reason, they speak to us in a few different ways. The gifts God gives tells us about God, Who gives them; they tell us about us, as individuals; and they tell us about what is most relevant and needed in the church at this time in history. They bring together the incredible combination of eternal knowledge with practical application in a way that is practical, understandable, and supernatural, all at once.

When it comes to the Ephesians 4 leadership gifts, the gifts given are no different. They speak of God, they speak to the individuals called to leadership who operate them, and they speak to each and every one of us who has the benefit and blessing of experiencing their gifts when they are operational. Leadership is just as much a gift to the Body of Christ as the charismatic gifts, open to all, which we will discuss in the next chapter. We should appreciate and receive solid spiritual leadership as a gift, both from God and those who operate in their respective callings, because they are a necessary gift and purpose for us in this hour.

The gifts spoken of in Ephesians 4 are known as "ascension gifts" because Ephesians 4:9-10 speaks of their bestowment in connection with Christ's ascension into heaven. When He returned to the Father, He left the bestowment of His leadership abilities and gifts to His church so it could efficiently function. If we look at the Scriptures, we see that Jesus was the only One Who functioned as all five of the offices mentioned in Ephesians 4:11: He was an apostle, prophet, evangelist, pastor, and teacher. Now that He has ascended, those different offices flow and function through the church so it can continue. To this very day we see people gifted to be apostles, prophets, evangelists, pastors, and teachers. These gifts are from the Greek word *didomi*, which refers to this specific gift of leadership. While everyone in the Body has gifts, not everyone has received this special ascension gift as purposed.

Receiving an ascension gift doesn't make someone better than someone else. Ascension gifts are there for a purpose, which we will examine momentarily. It just makes someone's calling and purpose in the Kingdom different from someone else's. If we desire to see the Kingdom advance, we have to have structure and guidance to do it. Through these different leadership gifts, we find the perfect needed balance to both advance and sustain the Kingdom until the time when Jesus comes back.

Ephesians 4:12-16 outlines the important reasons why we need His leadership in the church:

- To equip God's people to do His work.

- Build up the church.

- To mature the church.

- To keep us from succumbing to false and "trendy" teaching that does not lead to life (deceptive teaching).

- Speak the truth in love.

- Grow us in every way to be more like Christ.

- Learn more about Christ.

- Embrace Christ as the head of the church.

- Help us to figure out how we best fit together, so we can fit together perfectly.

- Help one another to grow.

- Keep the Body healthy, growing, and full of love.

These important duties and responsibilities are essential aspects of leadership that give the church a presence of continuing knowledge and guidance as we go through the different phases, trends, ideas, and yes, battles throughout the ages. If we will only embrace God's establishment for leadership, the church has the potential to be deeply powerful and transforming, even in our modern times. We can't deny we are up against many odds today, and that is why we need all the help we can get. Thank God for His gifts! They give us the power to keep going, even when it seems like we can't advance. His Kingdom will not be defeated!

LIVING WHAT YOU'VE LEARNED

With the Lord's authority I say this: Live no longer as the Gentiles do, for they are hopelessly confused. Their minds are full of darkness; they wander far from the life God gives because they have closed their minds and hardened their hearts against Him. They have no sense of shame. They live for lustful pleasure and eagerly practice every kind of impurity.

But that isn't what you learned about Christ. Since you have heard about Jesus and have learned the truth that comes from Him, throw off your old sinful nature and your former way of life, which is corrupted by lust and deception. Instead, let the Spirit renew your thoughts and attitudes. Put on your new nature, created to be like God—truly righteous and holy.

So stop telling lies. Let us tell our neighbors the truth, for we are all parts of the same body. And "don't sin by letting anger control you." Don't let the sun go down while you are still angry, for anger gives a foothold to the devil.

If you are a thief, quit stealing. Instead, use your hands for good hard work, and then give generously to others in need. Don't use foul or abusive language. Let everything you say be good and helpful, so that your words will be an encouragement to those who hear them.

And do not bring sorrow to God's Holy Spirit by the way you live. Remember, He has identified you as His own, guaranteeing that you will be saved on the day of redemption.

Get rid of all bitterness, rage, anger, harsh words, and slander, as well as all types of evil behavior. Instead, be kind to each other, tenderhearted, forgiving one another, just as God through Christ has forgiven you. (Ephesians 4:17-32)

Ephesians 4 now goes on to discuss matters of living the faith that come as a result of abiding by and receiving the blessed instruction of God's leadership, given to all in the church. We've discussed belief, we have discussed leadership, and now to round out the chapter, the Apostle Paul starts to address the results of such things. As we've already discussed some, there should always be a result, or product, for the things you are learning and experiencing in your faith. Our faith shouldn't be something we keep to ourselves!

Thus, we learn here we shouldn't be living like we used to, any which way we please. We should live in a different way than those who haven't come to empowerment and change of faith. Instead of filling our minds with things that take us further away from God, we should be led into a place where we desire to please God and focus on things that bless and renew us spiritually. Our attitude should be different! We should focus on doing the right thing and on doing in all things, what pleases God.

What does this kind of living look like? It is easy to break down into simple points, based on this chapter:

- Transform in our attitudes and behavior, so we are no longer living like we did before we came to know Christ.

- Come from a place where we don't understand the ways of God into walking better in God's ways, understanding Who He is and how we can live as He would best desire.

- Open our minds to the truth God offers us.

- Walk away from the lusts we pursue (whatever form they might take) and the deception that goes along with them.

- Stop telling lies, to both believers and non-believers alike.

- Don't allow your strong and uncontrolled emotions to lead you into a place of sin.

- Work through your strong emotions on a regular basis.

- Do not steal.

- Be willing and able and eager to work, even if you have to work hard.

- Give generously to others.

- Avoid using foul language or language that is abusive or offensive to others.

- Make a point to use your words to be helpful and edifying to others.
- Avoid using your behavior to grieve the Spirit.

- Work through the things in your life that cause you to be bitter, raging, angry, harsh, or slanderous.

- Be kind to one another, forbearing, and forgiving, because we have been forgiven through the work of Christ.

Look over this basic list and think about your life. Where can you improve? How can you allow the Spirit to bring to mind the practical and great teaching you've received? How can you better live what you are learning in your faith? No matter where you are at on your walk, we can all use improvement. Embracing and receiving greater revelation on these spiritual foundations will help you to run this race with a greater sense of joy and understanding.

⸺ CHAPTER FIVE ⸺
OFFERING WHAT YOU'VE RECEIVED

IT'S great – and desirable – for us to come together in church and offer our different gifts and abilities for God's purposes. That's the way church is supposed to be…but what happens when we don't know what those gifts or abilities are? What happens when we don't understand just what we have to offer, and it feels like we screw it up? Better yet, what happens when we have limited examples of the gifts we have, and we aren't sure how to implement or offer them in different settings?

It's not uncommon to hear gifts mentioned today, but in-depth study on just what spiritual gifts are, how they manifest, what they look like, and how to properly implement them in a ministry setting and one's life are seldom seen. This means there is a great amount of confusion among many over just what the gifts are and how to operate them.

Here we will sort out some of the confusion about spiritual gifts and other abilities, talents, and functions we can bring to the table in church settings. While nowhere near the full, comprehensive approach that can be had with this topic, this overview will sort through the confusion and invite powerful discussion and interest in all things we can offer in the Kingdom.

SPIRITUAL GIFTS

In the last chapter, we discussed one form of spiritual gifts: the *didomi*, or leadership gifts. These gifts are open exclusively to those who are called to leadership, because it gives those who have them the ability to lead, and lead well. These aren't the only gifts that exist, however. There are also the *charisma* gifts, which are from the work of the Holy Spirit and open to anyone in the Body of Christ. We will look at these gifts in this chapter to gain a better understanding of the way spiritual gifts work in all of us. Learning about the charismatic gifts helps us recognize the Spirit at work within us and within the Body of Christ as a whole and identify the Spirit's movements.

Like we discussed earlier, spiritual gifts are gifts, meaning God gives them to us without respect of who we are and without any sort of negotiation or cost to us. This doesn't mean having a spiritual gift doesn't require anything from us. We are responsible for developing spiritual gifts within ourselves and we are required to operate in the necessary discipline, maturity, and insight to properly walk in them. It does mean that we work with God, God works with us, and not everyone understands that process or product all the time. This isn't an excuse to go rogue, but a demand that spiritual gifts do require us to learn self-control, tempering, and are subject to the gift of discernment (which we will discuss shortly).

Now, dear brothers and sisters, regarding your question about the special abilities the Spirit gives us. I don't want you to misunderstand this. You know that when you were still pagans, you were led astray and swept along in worshiping speechless idols. So I want you to know that no one speaking by the Spirit of God will curse Jesus, and no one can say Jesus is Lord, except by the Holy Spirit.

There are different kinds of spiritual gifts, but the same Spirit is the source of them all. There are different kinds of service, but we serve the same Lord. God works in different ways, but it is the same God Who does the work in all of us.

A spiritual gift is given to each of us so we can help each other. (1 Corinthians 12:1-7)

This passage of Scripture affirms again that spiritual gifts are from a common source: the Holy Spirit. There are different ways we may use these gifts and different ways we may serve in the Kingdom, but we are all serving God. There are different ways God works, but it is still the one God, Who is the source of all we do for Him.

It is evident from verse 7 why we have these spiritual gifts: to help one another. As we go along on our faith journey, we will all need the reception of spiritual gifts and the benefit of them, for the good of our faith and the good of one another. They prove God knows our personal spiritual needs, the needs for the whole of the Body, and need in general that helps inspire all of us to edify, encourage, and build up this Kingdom until the time when Jesus comes again.

There is considerable debate over the specific ways that spiritual gifts work and how many spiritual gifts someone can have. It isn't my intent to discuss or debate these matters, because I don't think these arguments resolve much. The Scriptures tell us spiritual gifts come as the Spirit moves upon the people, which means any number of situations can result from such spiritual power. There may be times when we operate a spiritual gift on a regular basis, or times when we operate a spiritual gift once or a few times, out of a need that exists. It is probably safe to say that some believers will operate in a few gifts, some will operate very strongly in one or some stronger than others, or that others will operate in every gift at some point in time, diversified over the years. The point isn't how many gifts we have or what they are; the point is what we do with them. We don't have these gifts to edify ourselves or to be noticed, but as the Scripture says, to help one another.

The Bible identifies seventeen different gifts as "spiritual gifts" in the New Testament, open to anyone in the Body of Christ:

- **Word of wisdom** (1 Corinthians 12:8)
- **Word of knowledge** (1 Corinthians 12:8)
- **Faith** (1 Corinthians 12:9)
- **Healing** (1 Corinthians 12:9)
- **Miracles** (1 Corinthians 12:10)
- **Prophecy** (Romans 12:6, 1 Corinthians 12:10)
- **Discernment of spirits** (1 Corinthians 12:10)
- **Speaking in different tongues** (1 Corinthians 12:10)
- **Interpretation of tongues** (1 Corinthians 12:10)
- **Helps** (1 Corinthians 12:28)
- **Administration/government** (1 Corinthians 12:28)
- **Ministry** (Romans 12:7)
- **Teaching** (Romans 12:7)
- **Exhortation** (Romans 12:8)
- **Giving** (Romans 12:8)

- **Leadership** (Romans 12:8)
- **Mercy** (Romans 12:8)

We can group different gifts into four different categories, to make our study a little easier to understand:

- Prophetic gifts
- Administrative gifts
- Instructional gifts
- Transformative gifts

PROPHETIC GIFTS

- Word of Wisdom
- Word of knowledge
- Prophecy
- Discernment of Spirits
- Speaking in different tongues

To one person the Spirit gives the ability to give wise advice; to another the same Spirit gives a message of special knowledge. (1 Corinthians 12:8)

In His grace, God has given us different gifts for doing certain things well. So if God has given you the ability to prophesy, speak out with as much faith as God has given you. (Romans 12:6)

He gives one person the power to perform miracles, and another the ability to prophesy. He gives someone else the ability to discern whether a message is from the Spirit of God or from another spirit. Still another person is given the ability to speak in unknown languages... (1 Corinthians 12:10)

Prophetic spiritual gifts relate to prophecy in some way (such as one speaking for or representing the message of God). There are different ways this prophetic message can be conveyed through these gifts, and for this reason, the different prophetic gifts reveal different aspects of prophetic experience. Operating in these different gifts does not mean one is a prophet, but that one has been given a spiritual insight from God through that gift that is to be shared. The different prophetic gifts are word of wisdom, word of knowledge, prophecy, discernment of spirits, and speaking in different tongues.

- **Word of wisdom:** The word of wisdom is an instance where someone is able to convey wisdom through insight, especially when one isn't familiar with the situation themselves. It is a revelation from God Himself, offered through an individual to another individual or a group. It might fall in the form of a general message, word of advice, word of guidance, revelation for someone or for a group, correction, counseling, or an instructional message.

- **Word of knowledge:** The word of knowledge conveys information through the impartation of applicable knowledge. It might relate to a specific situation or in a general sense, might be educational or personal, and is received by divine revelation. A word of knowledge comes from God, and might come through a message, a teaching, a word of advice or guidance, a revelation, or correction. It might call out an issue, offer situation or advice, or convey divine information to the hearers.

- **Prophecy:** Prophecy is a very weighty subject, one that is more than we can cover in a paragraph. Prophecy is one of, if not the oldest, spiritual gift, existing from Old Testament times. Today, however, prophecy is not exclusively limited to the prophets. The work of prophecy is not just to foretell the future, although that is sometimes part of it. Prophecy reveals the word or revelation of God, thus making the will of God known to the people. Prophecy may be made known through revelatory word, instruction, message, or teaching. It also helps us to understand Biblical prophecy, foretell where we are going, and work in the different areas of prophetic arts, such as dance, music, or writing. A prophetic gift should always be tested, and subject to the discernment of the prophets.

- **Discernment of spirits:** Discernment of spirits is the ability to tell apart different spiritual origins behind issues, people, words, or claims. It is the "sorting out" process of what happens behind the scenes in spiritual origins. Discernment helps us to recognize what is true from what is false, and people with the discernment of spirits can know what is evil, wrong, demonic, good or divine, carnal, or cultural. In summary, discernment is knowing what is God from what is not. Someone who has the gift of discerning spirits might educate on spirits, recognize what is behind a motive, intent, or action, judge between words and prayers, arbitrate situations, and detect truth, lies, and complications that might arise.

- **Speaking in different tongues:** Speaking in tongues was first seen among the believers during the feast of Pentecost. It connects to prophecy as both a fulfillment and introduction to it, as speaking in tongues was first seen on the official birthday of the church. This incredible experience sees the person so full of the Spirit, the language of heaven comes forth from their mouth. It serves to proclaim the Gospel, to utter secret truths and hidden things, for deep prayer purposes, intercede through the Spirit, give a message, or to prove the miraculous of God exists.

ADMINISTRATIVE GIFTS

- Helps
- Administration
- Ministry
- Leadership

Here are some of the parts God has appointed for the church... those who can help others, those who have the gift of leadership... (1 Corinthians 12:28)

If your gift is serving others, serve them well... (Romans 12:7)

...If God has given you leadership ability, take the responsibility seriously... (Romans 12:8)

An administrative gift is the ability to organize and govern the church, especially when it comes to the regular needs and governing issues that arise within church settings. Administrative gifts show someone can lead and impact in a leadership capacity, without being a full-time church leader (such as an individual in an Ephesians 4:11 position). The administrative gift assists established leadership by helping in the assistance and oversight of different works and ministries that demand management and maintenance. We might more commonly refer to the gifts of administration as "lay leadership positions." They give those who are not called to ministry but do have leadership abilities the opportunity to offer their gift for the good of the Kingdom.

- **Helps:** Helps is a broad category of church service used to describe all aspects of church ministry that help the church consistently function regularly. Helps ministry covers those works of a church that are necessary to run, operate, and function as a part of general help or service in a community. For helps ministries to function properly, they require structured operation, service, work, and assistance. There are so many examples of helps, we cannot list them all here, but some include altar work, children's ministry, audio/visual ministry, singing on the worship team or choir, or community outreach.

- **Administration:** The gift of administration is a gift of governance, one that stands forth as a leader with organizational and implementing abilities to execute structure and efficiency. Someone with a gift of administration can administrate, continuing in the facilitation and structure put in place by the apostle of a church. They help to put organization in a situation, along with day-to-day work, office work, scheduling, planning, assisting and overseeing special events, personal assistance to a spiritual leader, and shaping of the flow and vision of a church and ministry.

- **Ministry:** Ministry, sometimes called "ministry service," is a gift of service. We aren't told how to specifically be of service, because there is no long list of ways to do the work of God. In service, we are asked to rise in our abilities and bless others with them, meeting the needs that exist. Service may involve service for a ministry leader, hospitality after a service, assisting in social outreach, making visits to a shut-in, prison ministry, or any other way we can bless the Lord through service to others.

- **Leadership:** Also called the gift of leading, leadership is the ability to stand and lead in any given situation, most especially in an organized setting. When one has a gift of leadership, someone might lead a class or some other structured setting without the call to be a full-time leader. In contrast with an administrator, a leader helps in making sure the needed structure is present and carried out in whatever context of one's leadership sphere. Leaderships are a part of ministry and church teams, assisting in working out issues and governance, helping to execute and oversee social ministry or needed programs, and offering needed leadership maintenance, wherever it might be.

INSTRUCTIONAL GIFTS

- Teaching
- Interpretation of tongues
- Exhortation

...If you are a teacher, teach well... (Romans 12:7)

... while another is given the ability to interpret what is being said. (1 Corinthians 12:10)

If your gift is to encourage others, be encouraging... (Romans 12:8)

The instructional gifts help us to figure things out that require more direction than just general prayer or spiritual insight one can obtain on their own. We all need help figuring things out from time to time, because it's not always clear what direction we should take or where we should go when left to figure things out ourselves. To remain on the right way, God provides us with educational and directional gifts.

- **Teaching:** Teaching is relatively self-explanatory; it is the ability to impart knowledge, wisdom, and instruction into a group or student who are taught. Varying from a teacher in Ephesians 4:11 ministry in that it is not a pursued ministry, teaching has many different applications in the church, even today. One with a teaching gift might fill in for a leader who is unable to teach a class, they might handle instruction of new members, offer expertise on a specific area of specialization, lead a Bible study or group class, teach Sunday school, write programs or curriculum or teach such, or offer any sort of instructional base that's needed in a teaching situation.

- **Interpretation of tongues:** When one receives the gift of tongues in front of a group or a church meeting, the interpretation of tongues is necessary to bring into focus just what is said and why that spiritual word has gone forth in that time. Because speaking in tongues is a spiritual process, reflecting and speaking the language of heaven, it is possible no one will understand it, someone might hear it in their own language, or that further explanation of tongues is necessary for those who are present. It is essential the word spoken is understood, and thus the public delivery of tongues should follow with an interpretation. As a spiritual process, one can interpret the words of tongues and offer explanation for those who hear through the work of the Spirit. An interpretation of tongues captures the heart and words of heaven, imparting mysteries and ideas we do not yet fully understand, and making them purposed for those who hear, recognize, and see them are able to do so.

- **Exhortation:** Exhortation is a word that means "to build up" or "to edify." When one has a gift of exhortation, it means they can see things on a practical level, break them down to be understandable, and then help keep someone motivated, interested, and determined through their process. When we think of exhortation we often think of verbal praise, but the gift of exhortation is more than just telling someone they've done a good job. Those with the gift of exhortation are great at explaining context and content, helping people through the "how-to" of spiritual life and matters. It may show up in counseling, a personal word or advice, giving a word of exhortation before a group, a seminar or class, or maybe even specified preaching or teaching.

TRANSFORMATIVE GIFTS

- Faith
- Healing
- Miracles
- Giving
- Mercy

The same Spirit gives great faith to another, and to someone else the one Spirit gives the gift of healing. (1 Corinthians 12:9)

He gives one person the power to perform miracles... (1 Corinthians 12:10)

...If it is giving, give generously...And if you have a gift for showing kindness to others, do it gladly. (Romans 12:8)

Transformative gifts are those that promote spiritual change, or transformation, in an individual's life. Transformation calls to us beyond what we experience in the flesh, in our problems this side of heaven, to look at things from a deeper spiritual perspective. They are an inspiration both to those who operate these gifts as well as those who receive from them, and the power of the transformative extends what we can easily understand in this realm. They prove to us that God desires to give good to His children, and that if we are willing to look, our spiritual lives are there, before our eyes.

- **Faith:** We know about "faith" as believers, because we can see faith is the substance (or stuff) of things hoped for but is the evidence (or proof) of things we can't see right now. In other words, this means that faith, in and of itself, proves itself. It stands as its own evidence, essence, and argument. To have a gift of faith means that one has an enduring, solid confidence in God and the things God can do, beyond the level of faith we have as we believe in God for salvation, as a Christian. It is a focus on God that supersedes everything else that comes along, as one with this gift believes in the Scriptures and the promises of God unto total life. The gift of faith stands as an inspiration to all believers, and reminds us that with God, all things are possible. Individuals with this gift are an encouragement in faith, extend their confidence in God to all of us, enthusiastic about what God is doing, and offer their unique perspective to all they encounter.

- **Healing:** The gift of healing is relatively self-explanatory. It is a gift by which God moves through an individual to heal another. Healing is about more than just symptoms, however. It works to transform lives by making God's power known. When one has the gift of healing, they can offer God's presence, His touch, and His power wherever it is needed: physically, emotionally, mentally, or spiritually. This is often done with the laying on of hands and prayer, but a healing gift can manifest in many ways: anointing with oil, offering comfort, prayer, counseling, or general assistance.

- **Miracles:** A miracle is any occurrence outside the order of nature and science that has its origins in the spiritual realm, coming exclusively from God. We can't pull apart a miracle and figure out some sort of natural reason for its occurrence. Miracles belong to

God alone; to bring Him the glory and prove He is God. Miracles as a spiritual gift cover a lot of ground, but we could say that miracles cover supernatural happenings outside of the gifts already mentioned. Such would include raising the dead, casting out demons, not being harmed by poison, and the ability to withstand and overcome evil. A worker of miracles may do so in front of or with a group or privately with one person, at any time.

- **Giving:** Like the gift of faith, there are some individuals who are endowed with a divine heart to give. They are excited and willing to do so beyond giving out of obligation, as we are called as believers. Givers desire to contribute to a work however they can, giving from whatever they have, and are excited to do so. Givers are one of the most powerful foundations to the Kingdom of God, because it costs money and offered time to keep things going. They know how to encourage others with their giving, because sometimes a pep talk and an action plan is simply not enough. A gift of giving will give of finances, of time, resources, gifts, and attention, without having to constantly remind or ask for those things.

- **Mercy:** A gift of mercy taps into God's very own heart to desire an end to suffering. Those who have a gift of mercy don't desire to see others get "what they deserve," but instead, desire to show empathy, compassion, and sincere concern. In mercy, an individual walks through things with others instead of throwing them aside and recognizes when someone is having a hard time or going awry rather than foundationally wrong. They respond with love and empathy, a heart that comes from the Father Himself. Those with a gift of mercy are quick to exercise this gift anywhere and will exemplify it in their relationships with others. They are supportive, helpful, and loving, showing love and appreciation in all they do.

THE FUNCTIONS OF THE CHURCH

Help me understand the meaning of Your commandments,
and I will meditate on Your wonderful deeds. (Psalm 119:27)

Spiritual gifts are an important foundation to what we do and see in church, but they are not the only ways God works in His people. There is also a group of specified works known as the functions of the church. These are so-called because they help the church to "function" and are specified as existing in the Scriptures, but not identified as spiritual gifts, offices, or appointments. They can operate in connection with a spiritual office, with spiritual gifts, or on their own. Usually, however, a function typically is seen as many spiritual abilities combined into a functional purpose. Anyone in the church can operate a function, or multiple functions.

The ten functions of the church are:

- **Preacher:** Preachers carry the message of God's Word. Preaching is distinguished from teaching through its nature and style of message. The goal of preaching is to make a message known and open it up in a way that commands attention. Often other things come with preaching, including signs and wonders to confirm the message. Through preaching, the world has the chance to come to know God through eternity. As the command to proclaim the Gospel to all creation is open to all believers, the function of a preacher is open to all.

- **Missionary:** A missionary, as "one with a mission," is an individual who, as moved by their faith or specifically by the call of God, goes into a foreign country or new territory to proclaim the Gospel and establish a long-term plan to teach the people present there and establish centers for worship. Missionaries may travel in their work on their own, or they may work and operate with a missions group. Someone may go on missions out of their own desire to do so or may go because God Himself directs them to go. Missions are a difficult challenge, and a missionary may desire their mission, or avoid it. Missionaries, however, reveal the important universal nature of the church and the importance of going into all the world to complete the Great Commission.

- **Dreamer and Visionary:** Combined as one function because the purpose behind the two is the same, a dreamer is an individual who dreams and receives divine messages from them, while a visionary is an individual who experiences divine messages from visions. The difference is the state of being one is in when they receive such: dreamers are asleep, while visionaries are awake and enter a spiritual state that shows them something from outside of this world. Dreams and visions can happen to anyone, anywhere in the world, at any time. The purpose of a dream or vision is to convey a divine message, and that message may be personal, national, or worldwide. Tending to be largely symbolic, dreamers and visionaries may not always understand the contents of their dreams, and such may require interpretation.

- **Interpreter of dreams and visions:** For those times when a dream or vision just doesn't make sense, someone with the ability to interpret a dream or vision is most helpful and useful. An interpreter of dreams and visions may ask questions, listen to the entire expanse of the dream's or vision's contents, and handle the complicated matters that may be present in a dream or vision. Dream and vision interpretation cannot be taught from a book, because dreams and visions can be specific to the individuals who receive them or generalized in a larger sense. This means dream and vision interpretation must come from God, because the same symbolism can mean different things in different situations.

- **Intercessor:** An intercessor is an individual who engages in intercession. While intercession is a ridiculously huge topic right now, it is often taken out of context. Intercession is different from regular prayer as it is meeting with and falling in line with heaven for the sake of earth and also meeting with the needs on earth for the sake of heaven. It is this wrangling, in-between job, considering both the practicality of earthly need and the spirituality of heaven. Intercessors show the way the natural and spiritual are interconnected, as they intervene in a deeper way to bring forth divine justice in this world. Intercession is mentioned along with prayer, but it is a deeper spiritual positioning, one of spiritual warfare on behalf of another, a group, a nation, or the needs of this world. Being an intercessor is not limited to prophets, and being an intercessor does not necessarily mean one is a prophet. It is its own function, one that shows an aggressiveness in spiritual warfare for the benefit of both God and humanity.

- **Watchman and Gatekeeper:** Combined as one function because their positions are very similar, the work of watchmen and gatekeepers provide a dual defense to monitor and prepare for anything that seeks to approach or invade a place. The two work together, with the watchman on a perimeter alert and a gatekeeper on alert at the door or gate. In ancient times, these positions were both sacred and secular. They monitored both literal invasions and spiritual ones. A watchman may work to guard a church or ministry they are part of, over immediate households, cities, nations, or regions. They are accustomed to spiritual disruptions and disturbances, in order to make sure spiritual watches are kept. Gatekeepers keep watch over the temple, or house of the Lord. They are accustomed to preparation work, such as sacred items, church security, protection of church leadership, and monitoring of the "gates," or doors. Gatekeepers also work to prepare and protect the church from a spiritual perspective.

- **Handmaiden and menservant:** Combined as one function because they perform the same duties and responsibilities, Handmaiden and menservants were a specific type of servant spoken of in Acts 2:18. They were so-called because they were literally "at hand" any time their master needed them. Often working as personal attendants, handmaidens and menservants handled all the personal needs of their masters: running errands, handling the household, keeping things in order, and seeing their master was properly cared for. This depicts the type of servanthood we are called to exude in the Kingdom: being this available and that important for the work of God, today.

- **Scribe:** Scribes are gifted writers and commentators on Scriptural ideas, positioned to influence others with the ideas and understandings of God. Scribes were individuals who calculated, counted, called to attention, kept records, handled dictation, read what was written, wrote their own words, and kept sacred records. Today, a scribe would be an individual who is a serious scholar of the Scriptures, well-versed in its context and interpretation, to write and educate others on their divine contents.

- **Spiritual father and mother:** Combined as one function because they perform the same purpose, a spiritual father or mother is an "originator" of one's faith, somehow standing as an original or foundational teacher in one's life. This indicates they provide something essential on which faith can develop. This is distinguished from our personal leadership, which may educate and bless us, but is not foundational in some form. A spiritual parent may be part of our walk when we start believing, when we shift into something else, when we embrace a new calling, or when we move into a new spiritual dimension and are properly taught for this phase by our spiritual "originators."

- **Mystic:** A mystic is an individual who has a mystical experience with God, one that is beyond a dream or a vision. Mystics do not just see what is to come but have an entire sensory experience by which they can hear, see, smell, touch, and taste whatever they experience. It might be experienced in part, or in full. This is a complicated and deep aspect of spiritual life and in truth, most mystical experiences are not fully understood this side of heaven. They reveal eternity to us and show us the promise that God is still working in ways we cannot always see, even today.

Abilities, Talents, and Skills

Under a final general heading of things we can offer from our own personality and ability resources are abilities, talents, and skills. Sometimes people call these things "gifts," but I am referring to them by a more official name to distinguish them from spiritual gifts, thus avoiding confusion. Abilities, talents, and skills are aptitudes that we are either born with, develop, or a combination of both that enhance our lives and the lives of others as we offer these different things for the benefit of all. There are many things people can offer as part of an ability, talent, or skill to the Kingdom that aren't all about spiritual gifts or functions. Some people play an instrument, some people sing, some are great with financial plans, some are gifted business consultants, some are great with crafting or building, and so on and so forth. These abilities are just as useful to the Kingdom as anything else, because such offers a necessary contribution to Kingdom edification. They help to meet practical needs and stand as an encouragement in the faith.

*So the whole community of Israel left Moses and returned to their tents. All whose hearts were stirred and whose spirits were moved came and brought their sacred offerings to the L*ORD*. They brought all the materials needed for the Tabernacle, for the performance of its rituals, and for the sacred garments. Both men and women came, all whose hearts were willing. They brought to the L*ORD *their offerings of gold—brooches, earrings, rings from their fingers, and necklaces. They presented gold* *objects of every kind as a special offering to the* LORD. *All those who owned the following items willingly brought them: blue, purple, and scarlet thread; fine linen and goat hair for cloth; and tanned ram skins and fine goatskin leather. And all who had silver and bronze objects gave them as a sacred offering to the* LORD. *And those who had acacia wood brought it for use in the project.*

All the women who were skilled in sewing and spinning prepared blue, purple, and scarlet thread, and fine linen cloth. All the women who were willing used their skills to spin the goat hair into yarn. The leaders brought onyx stones and the special gemstones to be set in the ephod and the priest's chestpiece. They also brought spices and olive oil for the light, the anointing oil, and the fragrant incense. So the people of Israel—every man and woman who was eager to help in the work the LORD *had given them through Moses—brought their gifts and gave them freely to the* LORD. **(Exodus 35:20-29)**

When it was time to build the tabernacle in ancient times, all Israel was called to bring forth the necessary materials and offer their skills to build and beautify their worship space. It's not so much the specific things they did, but the fact that everyone with an ability brought something and did so freely, as prompted by God's Spirit. This means everyone had a part, by contributing, in the product and purpose of the tabernacle.

I understand the temptation today to hire outside help to accomplish things or for leaders to take the expenses of an event unto themselves because they get tired of waiting for help. The problem with this is, though, that if people must put something in, they will get much more out of it rather than the leaders taking everything over on their own. The same is true with any ministry, on any level. The celebration and joy should come as everyone is willing to offer whatever it is they have for the betterment of the church or ministry community.

Whatever your skill is, apply it to your church or ministry. Offer it! If there isn't any need for it specifically right now, there will come a time when it will be needed. If it needs a little modification to fit a ministry perspective, figure out how it can work! Step out and offer these abilities, because doing so will help you stand far more involved and participatory than if you wait and stand back for someone to ask. In God's Kingdom, we are first in line to offer, always.

Financial Giving

We will be examining the matter of giving in a later chapter, but because we are talking about offering what we have in this chapter, we will do a short discussion on the relevance of financial giving in the life of the believer.

When we talk about "offering what we have," We always think about the generalization where we desire to "give our whole selves." We love the songs like *I Give Myself Away* because they tap into a concept we have about "giving ourselves" to God. The question becomes, however, what does "giving our whole selves" to God mean? Is it a strange abstract thing that happens during worship at church, or is it something that requires more of us? The answer, of course, is the latter. Giving ourselves to God means giving all of ourselves to God, not just the parts of ourselves that are easy or don't ask anything of us. If anything, giving ourselves to God means that sometimes giving will hurt, and God will ask things of us that we don't always want to do or give.

This becomes especially true when it comes to finances. Even though we are often just as stingy with our time and our abilities as we are with our money, it seems easier for us to talk about giving out of our ability than it is to talk about giving from our money. Somewhere inside, I think we like the idea of being pushed and prodded to give out of our abilities; it makes us feel good to talk about them, think on them, and have others try to draw them out of us. It's comfortable to talk about us, us, us. Yet when it comes to money...everyone wants to back out of the conversation. Money is a discussion that makes everyone uncomfortable, and in response, many in church today avoid having it. Sure, we want to talk about a financial miracle or a breakthrough (none of which is found in Scripture), but when it comes up that God simply expects we give...everyone wants to avoid it.

If we aren't having a conversation about money, however, we aren't talking about the full picture of giving. If we give to God in every area except giving, we aren't fully giving of ourselves. If we don't give where it hurts, is uncomfortable, forces us to examine our priorities, or challenges us...we aren't giving all the way.

Then the Pharisees met together to plot how to trap Jesus into saying something for which he could be arrested. They sent some of their disciples, along with the supporters of Herod, to meet with Him. "Teacher," they said, "we know how honest you are. You teach the way of

God truthfully. You are impartial and don't play favorites. Now tell us what you think about this: Is it right to pay taxes to Caesar or not?"

But Jesus knew their evil motives. "You hypocrites!" He said. "Why are you trying to trap me? Here, show me the coin used for the tax." When they handed Him a Roman coin, He asked, "Whose picture and title are stamped on it?"

"Caesar's," they replied.

"Well, then," He said, "give to Caesar what belongs to Caesar, and give to God what belongs to God."

His reply amazed them, and they went away. (Matthew 22:15-22)

We already touched on this passage earlier as pertains to earthly citizenship and governmental matters. On the inverse, however, this passage points to the same relevance and importance about not just paying what we owe our governments, but also, what we owe God. We should never, ever think when we walk into a ministry setting, it's acceptable to stand there empty-handed. It isn't acceptable to be a part of a ministry, recognizing its place in the Kingdom, and refuse to give. There are no viable or justifiable excuses for not giving, only reasons why we are simply stating that God and the advance of the work is not a priority for us. When we get that real about it – and admit we are not giving to God what belongs to Him – it changes our perspective of ourselves and the limitations we create to avoid giving in full.

GETTING INVOLVED

This entire chapter has been devoted to looking at different gifts, functions, abilities, and giving that can all offer you a way to participate in the ministry or church you belong to, in a new and different way. You may find it takes some time to learn just what gifts you have and just how you can best use them. This is normal, and to be expected. It might also take some time to figure out the best way to walk in every single gift, function, and ability you have. It's a true learning process to respect authority, discern when things are best used or best suitable in any given situation. We are also called to temper the spiritual gifts we have with the general call we have to live connected to one another in the Body and behave and interact in a spiritually mature and fruitful manner in each and every situation. Spiritual gifts, functions, and abilities are not an excuse for us to act however we desire. If we are led by the Spirit, we must operate by the Spirit! These things force us to work with others, connect and jump in, feet first, to the power and promise of Kingdom participation.

God has given each of you a gift from His great variety of spiritual gifts. Use them well to serve one another. Do you have the gift of speaking? Then speak as though God Himself were speaking through you. Do you have the gift of helping others? Do it with all the strength and energy that God supplies. Then everything you do will bring glory to God through Jesus Christ. All glory and power to Him forever and ever! Amen. (1 Peter 4:10-11)

One of the best ways to develop your spiritual gifts, functions, and skill set is to get involved. We can sit and read about all this stuff forever, and truth be told, we will probably study different levels and understandings of these spiritual matters from now until the time when Jesus returns. As we grow, our development of our gifts and abilities can change. Sometimes certain gifts or functions grow stronger, while others aren't as notable in our lives anymore. Sometimes we don't develop certain skills or abilities like we used to, and still, we develop new ones with new interests. There will always be something in your life to offer to the Kingdom, and as you go about the development of these essential aspects of life, keep going! Keep offering, keep growing, and keep offering these things so you can grow in them through practical experience and connect to the Body of Christ in a powerful – and lasting – way.

~ CHAPTER SIX ~
Receiving Guidance From God's Military Leaders

ALL of us have a relationship with leadership, whether we like to admit it, or not. Relationships with leadership can be complicated, often because we have more than one story of leadership to share. Some are negative, some are positive, and no matter how we approach it, some send us into states of anxiety or distrust. There's no question there are bad leaders in this world, even in church. This is why it is even more important to understand some of the important boundaries both leaders should have and we should have when dealing with leadership. If we know more about what defines leadership right, we will know better how to conduct ourselves and what signs to look for when selecting, interacting with, and developing relationship with a leader.

Our approach to leadership and our long-term relationship with spiritual leadership relate in many ways to our experience and involvement with church, how apt we are to participate, and how extensively we involve our families and communities therein. No one wants to invite someone to church when we have doubts about the leaders, and no one wants to attend somewhere when there is conflict, strife, or difficulty that goes unresolved.

Perhaps the biggest area of conflicts arises when it comes to understanding the differences in perspective leaders have about a church or ministry and a ministry situation than those who are a part of that ministry may have. It is also true that many in leadership today don't properly understand their position and calling, and that those who are a part of their work don't always understand what they are supposed to do. Here, we are going to cut through some of this red tape and explain a bit about ministry leadership, thus helping you to recognize your leader's role in your life, the development of your faith, and why ministry connection is important, even when things aren't always well understood.

<u>Yes, you need to be a part of a church or ministry!</u>

We've already discussed the fact that our spiritual relationship with God is not just about God and us. Our relationship with God is also about transforming our lives and our outlook about life, and that doesn't happen if we avoid others or fail to interact with them. We are created for interaction and contact, and the best way to grow with God is to do it with other people. We need the support, the fellowship, the difficult people who make our head spin, our leadership, and our family of faith to help us grow and develop into all God has for us to be.

Let us hold tightly without wavering to the hope we affirm, for God can be trusted to keep His promise. Let us think of ways to motivate one another to acts of love and good works. And let us not neglect our meeting together, as some people do, but encourage one another, especially now that the day of His return is drawing near. (Hebrews 10:23-25)

Even though this chapter is about leadership, it's important to say that your church and ministry experience is in part about your relationship with your leader, but it's not all about you and your leader. We need the fellowship church offers – relationship with other believers – as much as we might need to connect with our spiritual leader. We discipline ourselves through church and ministry attendance because it is good for us to be with other believers and to experience the corporate praise, worship, Scriptural instruction, preaching, and fellowship with others. Attending a church or a ministry experience does more for us than just provide camaraderie, however. It also forces us to make commitments, give of ourselves in every sense (much like we talked about in the last chapter), get along with others, put into practice a true sense of Biblical submission, better our relationships and interactions with other people, provide an outlet for spiritual gifts and abilities, perform community service, and draw closer to God as we experience the principle of spiritual fellowship. The right church experience helps us to keep our faith strong, develop spiritual relationships, and do good works for other people.

Not unlike today, some people in the first century felt the church was becoming so problematic and corrupt, it was better to withdraw and practice one's faith alone, without the benefit and blessing of a church body. The passage above clarifies the importance of meeting together, of encouraging one another and learning more about our faith together, rather than going at it all alone. Yes, there is nothing wrong with studying one's faith and developing one's relationship with God privately, but we still need that balance of assembly, of corporate participation, rather than favoring one over the other and abandoning part of God's purpose for us all together. We can't be in a Kingdom by ourselves, and for this reason, it is vitally important we don't adopt the cynicism of many Christians and think there is nothing good or redeemable in the church. There is no question there are bad leaders, bad churches, and bad people who masquerade as legitimate ministries out there. Jesus Himself warned us about following such people, even in the days before the church started. We know these things exist, but we should never become so jaded by such that we don't feel it is possible to connect anywhere, with anyone. There are many groups out there, ministries out there, and churches out there, that although they may be small or not always fall on the mainline radar, willing and ready to help you develop into everything God has for you to be.

<u>What to Look for in a Church or Ministry</u>

When selecting a church or ministry, there are a few things that are very key to keep in mind. The first is that the leadership of such is very relevant to what you seek in that organization, and we will discuss leadership selection in the next section. Here, though, it's important to examine and address just what you want in a church or ministry. Many people pick church and ministry involvement based on factors that are downright wrong: the church is a megachurch, the pastor is on television, the nursey/children's church program offers free babysitting during service, everyone else seems to like this church, there are no rules about attire, there is free coffee in the waiting area, or it's not expected that one has to follow a giving structure or financial schedule. I'll never forget my shock while sitting in a service one day and someone testifying that he loved his church because nothing was expected of him!

So now you Gentiles are no longer strangers and foreigners. You are citizens along with all of God's holy people. You are members of God's family. Together, we are His house, built on the foundation of the apostles and the prophets. And the cornerstone is Christ Jesus Himself. We are carefully joined together in Him, becoming a holy temple for the Lord. Through Him you Gentiles are also being made part of this dwelling where God lives by His Spirit. (Ephesians 2:19-22)

We come together in God's house because it signifies what He has done for us and what He is still doing as He knits us together in His Kingdom. We are built foundationally on the work of apostles and prophets, with Jesus Christ standing as its cornerstone. As we are part of this dwelling where God lives, we should seek to connect, to come together, to share in this common eternal experience. It's important and vital we make the decision to belong, and we make that decision in full, all the way. Our experience in church or ministry should be five-fold:

- **Worship:** Our first – and primary – purpose in church participation should always be the sincerity of worshiping God as we come together with other believers. In this worship experience, we hear more than just our own thoughts and musings; we experience different dimensions of worship, through song, spoken word, prayer, the Word of God read, giving, and the preaching of the Word. When we experience baptism or communion, we also come into a new dimension of connection and spiritual insight. We learn the incredible multidimensional faceted ways of worship that encompass so many aspects of life: praising, praying, calling upon God's Name, learning, exploring, studying, listening, speaking, hearing, expanding, growing.

- **Praise:** Worship exalts God, while praise celebrates Him. In worship, we acknowledge God for God; in praise, we celebrate all He has done. As Christians, the heart of worship is who we are; praise is something we do. Neither one competes with the other; both are essential aspects of our spiritual walk. We need to praise God for all He has done, from eternity past to eternity future. We can do this on our own, but it is often most edifying when we do it with others.

- **Growth:** We should never, ever go to a church or ministry with the mindset that we can stay where we are at spiritually and remain comfortable. At some point in time, all of us should experience the growing pains of spiritual life, and such should reflect and advance from our experience in a church or ministry.

We should never, ever expect to find a leader or a church home that always validates what we do, without challenge or question. If we are to grow, we cannot expect everything to feel good or appeal to our innate nature to be right or validated. We must expect that growth is sometimes uncomfortable, and in proper growth, we are challenged that much more to not retreat to the place where we think we are correct, but study, examine, discuss, interact, pray, and develop into all god has for us to be.

- **Establish:** Church or ministry experience should serve to establish us somewhere (from a spiritual perspective). Sometimes we hear complaints about "church hoppers," or people who seem to gravitate between churches, one after another, because things get too difficult, too uncomfortable, or are not done in the way they desire. There's no question that you shouldn't stay somewhere if you have misgivings about the teaching you hear or some sort of mistreatment among the leadership or membership (especially if it's not being addressed), and there is also no question that sometimes we must see how we feel about a place before we commit to it. Not every church is right for everyone, and sometimes we can't tell this right away. It is true, however, that if you are at a point where you are considering membership and attending on a regular basis, it's understood this is somewhere you should consider more of a permanent establishment.

- **Connect:** Church is all about connection: connection with God, connection with your leader, a better connection with yourself and your identity, and connection with others.

- **Go:** Whatever our call and whatever we may seek to do, our connection to a ministry should motivate us that much more to live our faith, reach out to others, carry the Gospel with us, and take on new things in our spiritual lives. Instead of remaining stagnant, the establishment of church or ministry in our lives serves to provide essential roots so we can grow and thrive through everything we do.

When it comes to church and ministry selection, we must take into consideration these six essential areas. It's not a matter of preference or what we like most, but what helps us grow and discipline as disciples of

Christ. We should consider the spiritual atmosphere, the maturity of the leaders involved, the level of spiritual insight that is offered, the growth and maintenance of the congregation, and different ways you can be involved if that's where you decide to be. If you can't see yourself as a right fit, then it's probably not the right place. If you do know that this is somewhere worth pressing forward, then there you have the right place to grow and thrive in Christ.

SELECTING A LEADER

Selecting a leader is part of selecting a ministry, of course. It wouldn't make sense to have your spiritual leader over their own ministry while you are part of something else. So, the question becomes, why are these two headings separate? Surely the two are related, and yes, they do overlap in many ways. Things such as instruction, atmosphere, and involvement all relate to whoever oversees a ministry. In some ways, however, selecting your leader is about more than just choosing to go to a church or how you might feel visiting one. Since the two issues are connected, it's important to examine both issues together to see if this ministry, this church, is where God would have you to be.

One of the major reasons why people don't find themselves properly rooted and grounded in a ministry is due to leadership issues and challenges. Even if you love everything else about a ministry: the worship team, the coffee in the foyer, the children's church program, the small group Bible studies, or the overall idea of the group, you will find yourself falling short if you are unable to properly connect with the group's leader like you should.

Perhaps the first thing we need to establish is yes, you do need a spiritual leader. We've already clarified it's not practical to think you can go off and handle things on your own, without anyone else. Accepting leadership's authority and interest is for your good, because a true servant-based leader will attune to God's direction and voice in order to see that you are taught, guided, corrected, and encouraged in your faith. Good leaders help us to see our spiritual lives from a practical perspective, one we can relate to and understand and most importantly, apply, for ourselves. True leaders don't see themselves as any better than anyone else, simply that they have the spiritual gift, able to help other people find their way to the Father and develop whatever spiritual gifts and abilities lie within, waiting to be discovered.

Dear brothers and sisters, honor those who are your leaders in the Lord's work. They work hard among you and give you spiritual guidance. (1

Thessalonians 5:12)

Remember your leaders who taught you the word of God. Think of all the good that has come from their lives, and follow the example of their faith. (Hebrews 13:7)

Obey your spiritual leaders, and do what they say. Their work is to watch over your souls, and they are accountable to God. Give them reason to do this with joy and not with sorrow. That would certainly not be for your benefit. (Hebrews 13:17)

Maybe the most important thing to consider when selecting a leader is recognizing that different leaders do different things. Apostles aren't prophets aren't pastors aren't evangelists aren't teachers. Not every leader in the Body is appointed for covering leadership (and we will speak on the different types of leaders in the next section). Not every leader is right for every calling or purpose in the Body. If you are called to leadership (and you know that at this time), you need a different type of leadership training than someone who isn't called to leadership. Recognizing this fact helps you to go a long way in all you do, and to where you will be most able to establish and find edification in your walk. Different styles of leadership follow different spiritual calls, and this is most important to see in action when considering and selecting a leader.

    The next thing to consider with a leader is the concept of spiritual "drawing." Jesus said He would draw all men to Him, and I believe this is an important spiritual principle about all things related to the Kingdom of God. Through this, Jesus told us He would not force people to believe in Him, but through His countenance and the truth about Who He was, people would be drawn, even if they were different in culture than Him. It is my belief that when we are called to work with a leader, the same experience happens. We are drawn together by the power of the Spirit, because such empowers the work of the Kingdom. It is for our benefit that the Spirit draws us to competent leaders who are equipped to handle our situations, for no other reason than they help us stand prepared for the things we will encounter in this world.

    Just as the Bible says we have a "High Priest (Jesus) Who understands," our leadership should follow Christ's lead and also understand what we deal with and experience in our Christian walk. Contrary to popular belief, leaders do not have to go through everything we go through to understand what we deal with or experience. Leaders should reflect compassion in difficult times, joy in good times, and guidance at all times, but we should never, ever expect that it's acceptable to try and control our leaders with our behavior or threats or intimidation. Leadership is there to understand, to help watch over our souls, to help us stay saved and grow in the faith, and to serve the Christian communities (and by large, the world) with the Gospel. Thus, when selecting a leader, we should make sure to do the following:

- Match our leader to our spiritual call (leadership or laity).

- See their level of care and interest toward us.

- Discern their level of "understanding" as a leader.

- Watch their heart; is it that of a servant?

- Recognize their ability to encourage as well as to discipline.

- Discern their spiritual presence.

- See if we can see ourselves active and involved in this ministry.

Types of Leaders: The Ephesians 4:11 Model

One point we raised in the last section was about the existence of different types of leadership in the Kingdom of God. Most of us have heard about pastors and some have probably heard about some works, such as evangelist or maybe a prophet, but seldom have we heard – or seen – the Ephesians 4:11 model work in modern times to its fullest. This is in part because while some might talk about it, we don't study it properly to see it implemented. Many have tried to insert Ephesians 4:11 into a pastoral model of church understanding, which presupposes to work all offices of the church into different extensions of pastoral roles. Such is incorrect and eliminates the unique beauty of each office and their importance.

History is full of different church models, all of which have one thing in common: none of them have been very successful. They may be popular, confusing when aligned with Biblical protocol, and familiar to us, but all of them hit a wall, so to speak, the more that time goes on. Some systems have lasted longer than others, but all of them have reached a point in history, a time when societal and world changes have changed their effectiveness. While pastors serve a great purpose, their function isn't to train leaders. While evangelists serve an important purpose, their function isn't to go from church to church and preach all the time. While teachers are awesome, they aren't a substitute for apostles or prophets. When we eliminate important gifts from church function, we find the church lacking abilities that can take the Kingdom of God on earth from where it is to where it could be. Whenever we tell God, "Nah, we don't need what You have given us," we are shutting Him out of our faith process, only allowing Him access and influence in certain parts or areas that we desire. God doesn't work effectively in these situations, and that means when we look around, there are many churches and many denominations effectively dying for lack of motivation and focus. Embracing the full picture of Ephesians 4:11 means embracing the leadership vision of God's Kingdom and shows that we are on board with whatever – and however – God desires to work today.

Now these are the gifts Christ gave to the church: the apostles, the prophets, the evangelists, and the pastors and teachers. (Ephesians 4:11)

Given directly by Christ, the Ephesians 4:11 model for ministry includes those offices, or spiritual leadership positions, of apostles, prophets, evangelists, pastors, and teachers.

- **Apostle:** The word apostle means "one who is sent." To be sent is the essence of the apostolic work: an apostle is one who is endowed with a special message from God and is sent to go forth with that message wherever God sends them, within the world. Apostles are sent to reveal the mysteries of God to establish a proper foundation for the growth and development of the church. This insight stems from the revelation they have directly received from God, Himself. The mysteries of spiritual things relates to the unveiling of the Gospel in the world and is found in the apostle's teaching and preaching. Thus, the apostle's authority is universal, throughout the church, whether they have personally founded a local church (whether it is wise to exercise such authority in every situation is another matter altogether). Apostles implement structure in local churches and the church as a whole, through education and spiritual instruction.

  Apostles teach, train, establish, and install leaders in congregations. By doing this, apostles implement a powerful and necessary structure to help congregations thrive in their cities and regions. Apostles are ideally itinerant, rather than stationary, because they serve as a needed divine ambassador. As the administrators of the church, apostles see local leaders are properly equipped, that each church lacks nothing in proper teaching and spiritual understanding, and in their respective assignments, nothing is left undone.

- **Prophet:** The word prophet means "one who speaks for God." Yes, this might sound like a superpower, maybe it even sounds like the ultimate power trip…but true prophets do not find it to be such. It is an intense calling with great responsibility, because it requires the utmost in spiritual accuracy and ability. First and foremost, the prophet is a communicator: they convey deep spiritual knowledge and understanding from God and can present that information to others. Prophets speak God's word to individuals, nations, the church, and even at times, governmental powers. Prophets are uniquely gifted to bring forth prophetic word, interpretation, and understanding to different events. In all things, a prophet's work should help us understand God's word in our lives and see how it fits into the bigger picture of prophecy. Through the prophet's ministry, we receive God's word and understand the way it applies to our lives, and through this, we find ourselves better connected to God.

   Prophetic ministry is more mystical than administrative, bringing spiritual quality and purpose to everything in the Kingdom. Prophets work as educators of other prophets and stand as the guardian of spiritual gifts and movement in the church. It is their responsibility to educate us on discernment, prophetic history, times and seasons, and relationship with God as we grow in the spiritual. Like the apostle, prophets are universal in authority, working beyond just a local church. How a prophet operates is a discernment call, and as such, the way they may interact with others may be different, depending on the specific region, nation, or location where they are called to proclaim the Word of God.

- **Evangelist:** The word evangelist means "Christ bearer." This expresses the total fulfillment of what an evangelist does, as well as the very heart of who an evangelist is. Evangelists carry Christ within them and proclaim the Gospel of Christ, the essential message of salvation, with their mouths. While evangelists go forth as apostles do, they are not called to be administrative leaders. Evangelists preach beyond borders of churches, calling especially to reach the lost, the hurting, individuals separated from God, and those who do not know the Lord. An evangelist may teach an individual or a group, may prepare individuals for baptism or perform baptisms, and always preparing a person or group for membership in the local church. This means evangelists may not always be present in a church as a visible leader. It's not to say an evangelist can't preach in a church, but that such doesn't define the essence of evangelistic work. They are great communicators and powerful preachers, with the ability to explain and break down Scripture in a way that is understandable to others.

Evangelists are primarily itinerant preachers. This does not make them superior, nor inferior, to universal (apostle, prophet) or local (pastor) authorities, but instead, parallel to their work for the growth and development of the church. Evangelists may be involved in missions (along with apostles or other ministry workers), Gospel proclamation in a specific area or region, or a specific assignment. Evangelists are independent workers, but still accountable for their teaching and properly equipped before working in the field.

- **Pastor:** The word "pastor" means "shepherd." Just like literal shepherds who tend to and care for sheep, pastors are responsible to tend and care for the souls of those whom God entrusts to their care. Pastors spiritually feed and care for the flock entrusted to them, and ensure the flock remains together, protecting from invading forces that seek to destroy. Pastors take care of their congregations, seeing to it they have the best teaching, their spiritual needs met, and open the door for practical needs to be met.

  Pastors are limited authorities, which means they only work within their immediate local congregation. Pastors are led by apostles (and in some instances, depending on the nature of a church or ministry, prophets). Part of the work of the apostle is to install pastors, elders, and deacons in churches, recognizing that each local congregation needs such work and structure to see the work of ministry is met.

- **Teacher:** The word teacher means "one who teaches" or "one who instructs." Teachers teach things to others. In the context of the church, a teacher is one who serves the church through their gift of teaching. A teacher's operation is to teach spiritual things to whomever God calls them to instruct, and they may work with children, youth, or adults. A teacher may work in a local church as a regular teacher, they may work in an educational institution that relates to church, they may work in a seminary or a church school or may work on a level that empowers the universal church. Like an evangelist, a teacher is a parallel authority. They are not superior to other offices but work alongside both local and universal authorities to help manage, teach, and instruct the church.

The office of the teacher could be understood as a work of apologetics. This means they see the faith is understandable to those who believe in it as they provide tools to make sure the faith can be applicable and promoted by all in the church. Teachers can be very diverse, and one who serves as a teacher may function in their gift in different ways. Beyond direct individual or group instruction, teachers may also write curriculum or establish programs, work with various levels of church leadership to implement new programs or levels of instruction, assist in tests or examinations, or other areas of instruction related to the growth and development of the church.

Seeing these different gifts should go a long way in helping with leadership selection. If you are called to leadership, your best bet is to serve under an apostle or a prophet, if you are called to the prophetic. If you aren't called to serve in leadership, you will be best served by a pastor. If you aren't sure right now what you are supposed to do, a pastor is most suitable for you. As understandings of spiritual purposes may change, it's very possible there may come a time when you are better served by a different leader. This does not happen all the time or in every single season of one's life, but when it happens, it is handy to draw out this list, reading the descriptions, and figure out where you are best suited to be. With all things, prayer and divine guidance are most important and necessary.

Appointed to help: the appointments

Ephesians 4:11 ministers do not do their work without proper help. We focus on numbers and people who follow a ministry, but those are not the only people who help an Ephesians 4:11 minister. The work of the appointments, or the positions of bishop, elder, and deacon, are appointed in each and every minister to make sure every need is met and ministers are assisted in and out of season.

The saying is true and irrefutable: If any man [eagerly] seeks the office of bishop (superintendent, overseer), he desires an excellent task (work).

Now a bishop (superintendent, overseer) must give no grounds for accusation but must be above reproach, the husband of one wife, circumspect and temperate and self-controlled; [he must be] sensible and well behaved and dignified and lead an orderly (disciplined) life; [he must be] hospitable [showing love for and being a friend to the believers, especially strangers or foreigners, and be] a capable and qualified teacher,

Not given to wine, not combative but gentle and considerate, not quarrelsome but forbearing and peaceable, and not a lover of money [insatiable for wealth and ready to obtain it by questionable means].

He must rule his own household well, keeping his children under control, with true dignity, commanding their respect in every way and keeping them respectful.

For if a man does not know how to rule his own household, how is he to take care of the church of God?

He must not be a new convert, or he may [develop a beclouded and stupid state of mind] as the result of pride [be blinded by conceit, and] fall into the condemnation that the devil [once] did.

Furthermore, he must have a good reputation and be well thought of by those outside [the church], lest he become involved in slander and incur reproach and fall into the devil's trap.

In like manner the deacons [must be] worthy of respect, not shifty and double-talkers but sincere in what they say, not given to much wine, not greedy for base gain [craving wealth and resorting to ignoble and dishonest methods of getting it].

They must possess the mystic secret of the faith [Christian truth as hidden from ungodly men] with a clear conscience.

And let them also be tried and investigated and proved first; then, if they turn out to be above reproach, let them serve [as deacons].

[The] women likewise must be worthy of respect and serious, not gossipers, but temperate and self-controlled, [thoroughly] trustworthy in all things.

Let deacons be the husbands of but one wife, and let them manage [their] children and their own households well.

For those who perform well as deacons acquire a good standing for themselves and also gain much confidence and freedom and boldness in the faith which is [founded on and centers] in Christ Jesus. (1 Timothy 3:1-13, AMPC)

[These elders should be] men who are of unquestionable integrity and are irreproachable, the husband of [but] one wife, whose children are [well trained and are] believers, not open to the accusation of being loose in morals and conduct or unruly and disorderly.

For the bishop (an overseer) as God's steward must be blameless, not self-willed or arrogant or presumptuous; he must not be quick-tempered or given to drink or pugnacious (brawling, violent); he must not be grasping and greedy for filthy lucre (financial gain);

But he must be hospitable (loving and a friend to believers, especially to strangers and foreigners); [he must be] a lover of goodness [of good people and good things], sober-minded (sensible, discreet), upright and fair-minded, a devout man and religiously correct, temperate and keeping himself in hand.

He must hold fast to the sure and trustworthy Word of God as he was taught it, so that he may be able both to give stimulating instruction and encouragement in sound (wholesome) doctrine and to refute and convict those who contradict and oppose it [showing the wayward their error]. (Titus 1:6-9, AMPC)

I warn and counsel the elders among you (the pastors and spiritual guides of the church) as a fellow elder and as an eyewitness [called to testify] of the sufferings of Christ, as well as a sharer in the glory (the honor and splendor) that is to be revealed (disclosed, unfolded):

Tend (nurture, guard, guide, and fold) the flock of God that is [your responsibility], not by coercion or constraint, but willingly; not dishonorably motivated by the advantages and profits [belonging to the office], but eagerly and cheerfully;

Not domineering [as arrogant, dictatorial, and overbearing persons] over those in your charge, but being examples (patterns and models of Christian living) to the flock (the congregation). (1 Peter 5:1-3, AMPC)

The appointments are so-called because they are a desired work that someone seeks to do to serve in a leadership position in assistance to Ephesians 4:11 ministers. They are not a calling, nor an office, they do not operate their own independent ministries within the function of their work, and they do not represent a formal ordination (although they certainly can be ordained to something else in addition to their appointment position). The work of bishops, elders, and deacons are not superior to those of the Ephesians 4:11 work of ministry, nor are they parallel; they are entirely subordinate, a work of helps and assistance therein. They are unique and different from those found in Ephesians 4:11, and are just as important, and necessary, as those found elsewhere.

- **Bishop:** The word bishop literally means "overseer." This definition literally relates to what a bishop does: they oversee something. Unfortunately, history has often confused what a bishop is, making it something superior even to the Ephesians 4:11 office or claiming it is the same work as an apostle, pastor or elder. In New Testament times, bishops oversaw and maintained the work of a ministry or a group of ministries, ensuring they properly functioned and operated correctly. They work to oversee some branch or aspect of church ministry that requires a level of consistent, regular oversight an apostle cannot always offer (as they cannot be in more places than one), and report back to the apostle about new or continuing issues that need work or address. As part of helps, a bishop may be the overseer of a specific ministry, may oversee the finances, work in the liaison capacity, or assist with a group of ministries in a locale or region.

- **Elder:** The word elder literally means "an older person with seasoned judgment." In the example of an elder, it does not have to necessarily be a person who is a senior citizen, but one who is old enough and mature enough to display seasoned wisdom, judgment, and instruction in spiritual guidance. Elders are individuals appointed in each congregation by an apostle to assist the pastor in the care of the congregation. The work of an elder is governmental in guidance and leadership, instruction, and meeting the spiritual needs of a congregation on a regular basis. Unlike deacons, elders are specifically assigned to assist the needs of a church or ministry rather than social lack or injustices.

- **Deacon:** The word deacon literally means "minister" or "servant." Deacons work to meet the social and practical work of a congregation's laity, general membership, or leadership rather than the spiritual needs they may have. Deacons are about service and remind us of the importance of "doing" in a church. For example, deacons may assist widows or impoverished church members as they need practical help. A deacon may also serve as an armor bearer or church leadership assistant. Deacons are also often the first to engage in shut-in ministry, hospital or home visits, or other words that ensure the practical needs of a church or ministry are always met.

Those who work in the appointments provide an essential and invaluable service to the Body of Christ by helping others. This shows us just how important help is in the Kingdom of God. We should, therefore, always show proper respect to those who serve in the work of the appointments, as additional leadership representation for the ministry to which we belong. If you desire to help out with one of these works, it would be great to talk to your leadership about it and find out what is involved, how you can best assist, and what training is available.

WHAT IS COVERING?

It's likely that the longer you are in church, you will probably hear the term "covering" from time to time. "Covering" is used interchangeably as a term for leadership. It is used to describe the type of leadership that one exercises, understanding it as a relationship whereby a leader takes a protective role over another person. Some use it, some do not, and some argue over whether the term – and the concept that sometimes goes along with it – is Biblical. While it is true it sometimes is used to refer to a leadership system that can be disordered and confusing, a true concept of covering as leadership can be found in Scripture.

Most important of all, continue to show deep love for each other, for love covers a multitude of sins. (1 Peter 4:8)

When a leader truly cares about those they lead (and they make a point to lead in love), that leadership covers the things we do that are wrong, or imperfect, or problematic. This doesn't mean our leader hides our sins or wrongdoing. What it does mean is this: a true leader makes the effort to work with us, recognizing the principles present through love and grace as an extension of spiritual love. They work with, they correct, they guide, and they encourage. Our leaders don't give up on us unless we desire to walk away. They hope, they persevere, and they continue to know us, working with us through our challenges or flaws.

If you aren't comfortable using the word "covering," it doesn't change your relationship with your leader. You don't have to use it. It is just a term that describes a spiritual connection we have with our leaders, and nothing changes that connection when we are properly connected in Christ. It just helps to give a visual idea of what exactly a leader does in the spiritual realm, and how we can better emulate that when we deal with others.

Understanding What Ministry Means to Your Spiritual Leader

When you think of ministry, you probably think of it in terms of attending services, studies and classes at your church or weekly congregational gatherings. The "ministry" that you receive is thanks to the work of your spiritual leader, and you most likely acknowledge that. It's something done out of service and to better the lives of others. You might even define "ministry" as some of the service you have done for the church or ministry of which you are part. There's nothing wrong with seeing ministry from this perspective, because it is the angle of ministry you are most familiar with and that you understand from your own walk and call from God. Ministry is different for different people and is different within the specific and unique call that each person has. This is even true for people who walk in the same office or appointment: while what they might do overall is the same from a definition standpoint, there are unique and purposed nuances that make their ministry call unique and different from someone else's.

To you, ministry is something you benefit from and receive. It may seem possible for you to be tired and desire to skip a service or a class or may sometimes even seem like something you can take or leave in your life. You may go through periods where you aren't sure how you fit on the bigger spectrum of things and just want to hang back. These are obviously feelings you should discuss with your leader and push through, but the point of this is that you, most likely, don't feel connected to the ministry benefits you get all the time. Sometimes your desire to receive is stronger than others, and with the other things present in your life, ministry may wax or wane in your view of importance.

What I've just described is not at all how your leader sees ministry. It is so far from how your leader sees ministry, it isn't funny. The nominal perception of ministry fails to echo the realities of what your leader deals with and experiences as a minister of the Gospel. The reason you do not recognize this is because your leader's ministry is so commonplace to them, it's not something they can easily describe to other people. In lines of professionalism, they probably do not complain to you about the things they deal with and the level of spiritual difficulties and emotional pain they often confront. With the unique nuances of a ministry, it's almost impossible to get others to understand it if they haven't experienced it for themselves. As a result, your leader probably doesn't talk about the very heart or understanding of what they do because they feel they won't express it right or it won't make sense to someone else.

It is my personal belief that for us to properly respect our leaders, we need to have some understanding of what this thing called "ministry" means to them, so as best as I can, I am going to try and explain it, here. We can't truly understand and respect the work that our leaders are doing if we don't understand it, and the truth about ministry is that this thing we call "service" comes at a high and heavy price for the average minister. While we can casually try and brush it away, saying that it's a choice to follow God or that the anointing makes what we do possible, none of these statements change the fact that ministry is a hard walk that if we understood it more, we would hold those who do it to the best of their ability in far higher honor than we typically do.

Now I, Paul, appeal to you with the gentleness and kindness of Christ— though I realize you think I am timid in person and bold only when I write from far away. Well, I am begging you now so that when I come I won't have to be bold with those who think we act from human motives.

We are human, but we don't wage war as humans do. We use God's mighty weapons, not worldly weapons, to knock down the strongholds of human reasoning and to destroy false arguments. We destroy every proud obstacle that keeps people from knowing God. We capture their rebellious thoughts and teach them to obey Christ. And after you have become fully obedient, we will punish everyone who remains disobedient.

Look at the obvious facts. Those who say they belong to Christ must recognize that we belong to Christ as much as they do. I may seem to be boasting too much about the authority given to us by the Lord. But our authority builds you up; it doesn't tear you down. So I will not be ashamed of using my authority.

I'm not trying to frighten you by my letters. For some say, "Paul's letters are demanding and forceful, but in person he is weak, and his speeches are worthless!" Those people should realize that our actions when we arrive in person will be as forceful as what we say in our letters from far away.

Oh, don't worry; we wouldn't dare say that we are as wonderful as these other men who tell you how important they are! But they are only comparing themselves with each other, using themselves as the standard of measurement. How ignorant!

We will not boast about things done outside our area of authority. We will boast only about what has happened within the boundaries of the work God has given us, which includes our working with you. We are not reaching beyond these boundaries when we claim authority over you, as if we had never visited you. For we were the first to travel all the way to Corinth with the Good News of Christ.

Nor do we boast and claim credit for the work someone else has done. Instead, we hope that your faith will grow so that the boundaries of our work among you will be extended. Then we will be able to go and preach the Good News in other places far beyond you, where no one else is working. Then there will be no question of our boasting about work done in someone else's territory. As the Scriptures say, "If you want to boast, boast only about the LORD." **(2 Corinthians 10:1-17)**

In this passage of Scripture, the Apostle Paul is not just defending his ministry; he is also trying to explain it. It's obvious that the Corinthians, though they knew him, didn't understand everything he went through or everything he was as an apostle. They only saw him and knew him in the context of their leadership, their help, their establishment, and their assistance. They didn't consider he had other thoughts, feelings, issues, needs, ideas, concepts, and beliefs. He was accused of doing things from a bad place or out of his ego, instead of seeing the truth and realities he offered to the people he led. He was accused of boasting; of being frightening; of measuring himself against others. Clearly, he was misunderstood, even by those who had benefited from his work.

When it comes to sharing about the essence of a ministry, words fail most ministers. Just as the Apostle Paul tried to share it to those he led, he couldn't describe it in full to them in a way they could embrace on the level where they were. As he described it, he was misjudged, much as your leader probably is, much of the time. Your leader's ministry is the heart and soul of what God has called him or her to do in this world. He or she has a personal investment in what they are doing. It defines a good portion of their lives: how they spend their time, where they spend their money, what they go to, what they are willing to do, what they refrain from attending, and what is most important to them. In many instances, ministry dictates just as much about our personal lives as it does of our professional lives, because it's hard to live with someone who just doesn't understand the work one is called to do. Ministry service hits home at the very heart of God and God's continued willingness to do for humanity even though humanity often did not do its best by Him. In receiving ministry, your leader has received an even greater sense of what it means to give, what it means to do for others, and all the ways that they, as a minister, are called to live their life. Your leader takes on the job of a role model; a trailblazer; a man or woman of purpose who is staunchly imperfect but serving a perfect God. Most likely, your leader strives for His excellence in all that he or she does and all that he or she is. This is a crazy combination of awe-inspiring, overachieving, intense, spiritual, accomplishing, and exhausting, all at once.

That is the more spiritual definition of the essence of being in ministry. The day-to-day experience of ministry is often far more practical and does not always feel nor sound so meaningful. Your leader has spent years of his or her life working their ministry, ironing out the details of it while trying to maintain the larger picture or vision. They have paid a high price with relationship or marital issues, sacrificing personal time or personal comforts, money, and desires in order to keep the vision that God has given to them alive. They work overtime to make sure you can attend those weekly services, classes, or events, all for your spiritual growth and benefit. Ministers know when to put on a good front for the cameras and the realities behind public events and social gatherings are that everything is, most likely, not really cushy at home due to stress and over-commitment. Those ministers who do have good home relationships make great efforts to practice what they preach and apply their own beliefs and principles to marriage and family life. Many are still unsuccessful but continue forward anyway because what God has called them to is greater than what they encounter in this life. Because they are still human beings, they confront their own personal insecurities when people they thought were friends do not turn out to support them for events and when they deal with the tremendous level of hurt they encounter from people who claimed to be there to support the vision and attend as members. On the natural level, ministers love big crowds, large audiences, large collections, and open doors for opportunities to grow ministries. Everyone wants to feel what they do matters to others. Ministers love things that signify progress, whether they are earthly or spiritual. Rejection, small groups, waning congregations, and hitting walls as things don't turn out as planned hurt a spiritual leader on a deep, unspeakable level.

Even though they might encounter disappointment, your leader probably wishes they could devote more of their time, attention, and efforts to ministry and doing the work they are called to do in ministry. It's very difficult to maintain a secular job and ministry positioning at the same time. They, most likely, want to do more than is sometimes feasible, and this can become both frustrating and depressing. See, every soul saved, every leader who sees the fruition of their own ministry work, every training that is successful, every healing and deliverance, and every person who walks in their fruitful gifts out of spiritual stagnation brings your leader back to their purpose, every time. To your spiritual leader, their ministry is their very life, the thing that keeps them going, and the thing that gives them hope in God's promises because they experience them with every victory.

I tell you all this for one reason: It's important you appreciate your leader, however they serve you. One of the greatest ways you can show your leader just how much they mean to you is by showing up, committed and regular, when they do things. Leaders don't hold services, classes, or events to feel good about themselves or to have something to do. All those things you reach a point where you could take or leave are things you should take – regularly – for your own benefit. Yes, it's awesome to have minister appreciations or events, but what the Apostle Paul expressed in 2 Corinthians 10 displays what he was really seeking from those he led. He desired they would follow his teaching and counsel. He desired they would follow God in the way they knew they were supposed to do so. He expected their spiritual support. He hoped he wouldn't have to keep explaining himself to others. It was his hope that those who were part of his work would step up and be part of it, doing what they were commissioned to do and be the church. The same is true for you today:

step up and be the church by being a part of the ministry you know you are called to, whether it is easy, convenient, or difficult. That makes a world of difference in showing proper respect to the work of your leader.

Losses in Ministry

Nobody wins all the time. As much as we like to puff people up and think that positivity will keep us going, nobody has an endless string of gains in their lives. We can positively confess all day long, but we all still have hits and misses. We all have those points where we miss God and fail to understand just what it is He is doing at times. These different experiences are all a part of balancing out life and give us the opportunity to hear what God has to say in our loss as much as our gain.

On top of the weight that is often ministry experience, ministers are expected to be a certain way all the time, no matter what is going on in their lives. It is considered very taboo for ministers to be truly "real" about the difficulties that they have. Many leaders go through down times, crisis, and hurts without saying a word to anyone and without handling their loss properly, in a way that offers true healing. Their own hurts and pains get stuffed down over the needs of others and without feeling like they can trust others with their issues, the issues go unresolved.

As a rule, circles of ministers operate through tightly-knit groups that have a couple of major things in common. One of those things may be a common superior leader or a city where one lives; the second is that they are all in alliance against someone or something. Gossip is common and often deeply hurtful. It doesn't help that if a minister chooses to refrain from such, they are left out of preaching engagements, conversation, and support. Such matters are also complicated when leaders or lay members leave a church or ministry and go to these other churches or ministries full of stories, however false, about their experiences where they are.

I've often said that leadership is not for wimps, and when I say that, this is the kind of matter I am talking about. No matter how much we might want to offer positive sayings or tell people not to worry about naysayers, negative and false reputations can damage a ministry, not to mention a leader as a person. It's very difficult to be the target, and when you are the target consistently, it can wear a leader down in a way that a positive Scripture or nice thought can't help.

These are all reasons that support the importance of your leader having a good leader they can rely on, as well as good friends and supportive people who can encourage them through difficult times and rejoice in good times. Such is a hard find, however, and that means a leader has to be assured of their call, personally encouraging themselves, and as solid as they have to be through good times as well as bad.

He chose His servant David,
  calling him from the sheep pens.
He took David from tending the ewes and lambs
  and made him the shepherd of Jacob's descendants—
  God's own people, Israel.
He cared for them with a true heart
  and led them with skillful hands. (Psalm 78:70-72)

In these difficult times, we see the true calling of a leader. No matter what they were called from or what they did before, they are able to be skillful leaders who weather the storms of ministry. We should all desire, however, to get behind the work of good leaders and make their lives easier, even if we don't know firsthand what they face. Your leader will, most likely, never confide in you about whatever is hurting or troubling them. You can help make their losses in ministry easier by refraining from gossip about your leader, by maintaining a sense of order and decency if you decide to leave a ministry, and by being an active participant in the ministry where you are. Sure, all ministers love to hear you appreciate them, but it means a lot more to a leader that you are present at service, follow through on what you say you will do, give financially on a regular basis, and keep your leader lifted up in prayer.

Your relationship with your leader

The ultimate goal of every spiritual leader – regardless of office – is to help those who are part of their ministry (whether leaders or laity) learn how to recognize God's voice and how to follow the leading of the Holy Spirit in their lives and unique circumstances. The way this goal is attuned and met varies depending on someone's calling and life situation, but it is the most essential and important part of any and all work in ministry. Why, you ask? Because you should never, ever hear your leader's voice more than you hear the voice of God. The voice of your leader should never shout out, drown out, or overshadow God; the two should enhance and complement one another. Even when you are just learning, it is your leader who is there to help you sort out what is you from what is God from what is the enemy, through their teaching and guidance. You may not always recognize God's voice in your life, you may have a hard time with it at times, but that direction is always there, and that is a big part of what your leader helps you to identify and sort out.

You call me 'Teacher' and 'Lord,' and you are right, because that's what I am. And since I, your Lord and Teacher, have washed your feet, you ought to wash each other's feet. I have given you an example to follow. Do as I have done to you. I tell you the truth, slaves are not greater than their master. Nor is the messenger more important than the one who sends the message. Now that you know these things, God will bless you for doing them. (John 13:13-17)

As a servant, your leader is available to serve you in this specific way, here for this very purpose. This means your leader plays a pretty big part in your spiritual life and development as a disciple of Christ. With your leader, you are a student, a disciple, one who is learning from this person placed and established to teach and train you in your faith. Your leader must be trustworthy and able to reach you, where you are, as you transform and develop through the different seasons of your life. You should be able to talk to your leader directly without having to go through an abundance of other people or channels (appointments are fine) and for the most part, they should be interested and attentive to your situations. Your leader should care about you, and what you are going through, even if you have to talk on the phone or via instant messenger sometimes. By working with your leader, you should know – and recognize – your leader's true heart toward you. Leaders should help you identify what is God from what isn't, sort out what might sound odd or strange, learn your unique symbolism with God, and teach you about how you can best study the Scriptures in a way you are able to understand.

This does not mean your leader is at your beckon call, nor does it mean you have the right to be selfish or demanding of your leader's time. It's important to realize your leader doesn't just have you to take care of, but others, as well. This can be an overwhelming task, and there are often many times in a leader's life where there is just not enough time – or energy – to go around for themselves or others in their lives. It is perfectly normal and acceptable for a leader to establish good boundaries with you. Your leader has the right to only accept calls or discussions after a certain hour in the case of emergencies, to make certain nights "off limits," or to decide that he or she needs family or personal time.

It also should be said that everyone's relationship with their leader is a little different. Some people require more individual attention than others. Personally, when I came up in church, I never had a personal audience with my pastor. I knew my pastor, my pastor knew me by name, but I never felt like I needed his personal time. I am sure if I'd needed it, he would have been there for me, but because I didn't, I never required it. When I grew into accepting my work as an apostle, however, my relationship with my leader was quite different. I spent many hours in discussion with her, studying and sorting out my call. I studied the materials she wrote and read the Scriptures on the topic. Because my position in church was different, my needs were different, and I needed something different from my leader. If you don't need a lot of personal attention, but get much out of public preaching and teaching, you aren't doing anything wrong. I am sure if you need something, your leader will be there. If you need more of your leader's time, I am sure that is something you are working out with them for the benefit of Kingdom growth.

Akin to this, which I think is vitally important: if you want your leader's time, you better be sowing into their ministry financially. If you want your leader's personal attention, they must take their time from something else to give it to you. If you want a leader who is available, you need to financially give so your leader can give you that time. If you aren't giving, your leader must make up his or her finances somewhere else, which means you are taking their time from their need to support yourself. If you are doing so without giving, you are being selfish. You are not considering their situation, finances, need, or issues, and expecting them to give without considering we all have to give in the Kingdom. If you require long-term, consistent professional services (such as for counseling, pre-marriage counseling, private leadership instruction, etc.), you should consider additional giving or fees in your ministry giving in addition to any regular tithes or offerings you supply to the work.

Some people are more connected to their leaders than others; some travel with their leaders or live where they can assist in ministry, altar work, recording, hear regular sermons, or other activities that help develop a different connection than others do. This doesn't mean your leader plays favorites; it means they know and are served in a different way by different people. If you would like to know and serve your leader better, get involved! Even if your leader is far away, I am sure there is something you can offer to do or some way you can participate that will help you to be closer and serve better, no matter where you are.

Ministry continuity

It is of the utmost importance that if you have made a commitment to be in a ministry, you are present and involved in that ministry. Only attending service or class when it's convenient, when you feel like it, when the mood strikes, or when it doesn't require any sacrifice equates to an inconsistent ministry experience that will become problematic later. If you only connect when it's easy or you find it convenient, you will take this same attitude to the difficult things in your Christian walk that won't be so easy to avoid. You will find yourself in constant warfare and difficulties, not because of the enemy, but because you haven't learned the principles of consistency and continuity in your spiritual life.

We are called to make a commitment to the ministry where we are called because commitment is good for us. It builds character and establishes us within a community that can stand supportive and engaged when we go through trials or difficulties. It's totally improper to go running from place to place and person to person every time you have a problem. By establishing firmly in a community, you are able to know who has your back, who is really your friend (this is not to say you can't have friends outside of your immediate ministry, but such should anchor you to know what to look for), and where to go for guidance and support when things arise.

A few years ago, I worked to establish a local church group that quickly fell apart in front of my eyes. The dynamics we needed to have to sustain our group were simply not present there, and no matter how much I tried to make them appear, they weren't. I worked primarily with a woman and her extended family, all of which lived with her. This woman had very lofty ideas and desired to do a ton of outreach work and wanted to be installed and ordained as pastor. I was fine with this arrangement, but we agreed to do such on the condition that she would have to train for an unspecified period to see how things went. It wasn't long before she became quite irregular in her church attendance and consistently failed to complete tasks or things I assigned for her to complete. In her constant absence, I had to do pastoral duties at the church, which meant my own gifts were not properly used and our spiritual outlook frequently fell apart. It was frustrating because when push came to shove, this woman desired the control and prestige of leadership, but didn't want to do the work she had to be in position. She was inconsistent and such reflected with her entire family.

Before and after participating in our ministry, this woman dragged her family through five ministries in three years. Every one of us had unique positions, some different governance structures, and different instructions. Her grandchildren displayed their theological and authority confusions as they went from church to church, and then inconsistently attended in the meantime. They would form attachments and friendships at one church, only to be ripped out when this woman didn't get her way. For a woman who wanted to be a pastor, her total inconsistencies and tantrum-throwing when she wasn't allowed to have her way trickled down into a negative witness for the young children in her life. She taught them from a young age that you don't need to make commitments to anything and that if you do not get your way, you should just pick up and move on to something else.

All the believers devoted themselves to the apostles' teaching, and to fellowship, and to sharing in meals (including the Lord's Supper), and to prayer. (Acts 2:42)

It's a mistake to think the early church had some sort of insight we just can't have today. Despite the difficulties and differences that existed in early church times, the focus of the very early church was on the movement, on being a part of this thing called Christianity for the first time. As we discussed earlier, that doesn't mean everyone understood everything the same or that they all agreed on the direction to take, especially as the years went by. Yet this passage in Acts 2, often quoted for the sake of unity, is one on the importance of commitment. It is a descriptive statement showing how dedicated the early believers were. They were so dedicated, in fact, they devoted themselves to the things that were most important in the development of their faith. There were no questions about how many days a week they could get away with missing church or how often they could skip events while still being eligible for advancement. Instead of being about what we want, we seek, and how we feel, our church experience should be devoted to something: discovering faith, upholding true teaching, fellowship with each other, and prayer. If we lack this connection, we will never find ourselves in a place that has a chance to change and transform us.

Those in our lives – children, spouses, partners, friends, co-workers, non-believers – are watching how we treat our leaders and the messages we give when we aren't really committed to wherever we are. If you don't feel connected to a ministry, then don't stay in the hopes that you will be able to maneuver things to your liking. Also, consider your own lack of commitment and why you seem unable to settle down and engage in a ministry like you should. Is it that you reach a place of having to face yourself, and that's uncomfortable? Is it that you are seeking a self-seeking experience in church? Is it that you seek your own good rather than the good of the entire church? Whatever it is, it's time to change it – and overcome it. You cannot ever receive spiritual promotion without first receiving the humbling to attend and remain consistent where you are planted.

Control and Respect

When it comes to leadership, we choose our leadership. Yes, I recognize that we have connections to our leaders and that ideally God sets us with a leader, but who we choose to follow is a choice we make. According to the Bible, those who are our leaders have "rule" over us:

Remember your leaders and superiors in authority [for it was they] who brought to you the Word of God. Observe attentively and consider their manner of living (the outcome of their well-spent lives) and imitate their faith (their conviction that God exists and is the Creator and Ruler of all things, the Provider and Bestower of eternal salvation through Christ, and their leaning of the entire human personality on God in absolute trust and confidence in His power, wisdom, and goodness). (Hebrews 13:7, AMPC)

If we choose a leader of our own free will and volition (not by force, coercion, or intimidation, but by our own spiritual drawing), we are choosing to follow their guidelines and regulations. We are recognizing their authority over a ministry, which we will discuss next. Most hopefully, we prayerfully expect to follow them as they follow Christ, seeing a proper imitation for spiritual life. We do not follow a perfect person, but someone who has been graced by God to stand as a spiritual leader over this particular ministry. If we choose to be a part of a church or a ministry, we recognize that by so doing, we are allowing our leaders to have that rule, or governance. Many times, we get lost when it comes to matters of governance or the concept of a leader being set in our lives, especially when we don't get our way or things change in our relationship with a leader. So, what does it specifically mean for a leader to have "rule," or authority, over us?

When we say a leader has "rule," or authority over us, that means a leader has a right to make decisions as pertain to us and our participation within that ministry. They have the right to establish guidelines, structures, and implement certain rules as pertain to ministry participation, and we must follow them to participate therein. In covering us, our leaders see who we are, and we trust them to determine our level of involvement, preparedness, and promotion as pertains to that ministry work. It is absolutely correct to say a leader does not have personal control over your decisions and actions, nor does a leader have the right to dictate what you decide to do personally. If a spiritual leader is "deciding" for you who you can or can't marry or date, whether or not you can take a job, making ministry participation unusually burdensome or raising up issues that are not in alignment with Biblical protocol to block your participation, what you can or can't do on your leisure time, or who your friends are, that leader is being controlling and is out of line. Whenever a leader starts telling you what you can or cannot do as pertains to your personal choices, a leader has overstepped a boundary. Leaders have every right to stand as guides, they have every right to offer advice or counsel or tell you that something isn't beneficial for you, but when it comes down to it, what you decide to do is ultimately your choice.

In your personal life, your leader serves as an adviser. They are someone you can go to, someone you can trust, someone who can give you guidance and a spiritual perspective on the things you seek to do and the ramifications that may be involved therein. This means a leader has an up-close-and-personal view of many things in your life, and they have the right to guide you therein. What you decide to do with their advice is your choice, but they do have the perspective to offer what they can within spiritual understanding to any situation you bring to them from your life.

A leader's sphere of control, however, is over the congregation or ministry that they are appointed to serve. This means a leader has the responsibility of keeping the ministry going, flowing, functioning, and growing. What this means is that while a leader does not have the right to force his or her choices on you and they cannot stop you from making those decisions in your life, a leader has every right to make decisions as to your level of participation based on the personal choices and decisions you make. This may not sound fair, but when we choose to be a part of a ministry, we are choosing to follow the guidelines that have been laid out, whether those guidelines come from God Himself or are just the personal directives of a leader.

For example: if you have confided in your leader that you are having an affair, a leader has the right to mandate you "sit down" from any positions you may hold in the church until the behavior stops and a reasonable period of repentance has followed. If you are admittedly using illegal drugs or abusing alcohol, a leader has the right to mandate you are not involved in church duties because you have become a liability to the organization. If you have been caught stealing or doing something otherwise illegal, a leader has the right to make their decisions properly and within decency and order. This is true with any issue that may arise that is contradictory to the principles of an organization, from gossip or slander to murder and theft.

A leader also has the right to mandate that a situation is somehow rectified before you can assume position in church. Depending on the situation, this may be nothing more than waiting something out, or it might be more involved, such as regular Twelve-Step group participation, counseling, rehabilitation, making financial restitution, serving out a legal sentence, making amends, or some sort of public apology or rectification. The required assignment should be compensatory to whatever happened, and there should be proper evidence that such has been and is being carried out before one even discusses restoration or elevation.

The same is true if a leader looks over your level of interest and participation in a ministry as pertains to certain involvements or elevations therein. If you are missing more church than you attend, your leader has every right to tell you that right now is not the time to place you in a position of appointment or Ephesians 4:11 ministry. A leader has the right to look over the things in your life and say that right now they are too chaotic, disordered, or problematic for you to focus on ministry advancement or position. By following God's guidance, a leader can, and should in fairness, make such decisions to ensure that the ministry is able to move forward. It is wrong to think they can place you in a position you cannot handle, or you are not ready for, and it is equally wrong to keep you in a position if you aren't able to handle it with the things that you are doing or experiencing in your life at this time.

It may seem contradictory or hypocritical for a leader to have this kind of governing authority, especially if you feel you know something about their personal lives or about them as people. The catch is that it's not, and you don't have the right to throw what you feel you know about a leader out there for all to see or in a leader's face. A leader has the specific purpose, the special gift of God to rule and lead God's ministry. To contradict or defame that when you know a leader walks in that gift of leadership is to defame Christ, Who gave it. Leaders don't claim to have it all together, but if you have given a leader rule over you, then they are exercising their God-given and your-given authority over the situation and doing what is best for a situation. If they aren't and they are acting out of the flesh, then you take that matter to them, to their leadership or to God, or you back away if reconciliation seems impossible and move on to wherever God has next for you. But if you remain a part of the ministry that they govern, you have given them rule over you and you have to respect that authority until the time comes when you know God has called you to remove yourself from the situation.

WAYS TO BLESS YOUR LEADER

Your leader performs an invaluable service to you in Christian ministry. There is no price tag for the hours, advice, teaching, life skills, discipline, encouragement, and most importantly, spiritual guidance your leader offers you. I've been asked many times over the years, how can we bless our leaders? What can we do that best shows just how much we appreciate and honor them, and how can that turn into a regular thing?

Give double honor to spiritual leaders who handle their duties well. This is especially true if they work hard at teaching the word [of God]. (1 Timothy 5:17, GW)

The Scriptures tell us that spiritual leaders who do their work well are worthy of double honor. Double honor includes financial compensation, respect, esteem, and distinction. The reason for this is simple: leadership is hard work. It requires a leader to not just take care of their own spiritual walk on a personal level, but to take responsibility for the spiritual lives of others. Leaders are doing double duty, twice as much as those not called to leadership must do. It is also relevant that they do not just handle moral issues, but good leaders also apply themselves to spiritual instruction, discipline, and wisdom when it comes to instructing the word of God. More than just for entertainment value, good spiritual leaders deposit something in the lives of those they lead.

The major thing all leaders seek is to know the good work they do is appreciated. Appreciation for that work is not as simple as recognizing your leader online during Minister Appreciation Month or having a yearly appreciation service. It's also nice to take a special offering for your leader on occasion, but much like an occasional special acknowledgement, these things aren't enough by themselves. They are nice, and I am sure your leader appreciates them, but they aren't what your leader is looking for, from you, to show that you appreciate their efforts on behalf of the Kingdom.

Here I am providing you with an ultimate cheat sheet of things you can do that show your appreciation for the things your leader does. Keep in mind: these things take continual effort. They aren't something you do one time and hope that it'll keep things until next time. If you want to make sure your leader knows you appreciate their work, these are the things that will let them know, no questions asked.

- Give financially without being prompted.

- Give without excuse as to why you aren't giving.

- Show up for services, events, and classes, and show up on time.

- Do what you promise and offer to do.

- Do what you are asked to do.

- Offer to help out and then show up when you are assigned to do something.

- Don't complain when assigned a task.

- Practice the principle of "pounding," where once a month a special offering of goods, services, or money are given to your leader.

- Show your leader your support on social media.

- Watch videos and purchase materials, such as books, that your leader produces.

- Speak well of your leader to others.

- Don't take opportunities to gossip about your leader.

- Spread the word about the ministry; don't keep it all to yourself.

- Invite friends, family, and others to church.

- Be willing to be of service to your leader, as is needed.

- Take your leader out for a meal, invite them over for one, or bring one to their home.

- Do something special for your leader, such as offering a special gift or taking care of something for them so they can focus more on ministry or take a break.

ABUSIVE LEADERSHIP

Today we hear more about the ills of abusive leadership than we hear about good leaders. This is often how things are. It is easier to lament a wrong situation and use it as the standing reason why we don't step out to do something else than it is to dive into something that may be good or right for us. This is one of the reasons why abusive leaders are so problematic, and such a problem for the church world today. One bad leader can cause someone to step back and stand on the sidelines for an indefinite period of time. They also make things that much harder and that much more time consuming for the leaders who will come behind them to correct and heal whatever they did. Abusive leadership is a serious problem, one with long-term consequences. As part of this chapter on leadership, we will address it briefly here.

There is no excuse for leaders who abuse and mistreat others. Most of us have met a leader who played favorites, mistreated others, or exerted too much control over their followers. Even if we haven't experienced such a leader personally, all of us have heard of extreme examples, such as the Jonestown massacre under the leadership of Jim Jones or the Branch Dravidian cult led by David Koresh. We know enough to know such examples of leadership are detrimental, and such encounters with a leader are morally and spiritually wrong, as well as legally reprehensible.

I've often been asked about the Biblical answer to bad or abusive leadership. The Bible's primary focus is not on bad leadership, but on building and developing spiritual leaders who lead God's people rightly and with integrity. This might sound flowery, but I don't believe it is such. If we build up enough good leaders, we won't have such a problem with abusive ones. When the Bible does speak of bad leadership, it's often in the context of governmental leaders, such as the bad kings in Israel and Judah's history. While these leaders weren't church leaders, I do believe they show us about the consequences of bad leadership. Much of what is said to them can apply to the church, and at times, various reprimands were for both governmental and spiritual leaders in Old Testament times. When they were unwilling to check abuses and bad moral character, both Israel and Judah fell into disrepair and eventually, occupation. When bad leaders control churches, the same things happen: they fall into disrepair and people go elsewhere.

Abusive leaders rise to power because they are charismatic enough and enticing enough to slip by the rules and fool existing people, who either place them in power or follow them with enough adherence to establish them in a following. Very few, if any, abusive leaders get there by rising through ranks; they often skip them because they know someone or charm their way through. If we maintain certain disciplines and regulations for rising leaders, this will eliminate the option for many abusive leaders to gain power under our watch. Instead of seeking short cuts, all leaders can help with this problem by adhering to existing guidelines and embracing them instead of trying to be the exception to the rule.

Beyond this, I do believe there is something to be said for not allowing anyone to elevate to leadership positions if they do not embody the Biblical standards for such. Every office and appointment lists criteria that helps us determine the calling and ability of each person who comes to us.

When the godly are in authority, the people rejoice.
  But when the wicked are in power, they groan. (Proverbs 29:2)

"What sorrow awaits the leaders of my people—the shepherds of My sheep—for they have destroyed and scattered the very ones they were expected to care for," says the Lord.

Therefore, this is what the Lord, the God of Israel, says to these shepherds: "Instead of caring for my flock and leading them to safety, you have deserted them and driven them to destruction. Now I will pour out judgment on you for the evil you have done to them. But I will gather together the remnant of my flock from the countries where I have driven them. I will bring them back to their own sheepfold, and they will be fruitful and increase in number. Then I will appoint responsible shepherds who will care for them, and they will never be afraid again. Not a single one will be lost or missing. I, the Lord, have spoken!" (Jeremiah 23:1-4)

Then this message came to me from the Lord: "Son of man, prophesy against the shepherds, the leaders of Israel. Give them this message from the Sovereign Lord: What sorrow awaits you shepherds who feed yourselves instead of your flocks. Shouldn't shepherds feed their sheep? You drink the milk, wear the wool, and butcher the best animals, but you let your flocks starve. You have not taken care of the weak. You have not tended the sick or bound up the injured. You have not gone looking for those who have wandered away and are lost. Instead, you have ruled them with harshness and cruelty. So My sheep have been scattered without a shepherd, and they are easy prey for any wild animal. They have wandered through all the mountains and all the hills, across the face of the earth, yet no one has gone to search for them.

"Therefore, you shepherds, hear the word of the Lord: As surely as I live, says the Sovereign Lord, you abandoned my flock and left them to be attacked by every wild animal. And though you were my shepherds, you didn't search for my sheep when they were lost. You took care of yourselves and left the sheep to starve. Therefore, you shepherds, hear the word of the Lord. This is what the Sovereign Lord says: I now consider these shepherds My enemies, and I will hold them responsible for what has happened to My flock. I will take away their right to feed the flock, and I will stop them from feeding themselves. I will rescue My flock from their mouths; the sheep will no longer be their prey. (Ezekiel 34:1-8)

When the ten other disciples heard what James and John had asked, they were indignant. So Jesus called them together and said, "You know that the rulers in this world lord it over their people, and officials flaunt their authority over those under them. But among you it will be different. Whoever wants to be a leader among you must be your servant, and whoever wants to be first among you must be the slave of everyone else. For even the Son of Man came not to be served but to serve others and to give his life as a ransom for many." (Mark 10:41-45)

I am shocked that you are turning away so soon from God, Who called you to Himself through the loving mercy of Christ. You are following a different way that pretends to be the Good News but is not the Good News at all. You are being fooled by those who deliberately twist the truth concerning Christ.

Let God's curse fall on anyone, including us or even an angel from heaven, who preaches a different kind of Good News than the one we preached to you. I say again what we have said before: If anyone preaches any other Good News than the one you welcomed, let that person be cursed.

Obviously, I'm not trying to win the approval of people, but of God. If pleasing people were my goal, I would not be Christ's servant. (Galatians 1:6-10)

Work willingly at whatever you do, as though you were working for the Lord rather than for people. Remember that the Lord will give you an inheritance as your reward, and that the Master you are serving is Christ. But if you do what is wrong, you will be paid back for the wrong you have done. For God has no favorites. (Colossians 3:23-25)

So, what should we do with abusive leaders? The first thing we should do is identify them. If someone comes with the presence of "lording," much like we find in the world, it is a safe bet they are a leader to avoid. There is a marked difference between upholding authority and flaunting it, using it for personal sport or gain. Another sign is they add to or edit what they teach with teaching that is not of God, doing so in order to sound novel, new, different, or exclusive. These are things we can watch for before we ever encounter a specific issue or problem in a ministry.

Outside of these more spiritually discerning signs, signs of abusive leadership include:

- Physical, verbal, emotional, or mental abuse.

- Financial control or manipulation.

- Deliberate manipulation or destruction of marriages or family relationships.

- Control of time; dominating one's life.

- Dictating who can or cannot be one's friends or how one spends their time.

- Playing favorites between members; pitting members against each other.

- Talking about members behind their back to other members to cause trouble.

If you are part of a ministry that displays any of these signs, the only option is to leave. It is improper and unproductive to think you are going to stay and change things, or stand up to such a leader. Abusive leaders only have as much power as their followers extend to them, so the best way to cut off an abusive leader is to leave that work. The best stand you can make for yourself and your spiritual development is to depart and pray for God's direction for be best possible place to heal, grow, and re-establish yourself in the true love and servanthood of spiritual blessing. Starting again is a powerful principle, and with abusive leaders, it is what is needed, every time.

Leaving a Ministry

The last thing we will examine in this chapter on leadership is what to do when you recognize it is time to move on from whatever church or ministry you find yourself to somewhere else. Believe it or not, there is a right and wrong way to leave a ministry. Leaving a ministry right sets many things in order and offers a certain sense of closure and purpose for your experience in that place, freeing you mentally and spiritually to move forward into whatever is next for you.

There can be any number of reasons why you feel it is time to leave a ministry. The reason may be for what we described just a few moments ago, dealing with abusive leadership. This isn't going to always be the situation, however. There may also be the reality that it's just time to move on from a place, as what it offers or focuses on is not where you are at, any longer. It might be that you are called into leadership, and you need a different type of leader, because you are moving away, because God is calling you in a different direction, or because you are ready for something else. Whatever the reason is, how you leave a ministry is very, very important. It shows the truth of what you say about moving on and displays your own level of personal integrity. When it's time to leave, how you handle it speaks a great deal about yourself, no matter the response you receive.

There are a few steps I recommend you take when leaving a ministry. The first is to make sure that you have a conversation, or if such is not possible, a written letter stating your departure from the work. Don't just up and leave or stop showing up. This is especially true when you have a position in a ministry that is important, and the leadership will have to find someone else to fill that role. Make sure your reason for leaving is clear and well-stated, and official in nature. Conduct yourself with God's grace, and expect to be treated, in kind.

Your leadership may respond favorably and release you, or they may desire more of a conversation or more information. If you feel comfortable, additional conversation may be warranted. Sometimes leaders are able to see miscommunication as prevalent and may want to try to rectify things, if there is a specific reason for your departure. If you find yourself out of place in church, a leader may not have anything else to add to that situation, except to perhaps wish you well or try to figure out what is going on. While I do not feel every situation warrants an additional conversation, if such is a consideration, it doesn't mean you have to stay in the church. If you feel it is time to move forward, then you still have the right to do so. Hopefully, a departure can be amicable and you can leave on good terms, with the door always open to return, if needed.

I also know from years of ministry that such does not always happen, and animosity can result from the leadership, from the one who is leaving, or from both. As one who has been in both positions, I will say that the way an individual leaves a ministry and treats a leader in the process can go a long way. I have been in the awkward position of dismissing people for their conduct who then retaliated, no matter how hard I tried to reason or talk with them. I've been in the position to try and rectify with leaders myself, only to get nowhere. But I can always say that in every situation, I have always done my best to communicate clearly to intention and whether the other person might have responded like I might have hoped, I was able to feel free from the situation and able to move on.

That is what I hope for each and every one of you. By leaving right and communicating such to your leader, I'm not telling you to ask for permission to leave or that you can't go if your leader doesn't approve. I am simply telling you to handle things the way you would want them handled, and to treat your leadership with respect, no matter how you might feel about them by that point in time. Whether they are where you are called to be, or not, at one time, they were your choice. You once felt called to be at that ministry and you did, hopefully, get some benefit from being there. Very few people have experiences in a ministry that are bad from the start. As with all experiences, your encounters in that church or ministry were mixed, and a time simply came when you were no longer getting what you were once getting out of attending that church and working with that leader. Now, unless your leader has done something direct to wrong you, is teaching or doing something unscriptural, or is somehow abusive, your decision to move forward isn't their fault, either. Leaving right shows your own growth, your own maturity, and your own desire to move forward with spiritual grace.

Get rid of all bitterness, rage, anger, harsh words, and slander, as well as all types of evil behavior. (Ephesians 4:31)

And I am certain that God, who began the good work within you, will continue His work until it is finally finished on the day when Christ Jesus returns. (Philippians 1:6)

So get rid of all evil behavior. Be done with all deceit, hypocrisy, jealousy, and all unkind speech. Like newborn babies, you must crave pure spiritual milk so that you will grow into a full experience of salvation. Cry out for this nourishment, now that you have had a taste of the Lord's kindness. (1 Peter 2:1-3)

Whether approved or not, when it's time to move forward, carry with you the lessons and insights you learned from all situations at that church or ministry. If things were bad, take the time needed to heal and move forward. Cast off the negative and abusive patterns you experienced, rather than picking them up and repeating them. Seek something better and greater for yourself. Have respect for your former leader, even when you've left. Avoid the temptation to badmouth that leader or tell stories that are less than ideal or slant you in a dishonest light. It's fine to tell the truth of your experience, but not to run rampant and lie or distort things to make yourself come off looking better than you were. Be honest in all things and find the needed perspective from bad situations. Grow from them and come to experience the Lord's kindness. This will ensure that, in the future, you won't be tempted to walk into such destructive places again.

CHAPTER SEVEN
BE A RADICAL GIVER!

EARLIER in this book, we looked briefly at giving and why giving is an important part of who we are as Christians. It isn't possible to be a Christian and not give. If you are receiving from the Kingdom, you must be giving something back to the Kingdom. While we love the idea of talking about giving talents and abilities, these are not the only things God expects of us. Like all things with God, He asks us to give of ourselves in ways that cost something from us. This is truer in no other place than His expectations of financial giving.

Financial giving is controversial in many Christian circles thanks to leaders who have used money to control and manipulate followers for their own gain. There is no question such behavior was and is wrong and is improper for Christian leaders. The resulting problem, however, is that people have gone to the other extreme, feeling such gives them the right not to give or to engage in what I define as "entitled giving" (I'll only give where or when it feels beneficial to me according to my own criteria). This wave of problematic attitudes toward giving has caused a total ruckus in the trends of giving in Christianity. Some don't give at all, some give outside of the church, and some only give when it is convenient or comfortable. Leaders often feel uncomfortable approaching the topic, as every time it comes up, someone out there is quick to accuse a leader of greed or being all about the money. Yet no matter what might have happened on a bigger scale, giving is still a requirement of the Christian faith, and it is something God calls us to do not just for the continuation of the Kingdom, but because it is good for us.

So, let's put ourselves aside for a bit and learn about this wonderful world of financial giving. It might not be the most fun aspect of our faith, but it is one that if we are willing to grow through our own discomforts and dislikes, we will find a whole new level of faith waiting for us as we push through to gain greater understanding.

STOP THE EXCUSES!

In his book, *Know God: No Fear*, my long-time friend and colleague Evangelist Anthony Sluzas makes the following observation in his chapter, "All The Lonely People:"

Multitudes in our world today miss out on the joy of knowing Jesus because of the pull of other things. They don't realize it but these folks chase after other (temporary) things in order to fill this void...

"Once I make this huge business deal, then I'll do it." Not gonna happen.
"Once I become financially stable and secure, I'll do it." Not gonna happen.
"When I finally get the problems in my marriage fixed, I'll consider it." Not gonna happen.
"Once I can afford to drive that awesome foreign car..." Not happening.[1]

In another book of his called *Escaping the Debt Pit: A Pocket Book About Debt and the Believer*, he discusses what he identifies as "the fear of generosity" in chapter 3. In this chapter, he compiles the following list of excuses he's heard over the years, called "You Know You Fear Generosity When You Say..."

- "I just tithe with my time. I don't tithe with my finances, just time."
- "Well, let me first talk with my CPA."
- "When the deal comes through, then I'll give."
- "I can't afford it."
- "I've already maxed out my charitable giving."
- "Two years ago, I really gave."
- When you proudly proclaim, "I am generous."[2]

What do these two sections of these two different books have to do with each other? Everything! Even if we claim to know Christ for ourselves on some level, a true fear of giving – of having to go above and beyond what is comfortable for us – often holds us back. We might say we believe, but we might not come to the full knowledge of Christ and the full joy of walking with Him because we don't want to give all of ourselves to Him. Finances are a particular area of contention with many believers who come up with all the reasons above not to give. The excuses start: they don't believe in tithing today, they don't tithe with their finances, they have to consult someone else, they'll give when they have it, they can't afford to give, they have already given somewhere else, they gave earlier in time, or that they simply can't give because they are just too generous and have nothing left. None of these statements are factual if we aren't, in fact, giving anywhere, but they are things we tend to hold to and believe when it's time for giving.

Over many years of ministry experience with financial wrestling, I can't help but acknowledge the validity of Evangelist Sluzas's statements. As leaders, we've heard it all when it comes to reasons why people don't give. They all amount to the same, tired, old, and boring messages time and time again, which filters down to us. They are spoken to us, and we are just supposed to embrace them as our own and accept them. The problem is when we hear these statements, we hear much more behind them than just that someone doesn't want to give (which is often at the very heart of the matter). We are hearing that the Kingdom of God is not important to you, the services we offer to you aren't important to you, and none of these things are worth your financial contribution. You can speak to us otherwise, but if giving is just not on your radar, that tells us something about your esteem for God, for the calling He has placed on our lives, for the fact that He has placed us in your life for your edification, and for just how much you want the ministry to continue. It tells us that you want these things, but you don't feel they are worthy of your giving, even if it comes at a sacrifice. In summary, you tell us these things don't really matter to you.

This may sound dramatic, but the reality of most ministries is that their financial survival relies on a small handful of people who are willing to make the necessary sacrifices to continue to give. A leader's ability to do the work, especially if they aren't taking a salary, can easily be tanked without the regular financial giving of everyone who is part of that work. It only takes a few bad months to close doors, shut down websites, or completely cancel all community outreach. Ministries can't sustain themselves, let alone thrive, on your desired intent to give or on your promise to give at some vague point later in the future. Your giving, whether it is a few dollars or a large amount is not only needed, it is essential to the continuation and growth of whatever ministry you are a part. If you aren't giving, you are participating in the possible demise of the ministry you're supposed to embrace and share with others.

If you aren't giving, it's for one of two reasons:

- You've been given the message you don't have to give, or
- You just don't want to give.

If the first is true, you most likely received that message because someone in your life valued relationship with you over financial giving, and you should be extremely grateful for that. Whether it was because your leader pitied your situation or believed you when you said you had no money, they gave something additional (beyond what is required of them to give) to you by not expecting you to step up and give. They put aside their own vision and desire for the work for your benefit. Maybe you made one of the promises above to them: You'd do it when you felt you were able to give, or you couldn't afford it, or you would do it when your big break came through. What do these statements mean? Where do you have to be at to feel like you are able to give? How much money will it take? How settled to you have to be?

All of us can understand that we go through periods where we just don't have the money we might like to invest in something in the way we might like. Having a leader who understands this can be a great thing. But if days, weeks, months, and maybe even years have passed and you still aren't giving or you only give when you feel able, you are taking advantage of that situation. Most likely, your leader knows it, but because they feel they made an agreement with you, they don't want to pressure you. Be advised, though, your leader is very aware of the things you are doing in place of giving to the ministry…and it is hurtful to them. Every time you run wild with your spending or buy something you really don't need, and you can't find even a few dollars to give to the ministry, that's a stab at the Kingdom. When you see yourself with things but aren't blessed, it's not because you didn't have every chance, you didn't have every opportunity; you didn't take it. Your leader wants you to give because you want to, out of a good heart, and if you just don't have it within you to do it…then enjoy your stuff, because you aren't getting anything else from it! To be abundantly blessed, we must abundantly give!

If the second option is the case, then I must commend that you are at least being honest with yourself about why you are really not giving. Point

a) is a cover for not giving, because whether we are told we have to give, we should seek to do it, anyhow. Giving shouldn't be something we have to be pressured to do or even ask for; it should just be done. But point b) drives home at the issue of giving, head-on: we don't want to do it. We like having our money for our own things, and we just don't like the idea that God tells us what we have to do with some of it. God, however, is our model for giving. We learn in the Scriptures that God loved us so much, He gave!

For this is how God loved the world: He gave His one and only Son, so that everyone who believes in Him will not perish but have eternal life. (John 3:16)

Even though we already examined this passage, it is worth looking at it again in this simple context. God's love was so overflowing, He gave. He could have kept Christ to Himself, for His own personal benefit, but that wouldn't have served a purpose. It wouldn't have expressed any love, because there would have been no cost to it. Instead, God showed His love by giving to us through Christ. The same is true for us, here: we show our love by giving. We display our love by giving of our time, our abilities, our gifts, and yes, our finances. If we aren't willing to give in any of these areas, we are missing the point of love.

TITHES AND OFFERINGS SYSTEM

In Old Testament times, Israel was a literal nation. They were not just a spiritual entity, a spiritual Kingdom like we are today. They had political boundaries, roads, buildings, a military, a king, and governmental responsibilities. As a spiritual entity, they had the tabernacle and later the temple for worship and sacrificial offerings. Those who operated the sacrifices were the priests, who shared in different responsibilities and duties to get the different jobs done. The priests of the temple were supported through the tithes and offerings of the people, because they were the only one of the twelve tribes who did not receive a land inheritance. Their call was to be of service, maintaining a special leadership relationship with the people and a powerful spiritual inheritance from God. Because the Levites were chosen to serve, it was mandatory the people of Israel supported them. Because the Levites served for God, the people knew – and recognized – that giving to them reflected their desire to give and receive from God.

This means the ancient Israelites didn't get the chance to debate over the convenience or legitimacy of tithes and offerings in their day. Even though Israel didn't always give like they should, there was no room for a disconnect between financial giving and society. When Israel stopped giving, God dealt with them, no questions asked, because not giving was not an option. Failing to give was a sign of Israel's disobedience in God's sight. It was more than just having a bad day or something being amiss; it was deliberately going against the commands of God. For this reason, giving – or failure to do so – was serious business. There were even requirements about just how to do what, where to bring it, and when:

"Do not worship the LORD your God in the way these pagan peoples worship their gods. Rather, you must seek the LORD your God at the place of worship He Himself will choose from among all the tribes—the place where His Name will be honored. There you will bring your burnt offerings, your sacrifices, your tithes, your sacred offerings, your offerings to fulfill a vow, your voluntary offerings, and your offerings of the firstborn animals of your herds and flocks. There you and your families will feast in the presence of the LORD your God, and you will rejoice in all you have accomplished because the LORD your God has blessed you.

"Your pattern of worship will change. Today all of you are doing as you please, because you have not yet arrived at the place of rest, the land the LORD your God is giving you as your special possession. But you will soon cross the Jordan River and live in the land the LORD your God is giving you. When He gives you rest from all your enemies and you're living safely in the land, you must bring everything I command you—your burnt offerings, your sacrifices, your tithes, your sacred offerings, and your offerings to fulfill a vow—to the designated place of worship, the place the LORD your God chooses for His Name to be honored.

"You must celebrate there in the presence of the LORD your God with your sons and daughters and all your servants. And remember to include the Levites who live in your towns, for they will receive no allotment of land among you. Be careful not to sacrifice your burnt offerings just anywhere you like. You may do so only at the place the LORD will choose within one of your tribal territories. There you must offer your burnt offerings and do everything I command you." (Deuteronomy 12:4-14)

When we read the Old Testament, understanding the different forms of tithes and offerings can be quite confusing. We are also further confused because many of the items presented were not always given in the form of currency or money. It's important to remember a couple of key things with this fact. The first is that crop or goods exchanges were common in Biblical times, and that crops or goods often had the power to work as currency in deals. This means when people brought food or other crop offerings to the temple, it was as good as offering money. Despite the form they came in, these different offerings served the same purpose: sustenance for the Levites. This ensured the Levites could attend to the duties of the tabernacle and the temple without having to hold down multiple jobs to support their families, and that the tabernacle and temple were properly supported, with plenty of finances to remain operable. The different offerings required in Old Testament times were:

- **Tithe:** A tithe was an ancient form of taxation common throughout different parts of the Middle East. It was one's "Kingdom tax." It is from a term indicating a tenth, and was that specific portion given from whatever the Israelites earned or produced throughout a year. Tithing was on financial earnings, produce, and possessions, and made sure the spiritual needs of Israel were properly financed.

    There appears to have been more than one tithe in Old Testament times: the general tithe, the tithe on specific agricultural items, and a tithe once every three years. There's some debate as to whether these were special tithes or a restatement on specific items, but at minimum, tithes were required by every Israelite on a regular basis. The tithes were paid to the Levites, who then also tithed, ensuring the High Priest also received the benefit of a tithe.

- **Offering:** Offerings were different financial, agricultural, or possession gifts beyond the mandatory ten percent tithe. I once heard it said that if an Israelite was giving as they were required, their total giving (including their tithe) was somewhere around thirty percent of their annual income. There are at least fourteen different types of offerings found in the Old Testament, with five major offerings noted: burnt offering, grain offering, peace offering, sin offering, and trespass offering. These different offerings point to different aspects of Christ's redemption and His sacrifice and teach us about the interworking of sin in our own lives.

- **Care for the poor:** Although often interpreted in the context of an offering, the Old Testament also commanded the Israelites saw to the required care of those who were without families or marginalized within society: namely, the poor, widows, orphans, the disabled, and the needy.

It's evident as we examine these two main headings that there is a distinction made between giving a tithe and giving a general offering. The two were set as distinct because they were associated with different purposes. A tithe was assigned as a tax, something that one paid as part of their benefit of belonging to Israel, while offerings were things that pointed to important spiritual realities and taught over and above about the importance of generosity and redemption in one's life. Often, tithes and offerings were required at the beginning of events, such as festivals and harvests, putting God and God's Kingdom first, before anything else. They enriched one's life twofold: one, the Kingdom and its spiritual dimensions were able to continue, and two, the individual learned the importance of giving from a sacrificial perspective. It was about more than just giving to get something else; it showed priorities in one's life. If God was to be first, giving had to be about more than just ascribing to prosperity or to have more than other nations. It had to be about doing what God said, even in the good years, or the lean years; when it was convenient or inconvenient. God commands us to give, thus giving teaches us about generosity, giving to the poor, about recognizing what we do have, thinking about others, and above all, considering and thinking about Him in everything we do – even how we spend our resources.

An additional note to the basics of giving a tithe or offering: we do not give our tithes or offerings to a person when we give it to a ministry. We are giving to God through that ministry. I say this because many feel they do not have to give a tithe or offering if they dislike a leader's personality or feel that by giving, they are opening the door for allowing financial fraud. When you give an offering or tithe, your tithe or offering is made out to and given to a church or ministry entity, which is an incorporated or charitable (or both) organization with legal standing, subject to certain financial regulations. Matters such as salaries are distributed therein according to the governance of that body, in accordance with the law. In many instances, leaders don't always take a salary or take something far more minimal than they should have. The only exception to such a situation would be if you are directly giving an offering, item, or financial gift to a leader, in their hand, made out to them, for a special offering or occasion.

CHEERFUL GIVING

I've been asked why God gave a specific figure for tithing rather than just allowing people to give whatever they wanted. I believe the reason for this is because human nature is greedy and selfish. It wants to keep back the best – and most – part for ourselves. God knew if He didn't give people a mandatory figure with specified offerings to give, people wouldn't do it. They'd come up with all sorts of reasons to avoid giving and act like they did a huge favor every time they did anything. There would have been no practical or conceivable way the Kingdom of Israel could have functioned with such inconsistency.

Sound familiar?

There are many who argue that giving today should be different, because we no longer live under the Mosaic Law. They are correct; we don't live under the law. It is true that while Jesus did mention tithing as a correct practice, the command to tithe was not spelled out in the apostolic church. We are, however, still commanded to give, just as people were commanded to do so in the Old Testament. The New Testament writers went on the premise that the early believers gave of their whole lives; some of whom gave everything they had, thus it wasn't necessary to reiterate the specified amount of a tithe all over again. The New Testament believers tithed, and then some, to keep the church going. What's more, tithing was a part of ancient taxation in societies beyond Israel, thus existing long before the Mosaic Law. We can see Abraham presented his tithe, or tax, to Melchizedek, King of Salem in the book of Genesis.

This side of the Law, we can safely understand giving to be a basic Christian principle, and as tithes are a part of giving, there is no reason a Christian shouldn't be encouraged to tithe. The needs of the Kingdom and of God's people haven't suddenly ceased now that the Mosaic Law has terminated. If anything, leaving people to their own devices with giving and not requiring disciplined giving of a specified amount makes sure people aren't sure where to start, and tithing, just as it did in Old Testament times, gives a great illustration for where giving should begin.

Because it is associated with taxation, I think of tithing as paying our "Kingdom taxes." As part of the wonderful privilege we have of living in God's Kingdom, we should never fail to be aware that the Kingdom this side of heaven does not function on angel wings and good wishes. It takes money to maintain the Kingdom, just like it did for the Levites of old. Meeting places, building maintenance, books, supplies, equipment, instruments, and the ability for God's ministers to live all requires finances. Tithing gives a rounded amount for one to properly budget and is a great way to encourage a starting place for giving.

Yes, I said a starting place for giving, not an ending point. We should consider that a tithe is a great place to begin, but it is not all the giving that God requires. Tithing is not the end-all, be-all of giving. Even the Old Testament addresses this fact. It is my belief that tithing is a great and most effective place to start when it comes to giving, but none of us should think our giving should stop at a tithe. If we think we are doing great just because we have done a tithe, we are mistaken. God asks us to be generous – to give beyond what might be required on paper – because such giving makes a difference for us.

Remember this—a farmer who plants only a few seeds will get a small crop. But the one who plants generously will get a generous crop. You must each decide in your heart how much to give. And don't give reluctantly or in response to pressure. "For God loves a person who gives cheerfully." (2 Corinthians 9:6-7)

Giving cheerfully means we do it with a good attitude, without hesitation and without having to be constantly asked, nagged, or reminded. It also means we give beyond what might be the tithe-requirement on paper. We give as much as we can, remembering the principle of generosity in our giving. We are generous – not being stingy – but sowing into a Kingdom that will reap a hundredfold whatever we put into it.

<u>How do you spend your money?</u>

There is a never-ending list of reasons why people refuse to give to a ministry in the Kingdom. Echoing Evangelist Sluzas's list earlier in this chapter, these are some of the reasons I've heard in my own ministry about why people don't give:

- I have too much debt.
- I amassed student loans.
- I must buy a new car (house, computer, clothes, shoes, etc.).
- I have a hard time budgeting my money.
- I have too many bills to pay.
- I have maxed out all my credit cards.
- I'm starting a new business.
- I'm moving.
- I want to go on a vacation and can't afford to do both.
- I have children.

- I just got married.
- I'm a single parent.
- My kids are in college.
- I live in an area where I am too poor to give.
- I'm back in school now.
- I don't make enough on my job.
- My spouse isn't working.
- My adult children are back at home.
- My adult child racked up debt on my credit card.

And the biggest one of all…

- I can't afford it.

Let's break this down simply: Yes, you can give, you just don't want to. By doing this, you are passing on your own irresponsibility or that of someone else to the church, and just expecting it's going to be all right with God.

It's not. There is no reason not to give. God has made giving income-based, accessible, and available to all. There is no excuse for not giving. It is just as simple as that people don't want to do it and want to get out of having to do it with the over-extended excuse.

These are my responses to the over-extended excuses:

- It's not the ministry's fault you have amassed debt and can't pay for everything.
- It's not the ministry's fault you have student loans.
- It's not the ministry's fault you bought a car, a house, or something else you can't afford.
- It's not the ministry's fault you can't budget.
- It's not the ministry's fault you have too many bills.
- It's not the ministry's fault you have maxed out your credit cards.
- It's not the ministry's fault you want to start a business you cannot afford.
- It's not the ministry's fault you are moving.
- It's not the ministry's fault you want to take a vacation you can't otherwise afford.
- It's not the ministry's fault you had children and did not plan for that expense.
- It's not the ministry's fault you just got married and did not sort out your finances prior to getting married.

- It's not the ministry's fault you are a single parent. We were not present when your child or children were conceived.
- It's not the ministry's fault your kids are in college and college is expensive.
- It's not the ministry's fault you live where you do.
- It's not the ministry's fault you decided to go back to school.
- It's not the ministry's fault you have the job you have.
- It's not the ministry's fault your spouse doesn't work.
- It's not the ministry's fault you allowed your adult children to live in your home without a financial arrangement.
- It's not the ministry's fault you gave your adult child a credit card when you should not have done so.

It cannot be expected that you are a part of a ministry, week after week, and benefit from the services provided and you just expect you should not have to give because of your own financial choices and irresponsible natures. If you are a part of God's Kingdom, you have the responsibility to spend your money accordingly, repaying debts you have and refusing to amass new ones. We are no longer trying to keep up with the neighbors or have the things everyone else has. Our focus is higher; our purpose is higher; and that means our money gets saved along with the rest of us.

It's been my experience that those who use the over-extended excuse usually don't have a problem spending money where they want to spend it. In fact, those who refuse to give or try to give meagerly to the Kingdom don't realize that what they do decide to spend their money on says a lot about them, as people. Where all of us spend our money says a lot about us as people, and it's important we learn just what our money has to say about us.

Don't store up treasures here on earth, where moths eat them and rust destroys them, and where thieves break in and steal. Store your treasures in heaven, where moths and rust cannot destroy, and thieves do not break in and steal. Wherever your treasure is, there the desires of your heart will also be. (Matthew 6:19-21)

This passage of Scripture glares right at a fact we might prefer to deny: Where we spend our money speaks to our priorities. Wherever our financial "treasure" (our money, our saved money, our income) is (where we spend it), there is where the very heart of our lives will be found. If we want the things of this earth, they come at the price of eternal things. If we want to know what is most important to any one of us – if it's God or something else – all we must do is follow the money. You can tell me all day long how God is first in your life, how you want to be in ministry, how much you love the ministry, how much it gives to you, how you want to do more for the Kingdom, but how you handle your money is going to be the deciding factor as to whether or not I believe what you say. If you tell me you are all about God's business but have to be pressured to give (and then still don't), or you always have money for the things you want to do for yourself – new outfits, new hairstyles, vehicles, special nights out, family events, or entertainment – and never have it for the Kingdom – then your heart is not for the Kingdom.

If we want to gain the Kingdom, we must make decisions that sometimes leave us a little uncomfortable. This is especially true when it comes to giving. If you want to grow in your faith, it's time to let go of the things that hold you back and trust God to take you into that next place. Maybe most importantly, it means making different financial choices that show you are serious about what you claim to desire.

<u>Sacrificial giving</u>

The basic principle of giving anything – whether it is finances, as we are examining in this chapter, time, goods, objects, or as they did in Biblical times, agrarian giving – is that by giving, we let something go. In giving, we give part of something for the benefit of something else. Giving is a part of unity; it is a part of spiritual fellowship; it is a requirement of the Christian life. If we want to be a part of something greater than ourselves, we must give away whatever hinders us from having that.

In the modern church, we talk about giving with the agenda of "increase" or always "getting" something back or more or greater from our giving. I do believe that when we give, we are blessed by God, but not every blessing means we get "more." Sometimes the blessing is the elimination of something to make room for something else. The answer to every situation, solution, and satisfaction we seek is not more money or more things. We can't unite if we never have a need; we cannot fellowship or worship if we have no room or time for others; and we cannot find God in our faith lives if we are so overtired by commitments, new businesses, jobs, or family that there is simply no space for Him. Discernment is birthed and wrought through the silence of God, through those periods of space by which the Spirit comes to indwell and fill the emptiness we find in our lives. If we are forever giving with the expectation of gain rather than sacrifice, filling rather than emptying, and materialism rather than spiritual gain, we must face the fact that we will gain the entire world, but lose our souls.

Somewhere in here, God asks us to lay down our demands, our expectations, and desire Him, looking to eternity rather than earthly gain. We are to give even if it's uncomfortable, even if we don't see the result in this lifetime, even if it is for a purpose we don't understand with our natural minds. Through giving, we learn how to become more like Christ, because Christ asks us to give in the areas of our lives where it hurts the most. Money represents power and status, which we lay down in bringing our finances to the Kingdom, for its advances. We are to give of our time, which means we don't get to spend it on something else we might rather do. We are to give of ourselves, which means we don't always get everything we want out of our lives or this situation. Giving equates to sacrifice, because it unites us to His sacrifice. It brings us closer to Him as we follow the end of obedience, because that end brings us to the place where we find the end of ourselves and the beginning of eternity.

Thus, giving forces us to make choices. That's why no one wants to talk about it. We have to choose between things when it comes to giving, and our choices become evident when confronted with the requirement to give. Giving signifies letting go of things that have the power to hold us bound, hold us captive, or hold us back. When we give, we prove those things don't have a hold on us. When we hold back, we prove they do. This evidence is seen nowhere better than in two Bible situations that Jesus used to illustrate the importance of giving.

Someone came to Jesus with this question: "Teacher, what good deed must I do to have eternal life?"

"Why ask Me about what is good?" Jesus replied. "There is only One Who is good. But to answer your question—if you want to receive eternal life, keep the commandments."

"Which ones?" the man asked.

And Jesus replied: "'You must not murder. You must not commit adultery. You must not steal. You must not testify falsely. Honor your father and mother. Love your neighbor as yourself.'"

"I've obeyed all these commandments," the young man replied. "What else must I do?"

Jesus told him, "If you want to be perfect, go and sell all your possessions and give the money to the poor, and you will have treasure in heaven. Then come, follow Me."

But when the young man heard this, he went away sad, for he had many possessions.

Then Jesus said to His disciples, "I tell you the truth, it is very hard for a rich person to enter the Kingdom of Heaven. I'll say it again—it is easier for a camel to go through the eye of a needle than for a rich person to enter the Kingdom of God!"

The disciples were astounded. "Then who in the world can be saved?" they asked.

Jesus looked at them intently and said, "Humanly speaking, it is impossible. But with God everything is possible." (Matthew 19:16-26)

Jesus wasn't telling this young man that his eternal salvation rested in his works. This wasn't an issue of money being dirty and everyone who has money is forced to get rid of it all to be saved. He was identifying a point of idolatry in this young man's life. He was young, he had the world at his beckon call, he was rich, he understood the basic demands of his religion, and he had exactly what so many of us look for – "it all." He had it all, and still, something was missing. This man had everything we all hope and seek to find, and he was still coming up short. He knew all those things he had and all those things he did were not going to lead him to eternity, and something else was needed.

    The problem was, there wasn't room for God in his life. He was so busy trying to uphold obligations and maintain the wealth he had; he was looking for something else he could easily knock off his to-do list. Jesus clarifies that's not what salvation is, nor should our approach to it be like we approach everything else in this life. This young ruler needed to make room for God to come into his life and make him aware of just how much he needed him, because to find salvation, he first needed to realize he needed God more than he needed all the stuff that surrounded him. When Jesus told him he needed to get rid of his possessions and follow the One Who was salvation – Christ – he didn't follow. Instead, he went away and went away sad. His sorrow wasn't genuine; it was self-serving. He wanted it all and salvation, too, and Jesus made it very clear he couldn't have it. To gain what he wanted, he had to give something up.

He was unwilling, and that was the end of that.

Jesus wasn't saying people who are wealthy can't be saved. He was saying that it is hard for those who have everything to genuinely give enough to find what they seek. Salvation can't be bought, nor can it be wrangled; it is something we find when we recognize we have a lack in our lives and need to follow Christ to the end, wherever that journey may take us.

In contrast, we find a widow whose experience in giving reflects the exact attitude God asks us to have:

Jesus sat down near the collection box in the Temple and watched as the crowds dropped in their money. Many rich people put in large amounts. Then a poor widow came and dropped in two small coins.

Jesus called His disciples to Him and said, "I tell you the truth, this poor widow has given more than all the others who are making contributions. For they gave a tiny part of their surplus, but she, poor as she is, has given everything she had to live on." (Mark 12:41-44)

This woman was noted as being without financial means. She certainly wasn't the rich young ruler who came to Jesus, demanding of how to find his salvation. Instead, this woman was a widow. That means she was living alone, without much to her name, and without an inheritance. Even though her monetary amount was less than what others gave, Jesus pointed out she gave more than everyone else. She gave from what she had to live on; she gave of herself. She didn't give a small check or even just a tithe, but a huge portion of what she had. She did this because she understood the importance of giving, and even with the little amount she had, she knew the work of the Kingdom had to continue.

It's God's desire that we get the revelation of the poor widow: that we give, even if it costs us something. We have no excuses not to give, even if we are poor. The true heart of giving, of life, of giving from a place of sincerity means we give something up. I believe even though this woman didn't have much, God saw to her every need, because she saw to His business. She was willing to make a sacrifice, and her giving showed that nothing she had held her captive.

Approaching Charitable Giving From A Balanced Perspective

I've met more than a few people who feel that churches are irresponsible with the resources they are given and defend not giving to a church or ministry (even one they attend) by saying they give it to charity. They feel their money is better spent in such instances, and that it is just as good as Kingdom giving. Is this a good approach to giving? Does this address God's outlined giving? Is charity a substitution for dedicated Kingdom giving?

The answer is no. Charitable giving is good and is part of the mandate of our faith. Just as we could see from the Old Testament, giving to those who were in need is a requirement. We should never step back and think giving to others is unnecessary. But charitable giving as a defense mechanism in place to avoid giving to a church or ministry doesn't wash. It avoids our own personal responsibility in discerning where God has for us to be and makes sure good leaders don't have the provision to meet the needs that exist. By painting every single ministry as corrupt, it ensures a good ministry won't be able to survive and thrive.

It is also misleading to assume that charitable organizations are more responsible with their funding than ministries. Large charities often suffer from what's known as overfunding. This means that while their focus might be on a specific issue, more and more of their resources go to things unrelated to their cause because they have more money than they know what to do with. For example, a cancer organization might present itself as being all about the fight against cancer, but your donation, most likely, goes into the overhead for expensive office space, commercial airtime, mailings, lobbying or political campaigns, and expansion, rather than toward the cause you desire to sponsor. Just because an organization serves a good cause or is about the things you claim to support does not mean that you are actually funding that cause, nor does it mean they are better governed or more efficient with their money than a church or ministry might be. There have been just as many scandals with charities as there have been with church organizations, and thinking it's better to give here or there rather than to the Kingdom is a mistake.

I am also careful to say that some causes and charities do good work, but they aren't necessarily works that focus on our immediate Kingdom focus. For every believer, the continuation and advance of God's Kingdom should be our first priority. It is our honor to participate in the Kingdom through the sacrifice of our giving, and that means however we first give – tithes, offerings, or both – should and must go to God's Kingdom.

"Then the King will say to those on His right, 'Come, you who are blessed by my Father, inherit the Kingdom prepared for you from the creation of the world. For I was hungry, and you fed Me. I was thirsty, and you gave Me a drink. I was a stranger, and you invited Me into your home. I was

naked, and you gave Me clothing. I was sick, and you cared for Me. I was in prison, and you visited Me.'

"Then these righteous ones will reply, 'Lord, when did we ever see You hungry and feed You? Or thirsty and give You something to drink? Or a stranger and show You hospitality? Or naked and give You clothing? When did we ever see You sick or in prison and visit You?'

"And the King will say, 'I tell you the truth, when you did it to one of the least of these My brothers and sisters, you were doing it to Me!' (Matthew 25:34-40)

When considering charitable giving, we should consider the outlook of Kingdom interest in such, as well. Whether feeding the hungry, providing for the poor, making item donations to thrift stores or places where needs exist, providing educational resources or something else, our purpose in charitable giving should not be political or to meet with a political end. Charity is about people; about being a means by which God can meet needs that exist right here on earth. If there are those who are without something, it should be our honor to find organizations or support groups that extend whatever is needed to those who are in a position to seek it the most. We become a living representation that God does care about others, and He does see their needs, right as we live and operate in God's charity.

WHAT ABOUT POLITICAL POVERTY?

Poverty as it exists in modern times is largely political in nature. What I mean by this is such is the result of the battle between the rich and the poor, imperialism and occupation by different nations, and the exploitation of some groups over others. It stares us in the face on the television news, on the internet, in our inboxes, in books, and in most private documentaries or cultural discussions in interviews. It seems like everywhere we look, we hear about poverty that exists as an insidious aspect of human cruelty. Poverty is blamed as the root of all human issues, and as a result, certain implications are made about one's ability to give when they are poor. If it is someone else's fault that one does not have anything, how can they ever get ahead? How is giving possible?

Over the past few years, I have radically changed my perspective of those who come to our organization with their hand out, but do not desire to give anything in return. This is true of those who live in poor nations as well as wealthy ones. If someone comes to a ministry wanting things – whether it is materials, teaching, guidance, leadership, assistance, membership, instruction, or something else – but they do not want to give, they will not be eligible to join our ministry. Many protest. Many get angry. Many accuse me of being unchristian or unfair, and some go as far as to question my calling. It doesn't change the regulations, nor does it change my mind. If you come with the attitude that you should receive and you absolutely have no intention to give, you cannot be a part of this ministry.

The reason I am doing this now is for one simple reason: giving isn't income-based. I do not in any way, shape, or form deny the politics of poverty, but such politics aren't new. They existed in Biblical times as well as modern ones, and God's command to give is still vital and living for any and all who want to be a part of the Kingdom. No matter what situation we live in, we still can be a part of God's Kingdom, but we must play by God's rules. This means we all give – even when what we have seems meager or small. If we come to the Kingdom to receive, we are also required to give. No one is so poor they can't give, because God has made every tithe income-based and every offering open to amounts and options available.

Heal the sick, raise the dead, cure those with leprosy, and cast out demons. Give as freely as you have received! (Matthew 10:8)

Often, we understand the principle of "freely receive, freely give" to refer only to the one who receives something from God, such as a spiritual gift. We expect that gift to be given freely and liberally, and many understand that to mean it should be given without cost. In theory, they are absolutely correct; but there is a catch to it. Free giving and receiving is not just exclusive to the one with the ministry or the spiritual gift! In order to keep things freely given, they must also freely receive of the resources and provisions others have so the cycle can continue. If those who give don't receive, they can't continue to give. Everyone is required to both give and receive, and if someone refuses to give, they are interrupting the cycle so it cannot continue.

In the Kingdom, everyone gives. When we let people off the hook for giving, even if it seems like there is a good reason why they can't, we aren't helping them to grow or develop the necessary faith to participate in Kingdom living. Being a part of God's Kingdom is about more than just what we receive; it's also about what we give out and what we give to others. In receiving, we give, and in giving, we can receive. The better we understand this, we create systems for Kingdom sufficiency. It is better to encourage ministries to develop good financial habits and patterns than to become a personal bank or needs repository, that never encourages them to do better. If you are having to fund everything, that means they aren't giving themselves and it denies them the opportunity to see God at work and actively giving and receiving at the same time.

No one is exempt from giving; not due to the nation where they live, not due to politics, not due to circumstances. We freely receive, and we freely give. If we all do this, we will find there is more than enough for whatever work God has ahead, and for all He desires to do in His Kingdom.

GIVING AND DOING IN GOOD FAITH

Sometimes we have those situations where we are giving our best and doing our best, and we still come up short. We might not have for a special offering or a registration fee for an event, but we still want to be a part of it. What do we do in such instances, and how can we offer to give something back?

Giving is not all about money, although as we've clarified in this chapter, we can't substitute our financial giving with something else all the time. If you are never offering to give financially, something is wrong. When it comes to those instances where we are giving our best, but we are unable to do more, we offer to give in good faith through volunteering, offering our talents or abilities, offering to help our, or offering a skill. We still bring what we have to the table, and do so without shame, even if it is not, in the end, accepted.

"And I have been a constant example of how you can help those in need by working hard. You should remember the words of the Lord Jesus: 'It is more blessed to give than to receive.'" (Acts 20:35)

In everything we do, we should continually remember how important it is to give, even when money isn't what we give. We should always keep in mind the important heart of giving and why it is better to give than to receive as we go about any and all situations that arise in our lives. Giving makes our lives meaningful. It frees us up to receive so much more in our lives, because we have room and place to receive whatever God wants to pour out upon us. The promise of open windows of heaven comes only through giving, because there is no room to receive if we are simply too full. Let your heart speak of your treasure in heaven, in the Kingdom of God, rather than in the things of here. Let God move in your life, over and through you, as you receive the powerful revelation on the importance of giving and the transformation it brings.

REFERENCES

[1]Sluzas, Anthony. *Know God: No Fear.* Columbia, South Carolina: CreateSpace Independent Publishing Platform, 2017. Chapter 2, All The Lonely People: Page 8.

[2]Sluzas, Anthony. *Escaping The Debt Pit: A Pocket Book about Debt and the Believer.* Columbia, South Carolina: CreateSpace Independent Publishing Platform, 2017. Chapter 3, The Fear of Generosity: Pages 39-40.

Both references used by permission of the author.

‑ CHAPTER EIGHT ‑
You're a Solider in the Army of the Lord

SPIRITUAL warfare is a popular topic in many Christian circles. It seems like there are a myriad of books, ideas, thoughts, and teachings on this singular topic. It can be intimidating and overwhelming to study, especially when we consider that very few of the authors and teachers present information identical to each other. Much of it follows trends or popular ideas, many of which are not Scriptural and some even have the possibility to be dangerous. If we don't understand how something can apply for our lives and make sense for our situations, it doesn't wind up being of much value to us.

While spiritual warfare sounds exciting and maybe like a lot of fun, it is a serious discipline for the believer that takes insight and understanding. If we want to implement spiritual warfare properly in our lives, we need to do so with skill and spiritual application. The more we understand it in its proper context, the better it will serve us as we go through life.

In this chapter, we will examine the principles that help us develop proper spiritual warfare techniques in our lives without being spooky or scary in their approach. Most laity members won't have occasion for intense spiritual warfare on a regular basis, and it is, therefore, more prudent to examine the topic in a way that will help you apply it for your own circumstances. How can we use spiritual warfare in a practical way?

How does it apply to our everyday lives? What is the best way to stand ready without being paranoid or fearful? These are all questions that are important, and we will answer, as we learn the best ways to stand as a solider in the army of the Lord!

Understanding Spiritual Warfare

Spiritual warfare isn't the next best paranormal show on television. We're not ghost hunting or looking for Bigfoot. This is about using and applying Scriptural principles to outwit the enemy we have in Satan, also known as the devil. Just as there are good spirits who do God's bidding, there are also evil forces who do Satan's work. That means while we are here on this earth, we will have situations and experiences brought about by our enemy, because our enemy desires to draw us from God. This means he might make our spiritual lives difficult or make it take that much more effort to do the right thing or follow the will of God for ourselves. Just like God can work through people for good, correction, or encouragement, the enemy also works through people, but for a different purpose. The enemy's goal is to make us think God is far from us or doesn't care, and bring discouragement, secretive sin, or bad things into our lives. It's through those states that we start to distance ourselves from God and others, and that we wind up losing the battle of spiritual warfare.

This summarizes the spiritual battle that exists: there is an enemy who desires to lure us away from God and away from the things that will lead us to eternal life with Him. This means how we handle spiritual warfare relates much to the type of ideas military personnel have about battle: the ability to remain focused, despite distractions; strategy to handle oncoming fights as they arise; and ways to best navigate and overcome the enemy in our own lives.

"I tell you the truth, anyone who sneaks over the wall of a sheepfold, rather than going through the gate, must surely be a thief and a robber! But the one who enters through the gate is the shepherd of the sheep. The gatekeeper opens the gate for him, and the sheep recognize his voice and come to him. He calls his own sheep by name and leads them out. After he has gathered his own flock, he walks ahead of them, and they follow him because they know his voice. They won't follow a stranger; they will run from him because they don't know his voice."

Those who heard Jesus use this illustration didn't understand what He meant, so He explained it to them: *"I tell you the truth, I am the gate for the sheep. All who came before Me were thieves and robbers. But the true sheep did not listen to them. Yes, I am the gate. Those who come in through Me will be saved. They will come and go freely and will find good pastures. The thief's purpose is to steal and kill and destroy. My purpose is to give them a rich and satisfying life."* (John 10:1-10)

Spiritual warfare doesn't entail some sort of special defense or posture that we can only understand from a special instructor or teacher. Rather, it is best won as we come to know Jesus in a better way for ourselves. Some people spend so much time studying about the devil and trying to devise special prayers or spiritual defenses in spiritual warfare, they start to forget about Jesus Himself, the One Who comes to give us the abundant life. It's not God's will for us to spend all our lives in fear of Satan or of doing or pursuing the wrong things that we lose sight of the true life He has for us to live. Spiritual warfare is understanding what we see written in the passage above: anyone or anything that tries to take us away from God is working under the power of the enemy. Recognizing Christ's voice in our lives keeps us away from the enemy – and those who work for him – and keeps us on the right track. If we are willing to set ourselves aright each and every day, we may even go through periods where the enemy is the last thing on our minds.

We will discuss the basics of our enemy, Satan, shortly. First, there is something along our current lines of thinking we need to examine…

BEING A GOOD DISCIPLE

I bet some of you are reading this section's headline and wondering, why are we suddenly talking about discipleship? Isn't that something better served in another chapter? Admittedly, we have already talked about discipleship. It's important to be a good student of the things of faith on a regular basis and to understand the principles of discipleship for our spiritual development. Beyond this, however, is the reality that being a good disciple helps us to understand many things of our faith that otherwise seem confusing and overwhelming. Staying connected to Christ through right teaching and instruction goes a long way in developing the necessary skill to defeat the enemy.

I meet many, many sincere Christian people in my ministry who I believe love God and desire spiritual development in their lives, but who often complain of missing something in their walk with God. They just don't feel they get a lot out of it. When I inquire more about why this is, it's usually because they are relying on their faith experience to come exclusively through whatever their pastor or leader teaches, hoping God will reach out to them through someone else, or by waiting for signs to appear for direction or meaning. Don't get me wrong; it's awesome to know you can rely on your spiritual leader for a great and inspired word, or to get a message through someone else, or to even receive a divine sign. The catch is our pastor, our friends, and divine signs aren't around all the time. We can't hope and pray for one in every single situation we face. Other people can't fight our spiritual battles for us and no one can live the Christian life for you except you. At some point in time, you will have to take the affirmative interest in your faith and your life and develop it with God in a way that makes sense to you and works with the calling you have and the vision God has placed on your heart.

Those who often feel something is missing in their spiritual lives are often very consistent with the application of their faith. They might be serious and dedicated one day, and in a totally different place the next. They might be partially obedient to God's will but do things in other ways the rest of the time. This inconsistency often means they won't be ready when the enemy comes for them and will have a hard time fighting and resisting the temptations that come along or withstanding to do right in difficult situations. Inconsistency can make one feel an almost "whatever" sense of their faith and means that the enemy's eagerness to get them away from where God would have them to be becomes that much easier.

Examine yourselves to see if your faith is genuine. Test yourselves. Surely you know that Jesus Christ is among you; if not, you have failed the test of genuine faith. (2 Corinthians 13:5)

Discipleship is an absolute must for every believer who desires to be victorious in spiritual warfare. You can spend as many hours as you like reading about various demons and spirits, you can anoint every surface of your house until they're all greasy, you can spit and scream and run in circles and sweat and curse the name of the devil, but until you take those steps to be serious about your faith in Christ, it's going to all be a big jump into paranormal craziness. Your consistency in your faith gives you the best and most foundational way to approach spiritual warfare from a balanced perspective and in a way that will fit into your life, rather than overtake it.

This means…be serious about your faith! The best defense is a good offense. Devote yourself to the study of Scripture. Embrace a regular pattern of prayer. Learn the ways of God in your life and how God reaches out and speaks to you in your circumstances. Let Christ work through you and attune yourself for better obedience. Be of service and support to others. Monitor your own behavior and watch for the development of spiritual fruit. Let God convict you when it's time for a change to happen and let that change happen. Let the world know your discipleship is real and do so consistently. Most of all, let yourself know your faith is real. Stop doing it and then not doing it and make the point to dedicate yourself to your faith in a way that changes and transforms everything within and around you.

About Your Enemy

The understanding of Satan, also called the devil, has a complex evolution in the history of faith. It hasn't helped that the imagery and concept of Satan have been riddled with folklore and cultural superstitions. You've probably seen the results of these influences at some point: a red being with pointy ears and a pointy tail, carrying a pitchfork. There are many who believe the devil is equally powerful to God, just as an evil counterpart. Some almost take a cartoonish approach to the devil, treating him as if he is a superhero villain or menace. Understanding Satan is a little more involved than the way we often approach him, but at the same time, he is not nearly as complicated – nor as powerful – as some make him out to be.

The Bible doesn't give us a lot of detail about Satan, beyond he is known by a few names, all of which describe his nature. The name "Satan" is from a Hebrew word that means "adversary" and is so-called because it is his desire to be the enemy, or problem, of God's people. Satan wasn't always Satan, however, and he wasn't always an adversary. He is an adversary by choice; prior to his decision, he was an archangel, ruling over the choirs of heaven in glory and splendor. He was so notable, in fact, he thought he could do God's job better than God could, and desired to take the place of his Creator.

"How you are fallen from heaven,
  O shining star, son of the morning!
You have been thrown down to the earth,
  you who destroyed the nations of the world.
For you said to yourself,
  'I will ascend to heaven and set my throne above God's stars.
I will preside on the mountain of the gods
  far away in the north.
I will climb to the highest heavens
  and be like the Most High.'
Instead, you will be brought down to the place of the dead,

*down to its lowest depths.
Everyone there will stare at you and ask,
'Can this be the one who shook the earth
   and made the kingdoms of the world tremble?
Is this the one who destroyed the world
   and made it into a wasteland?
Is this the king who demolished the world's greatest cities
   and had no mercy on his prisoners?'"* (Isaiah 14:12-17)

Spoken of in personification and comparison to the King of Babylon (because Babylon is often used in Scripture to illustrate the conflict between the world and God's Kingdom), we learn that Satan was bright and shining before he was cast down to earth, due to his rebellion. In his state as the angel Lucifer, Satan desired to be as God, and through a revolt in heaven, was kicked out, along with the angels that desired to follow him in revolt. Those angels are now demons who assist Satan in his ultimate plan, and Lucifer is now the devil, also known as Satan.

This is important for one very central reason: Satan's desire was to be more than like God; it was to become God, to be better than God. In many ways, that is just how Satan works through people today as well as in each and every one of us. Satan challenges our humility before God and tempts us with things that bolster us up, make us feel good temporarily, help us temporarily escape the problems of this life, inflate our egos, or lure us into the idea that we know better than God and can do better than God for ourselves. Because we don't consider the results of Satan's fall, we fail to realize that Satan's end – as well as ours with him – leads to desolation, or nothingness. It feels good in the immediate and might even seem like something great and fun initially, but in the end, it doesn't take us anywhere near where we desire to be.

Satan hates the people of God simply because they are God's people. He chose a rebellious path that led him to a huge fall, and he knows it. So not unlike what many people do when they do something wrong…instead of making it right, they try to get others involved in their wrongdoing. That means those who reap the benefit and blessing of God's life are of particular interest to him. It's his desire we will all rebel against God, too, and he attempts to manipulate the believer by causing them to think God doesn't care about them because bad things happen, or difficult times come. He tempts believers with grandiose ideas, things that will solve nothing and yet make us feel better right now, or with things that will help us escape the realities God desires us to face. Not everything about being a Christian is roses and fun, and not everything God brings us to is always easy to maneuver or navigate. There are things we need to change as much as things we need to improve, and we can't do that if God doesn't force us to deal with ourselves. Thus, Satan's answer to things is to try and handle them with methods that will lead to desolation – to the wasteland – we will find if we but follow him. It won't feel like it initially, but eventually, we will find ourselves in a place of total abasement. Why? Just as Jesus comes for life and life abundant, Satan comes into our lives to steal, kill, and destroy.

Much like thieves, however, Satan doesn't come into our lives jumping up and down, and saying, "Hey, over here, look at me, I'm the devil!" He doesn't announce his presence. Satan works his way in and works havoc on our situations and lives, all looking like everything we hope for or desire.

But I am not surprised! Even Satan disguises himself as an angel of light. (2 Corinthians 11:14)

We need to watch for the things we come to idolize or think we simply can't live without, no matter what they might be. That's where Satan comes in to try and divide us from God. Whether it's a person, a thing, an aspiration, an ideal, or a situation, Satan knows how to either destroy us or bring it into our life just enough to get us away from God's precepts and ultimately, from God. God knows what we need and what we can handle, and if we are in a period where we must wait, that's what we must do. It's important to know and recognize some things are just not for this point in time, and seeking, lusting, and idolizing other things opens the door for the enemy to come swoop in and start taking from us.

Knowing our enemy is important; obsessing over our enemy will cause us to lose focus and, therefore, lose power. It's important to know Satan doesn't come with a pitchfork and red onesie outfit, but instead, with promises to take us to a different place through the things that hold us most bound. The more we realize how Satan works, the easier it is to identify his movements in our lives and learn ways to resist his tactics and stand strong in the spiritual battle.

SOME THINGS...JUST AIN'T THE DEVIL!

In the last section, we learned who Satan is and what he does. Now, we are going to deal with a whole other reality about Satan: there are too many out there who give Satan far more credit than he deserves. We've all met someone who does nothing more than run around all the time, screaming that everything is the devil. If they don't get what they want, it's the devil. If they have a problem, it's the devil. If they eat dessert, it's the devil. If they can't keep their diet, it's the devil. The devil, the devil, the devil!

One of my favorite examples of the true absurdity in blaming everything on the devil is the light bill. I've met people who don't pay their bill and then get a final cutoff notice from the power company, and call that the devil. They will spend hours praying, screaming, crying, running in circles, spitting, calling the blood of Jesus down over the power lines, cussing demons, and acting the fool...when none of that is necessary! If they want to keep the lights on, all they have to do is go pay the bill. It's not the devil that is turning the lights off; it's the power company. The lights are being turned off because someone agreed to pay for the electricity for their home or apartment and they failed to keep their end of the agreement. This is what happens when people don't keep their end of agreements. It has nothing to do with the devil, or Satan, or demons, and it certainly doesn't rate the ruckus that many cause. If you want to keep your lights on, you don't need a ridiculous prayer display; you need to keep your bill paid. It's that simple.

This is but one example of the way we often blame the devil for things that aren't the devil's fault, to divert attention away from the things that are our fault and are our responsibility in this life. The devil does not make us do anything; we make choices. The devil may tempt us or make things hard for us, thus influencing our decisions. The devil may even actively work in other people to bring us to a place where we feel like we have no other options but to follow or engage in behaviors that take us to those places, but the decisions we make are ultimately our choices. We must own those, not for the sake of fault or blame, but for accepting responsibility for the things we do.

Some things are the product of our responsibility. Some things are the product of others' responsibility. Sometimes things are the result of our culture or influences. Some things are just about our human weaknesses, our flesh. Sometimes, even the difficulties that come into our lives are from God, there to teach us something or help us examine our choices! Not everything is about the devil, all the time, and it benefits us to recognize the difference. By doing so, we can identify key points in our lives that raise personal issues and weaknesses we can work with God to rectify. They also help us to step back and realize we need to be true to our commitments, and careful in what we agree to do with other people. If we can't oblige a contract, we shouldn't enter it to begin with. If we can't maintain our faith and our integrity in certain relationships or connections with others, we should unite with those who can help us maintain such in our lives. It's not about being around people who are exclusively Christian all the time (because Christians can have character issues, too), but about being with people we can both lift up and who can lift us up.

One of the biggest secrets to spiritual warfare is setting yourself up for the best possible chance to succeed in your Christian faith. That means learning to live out the faith, maintaining connection with a great spiritual leader, and embodying good decisions in your personal life. This doesn't stop Satan from stepping in to try and cause his unique issues in our lives, but it does give us the fortitude to recognize demonic attack and withstand it through proper guidance and support.

A person standing alone can be attacked and defeated, but two can stand back-to-back and conquer. Three are even better, for a triple-braided cord is not easily broken. (Ecclesiastes 4:12)

There is power in setting ourselves up for success! Instead of trying to go at everything alone, stop blaming the devil for everything or looking for a devil around every corner and move into a place where you can team up with others to find the right balance to live your faith as only you can.

Why we battle

Behind spiritual warfare, we embrace a powerful message: the things of God are worth fighting for! Having the life God desires you to have, with everything that goes along with it, is worth everything we go through for it. Yes, the road of Christian faith isn't always easy, and there may be many things about it that aren't always a lot of fun and take a lot of discipline. But gaining spiritual growth, living in faith, seeing God come through for you, time and time again, and waiting things out to come to a better sense of yourself, are all things you can't put a price tag on, nor would you want to do so! Having all that God desires for us is so important, we need to be willing to fight through the difficulties to persist and have it. We stop holding onto the things that aren't for us and start embracing those that are. The more we do this, the more we realize just how important it is to grab hold of what God wants for us.

We are human, but we don't wage war as humans do. We use God's mighty weapons, not worldly weapons, to knock down the strongholds of human reasoning and to destroy false arguments. We destroy every proud obstacle that keeps people from knowing God. We capture their rebellious thoughts and teach them to obey Christ. And after you have become fully obedient, we will punish everyone who remains disobedient. (2 Corinthians 10:3-5)

Spiritual warfare gives us a spiritual, or non-material, approach to fight the things that come along in our lives and cause us trouble. It acknowledges that the enemy is behind the things that come along to try and seriously trip us up, and that we can't solve every problem of this life with human application and wisdom. It's wonderful to think we can sort everything out with a conversation or by expressing how we feel all the time, but this doesn't always help our situations find a constructive end. Yes, we do what we can to be peaceable with others and to work things out in the best ways we can, but sometimes the motives behind a situation or circumstance are more spiritually complicated than meets the eye. The Scriptures tell us the only way we can destroy false arguments, human reasoning, rebellious thoughts, and proud behaviors is through genuine, honest, and sincere spiritual warfare. How we may approach such situations may vary, but the end goal is for you to stand, with all God has for you at this point in time, so you can gain that much more victory for whatever is to come next.

We engage in spiritual battle because we have an enemy. We engage in spiritual battle because there are things that come along in this life that cause us to stand and stand firm. These are an opportunity to present our faith in a practical way, one that says, "I'm not going anywhere, and you aren't taking the progress I've made!" It connects us to God and teaches us that every strategy we need to take doesn't start with our brilliant ideas, but with genuine prayer and insight from God. This takes our relationship with God to a different level: one that invites God into areas of our lives that we might never imagine Him to serve for us: those of our losses, hurts, and conflicts. In spiritual warfare, we aren't just asking God to come and heal our issues or to fix them for us, but to give us the confidence to stand firm when such things arise, because such things will happen in our lives. If everything that comes along blows us over, causes hurt feelings, destroys our ability to focus, or causes us such extreme loss that we can't stand and deal, we will never, ever be able to withstand the general difficulties of life long enough to grow in Christ. Being a Christian is not about the removal of such issues but finding new ways to endure through unto a place of freedom.

PICKING YOUR BATTLES WISELY

We've all heard the old adage, "chose your battles wisely." This applies nowhere more than in spiritual warfare. Some battles are just not ours to fight, and some we are not qualified to fight. When it comes to fighting the battle or walking away and allowing God to fight that battle on our behalf, we must know how to hear from God in each and every situation and respond accordingly.

There are those who argue that God should fight our every battle; others believe we should stand and fight ourselves. We're told to let God fight things, then we spend all our time fighting the devil, focusing on haters, looking at enemies, and fighting everyone when we feel we've been wronged. Then we are told things will get better after this struggle or battle, and then someone tells us that when we get to the next level in God, there will be a new devil waiting for us. Sometimes we are told to be on the offensive, sometimes we are told to be on the defensive, and much of what we discuss in spiritual warfare focuses on people and personalities, rather than spiritual powers. In the midst of so many conflicting messages, what exactly should we do? Is the battle ours, or God's?

So God led them in a roundabout way through the wilderness toward the Red Sea. Thus the Israelites left Egypt like an army ready for battle. (Exodus 13:18)

Then Moses said, "If you keep your word and arm yourselves for the LORD's battles...all who are able to bear arms will cross over to fight for the LORD, just as you have said. (Numbers 32:20, 27)

"You are my battle-ax and sword,"
 says the LORD.
"With you I will shatter nations
 and destroy many kingdoms. (Jeremiah 51:20)

Be on guard. Stand firm in the faith. Be courageous. Be strong. (1 Corinthians 16:13)

He will go out to deceive the nations—called Gog and Magog—in every corner of the earth. He will gather them together for battle—a mighty army, as numberless as sand along the seashore. (Revelation 20:8)

The answer to the question is the battle is both ours and God's. The battle is ultimately God's, but it is our choice how we fight and when we fight. The battle is personal to us, and it is personal to God. This doesn't mean we run rampant, however, doing whatever we want in spiritual battle. Soldiers follow the guidelines of their superiors, and in this instance, we follow the directive of God. If God tells us to stand still and let Him handle it, then that's what we do. If He tells us to stand and fight, then that's what we do. The commands may be different based on the circumstances; and this is not at all a contradicton. This is part of why it's so important for us to draw to God and to know His voice, which we develop as we communicate with Him and learn about hearing from God from our leadership. We can't know what to do if we don't recognize the voice of our Commander.

Picking your battles wisely relates to just this: know when to go in, and when to step back. Know how to fight, strategically, in a way that will bring about victory. Don't let your own emotions or the enemy's tactics cause you to lose this focus in your life! Listening to God – and knowing what to take on and what to leave – will go a long way in helping you remain victorious in spiritual battle.

INTERCESSION

As we looked at previously, intercessors are a function of the church, here to help wrangle on behalf of both earth and heaven. Intercession is the name for this important spiritual work, which lifts petitions before heaven and also sees things from the heavenly perspective. Intercession is different from regular prayer because it forms that intermediary position, seeing the complicated ways that the natural world and spiritual world are interconnected. Intercession intervenes on behalf of God for His justice and mercy in this world, and on behalf of this world for the needs and issues that exist while we are here.

Intercession is part of spiritual warfare because within it we find this state of battle and wrangling, one that makes an individual aware of the spiritual issues that often fall behind natural ones. Individuals who operate in the function of intercession perform a powerful service as an advocate, one by which they not only fight in battle for themselves, but for others, as well. A spiritual intercessor is a battler on the front lines, fighting battles that they may know or not understand, all for the purpose of betterment; helping this world to be a little bit more on earth like it is in heaven.

Then the men got up from their meal and looked out toward Sodom. As they left, Abraham went with them to send them on their way.

"Should I hide my plan from Abraham?" the LORD asked. "For Abraham will certainly become a great and mighty nation, and all the nations of the earth will be blessed through him. I have singled him out so that he will direct his sons and their families to keep the way of the LORD by doing what is right and just. Then I will do for Abraham all that I have promised."

So the LORD told Abraham, "I have heard a great outcry from Sodom and Gomorrah, because their sin is so flagrant. I am going down to see if their actions are as wicked as I have heard. If not, I want to know."

The other men turned and headed toward Sodom, but the LORD remained with Abraham. Abraham approached Him and said, "Will you sweep away both the righteous and the wicked? Suppose you find fifty righteous people living there in the city—will you still sweep it away and not spare it for their sakes? Surely you wouldn't do such a thing, destroying the righteous along with the wicked. Why, you would be treating the righteous and the wicked exactly the same! Surely you wouldn't do that! Should not the Judge of all the earth do what is right?"

And the LORD replied, "If I find fifty righteous people in Sodom, I will spare the entire city for their sake."

Then Abraham spoke again. "Since I have begun, let me speak further to my Lord, even though I am but dust and ashes. Suppose there are only forty-five righteous people rather than fifty? Will you destroy the whole city for lack of five?"

And the LORD said, "I will not destroy it if I find forty-five righteous people there."

Then Abraham pressed his request further. "Suppose there are only forty?"

And the LORD replied, "I will not destroy it for the sake of the forty."

"Please don't be angry, my Lord," Abraham pleaded. "Let me speak— suppose only thirty righteous people are found?"

And the LORD replied, "I will not destroy it if I find thirty."

Then Abraham said, "Since I have dared to speak to the Lord, let me continue—suppose there are only twenty?"

And the LORD replied, "Then I will not destroy it for the sake of the twenty."

Finally, Abraham said, "Lord, please don't be angry with me if I speak one more time. Suppose only ten are found there?"

And the LORD replied, "Then I will not destroy it for the sake of the ten."

When the LORD had finished His conversation with Abraham, He went on His way, and Abraham returned to his tent. (Genesis 18:16-33)

Abraham is one of the most powerful examples of an intercessor that we find in Scripture. With the wickedness of Sodom and Gomorrah, it was Abraham who came in fashion to intercede for the people of these cities after God announced He would destroy them. Some consider Abraham's behavior to be "challenging" God, but that is certainly not what Abraham was doing when we recognize the work and role of an intercessor in a proper way. Abraham came and petitioned God, meeting with God in true intercessory fashion. He recognized both God's position and the sorry state of the people, and he petitioned God to have mercy on those who might have been righteous in the face of wickedness. Until it was evident there was none who was righteous in Sodom of Gomorrah, Abraham stood firm, calling on heaven for justice and praying for earth's repentance. He interceded for what he didn't know, for what he did know, and for the assurance he found present in God, his Creator.

Abraham's experience in spiritual intercession reveals that intercession is a warfare experience that is not always successful in the eyes of the intercessor or other onlookers. I am sure Abraham would have loved to see Sodom and Gomorrah saved for the sake of one or two righteous people, but there weren't any. God had information he didn't have, and that meant when it came to the ultimate decision, Abraham came to trust God. Intercession isn't all about the results we'd like to see on earth, but about that desire, that wrestling to wrangle between heaven and earth, and standing in the gap for what is right and just.

The work of intercession also works to connect the Body in unity and to bring people into the Body of Christ through spiritual insights, intercessory prayer, and power. Intercessors remind us of the ultimate intercessory victory of Christ on the cross, where His sacrifice worked to bridge the gap – bridge the wrangling of sin – between heaven and earth. Though intercessors are not Christ, they work in their position now to petition heaven for the salvation of souls, for the needs of those in the Body of Christ, for the continuation of the faith as we await the time when Jesus returns, and to stand as an agency representative of the issues that impact both earth and heaven.

Not everyone has the ability to function as an intercessor. Intercessors are given the specific ability to wrangle and represent as they do and are given certain insights in order to discern and recognize both heavenly and earthly perspectives. They must always remain on the watch, aware of the need to wrangle, battle, or engage in prayer for others (known as intercessory prayer). Intercessors need to know when they hear from God to act accordingly in intercession. As front-line soldiers in the work for spiritual warfare, intercessors are great people to know and connect with when it comes to difficult times or the need of spiritual breakthroughs in prayer or other issues. It is most important – and relevant – to embrace the importance of intercession, all the while respecting this unique work in the world of spiritual warfare.

<u>Armor of God</u>

The most common subheading for discussion on spiritual warfare is the armor of God. For this, we go to Ephesians 6:10-20.

A final word: Be strong in the Lord and in his mighty power. Put on all of God's armor so that you will be able to stand firm against all strategies of the devil. For we are not fighting against flesh-and-blood enemies, but against evil rulers and authorities of the unseen world, against mighty powers in this dark world, and against evil spirits in the heavenly places.

Therefore, put on every piece of God's armor so you will be able to resist the enemy in the time of evil. Then after the battle you will still be standing firm. Stand your ground, putting on the belt of truth and the body armor of God's righteousness. For shoes, put on the peace that comes from the Good News so that you will be fully prepared. In addition to all of these, hold up the shield of faith to stop the fiery arrows of the devil. Put on salvation as your helmet, and take the sword of the Spirit, which is the word of God.

Pray in the Spirit at all times and on every occasion. Stay alert and be persistent in your prayers for all believers everywhere.

And pray for me, too. Ask God to give me the right words so I can boldly explain God's mysterious plan that the Good News is for Jews and Gentiles alike. I am in chains now, still preaching this message as God's ambassador. So pray that I will keep on speaking boldly for him, as I should.

The spiritual armor spoken of in the passage above was very deliberately selected as an illustration designed to help the reader understand how prepared we need to be, on a daily basis, for spiritual warfare in our everyday lives. The catch is the illustration is very tailored to Biblical times, rather than what modern-day soldiers might wear. The Apostle Paul used the imagery of the Roman army to fill our minds with just how completely covered in spiritual preparations we need to be to face our enemy, day in and day out. We are encouraged to be strong in the Lord, and in His power, which shows where our priorities and direction lie. If our focus is on the Lord, we know He is the source of all we are able to do. As our source, we can trust Him for direction. We do this by remaining connected to God and living, growing, and loving as He commands us to do. It doesn't mean we have to be constantly forceful or aggressive, but that we will be able to withstand anything that comes along.

The need for spiritual armor is also illustrated well because we aren't fighting against the things we see in this world. This isn't a battle against people or personalities, nor is it over land territories. This is about spiritual authority and the battle between the Kingdom of God and the kingdom of the enemy. What we fight is often not materially tangible, and we must, therefore, acknowledge the invisibility of our enemy and know them by their movements. Thus, we stand firm, prepared with our armor on and ready to fight:

- **Belt of truth:** The belt of truth is buckled around the waist, serving as a central point to hold us upright. Truth has this impact on our lives, keeping us upstanding, holding ourselves up and together, and being able to stand without slouching or shame.

- **Body armor (breastplate):** The breastplate, or body armor, covers the chest area, especially the area of the body where we find very important internal organs, such as the heart and lungs. To keep God's righteousness within our heart and inward places signifies that we will always keep the ways of God in the deepest parts of us, desiring to do right and have right standing with Him at all times. This ensures we will be directed by God in all things.

- **The shoes of peace:** Shoes represent physical steps or movement, which represent spiritual movement in this instance. If our shoes fit us properly, we are able to run and move freely, with swiftness and quick movement. If they aren't a right fit, we can deal with slower movements and discomfort. We are to be fitted with the peace of the Gospel because it is something that fits us right and gives us the readiness of spiritual movement and purpose when we must act quickly and with grace. It shows us ready for our walk and our calling, and that we can answer life's issues with a greater spiritual purpose.

- **Shield of faith:** Shields are used to extinguish oncoming darts, arrows, or other objects that might be thrown at a soldier in battle. The shield of faith stands to extinguish the flaming arrows thrown at us by the enemy, who never plays fair and attacks us with fire, representing a battle often come right when we need it the least, right where we need it the least. Our faith in Christ has the ability to quench these fiery, unfair, and all-too-common darts thrown our way. Our faith can keep such invasions from entering too close into our personal space and helps us to persevere in battle rather than being taken out of the fight too early.

- **Salvation as your helmet:** Helmets protect the head from serious injuries that could cause a decline in cognitive function and bodily operation. Salvation as our helmet shows the transformation we undergo in our spiritual minds as we grow in faith. We need to pay attention to what we allow to enter our thinking, thought processes, images, concepts, and other things that can infiltrate our personal mental space and affect the entirety of our spiritual being. Remembering that our minds are saved, and we are of sound mind goes a long way in spiritual understanding.

- **Sword of the Spirit:** We learn the sword of the Spirit is the Word of God, which refers to any spoken word that comes from God. This relates to how we use and relate God's Scriptures to us, as well as how we relay God's revelation to each and every one of us as we go through spiritual directives in the battle.

- **Pray in the Spirit:** Prayer in the Spirit is more than just speaking in tongues, although that is definitely a large part of it. Praying in the Spirit is to be in touch with the Spirit's intercession and following that leading as we learn what to pray for, how, and when. By learning the different ways we best communicate with God, we are able and equipped to pray at all times, on many different occasions, and in all seasons. We must be alert and pray not just for ourselves, but for all in the Body of Christ, as prayer is needed.

The need for spiritual armor teaches us that God doesn't send us into battle empty-handed, thus we shouldn't run around in spiritual battle without the proper preparation. One of the major reasons people falter in their spiritual warfare is because they don't discipline themselves to realize this is a serious thing in our lives. No, spiritual warfare doesn't require us to stop living and start behaving in strange ways that are counterproductive to our spiritual goals. We are here, given every ability to properly focus and prepare for the battle, and to do and have exactly what God desires us to have: spiritual victory.

SPIRITUAL VICTORY

The ultimate spiritual victory over sin and death has been won by Jesus Christ. We might not see the results in full yet, as the kingdom of darkness rages against the Kingdom of God, but we know that one day we shall see the full results of this victory come to life when Christ returns. In the meantime, we enjoy seeing the results of this victory in our own lives, even though we may not see it on a large scale right now.

Victory is the ultimate result of salvation this side of heaven, and that means it manifests in any number of diverse ways for us. It is a sign that God is with us, and that ultimately, He oversees and directs any battle we experience. We can know, and rest assured, that God cares about us and loves us enough to lead us through to the very end of the different things we face.

Then, when our dying bodies have been transformed into bodies that will never die, this Scripture will be fulfilled:

"Death is swallowed up in victory.
O death, where is your victory?
   O death, where is your sting?"

For sin is the sting that results in death, and the law gives sin its power. But thank God! He gives us victory over sin and death through our Lord Jesus Christ.

So, my dear brothers and sisters, be strong and immovable. Always work enthusiastically for the Lord, for you know that nothing you do for the Lord is ever useless. (1 Corinthians 15:54-58)

The Christian life is one full of reminders of God's ultimate promise to us. It's important we remember that whatever we experience, go through, or face is temporary. All these things we see, that seem so vital and brutal, will one day be no more. Our focus in spiritual battle keeps us looking at God and believing in Him to transform everything we see for His glory. This transformation includes us as much as it includes our circumstances. Through spiritual battle, God brings new things out of us as we apply our faith and grow through what we go through. This, we are able to see, is the ultimate victory of every smaller battle we encounter. As He increases and we decrease, we are able to see a whole new beginning from the end of a Kingdom fight that God walked us through, step by step.

CHAPTER NINE
TAKING OUR PLACE IN HISTORY

W E'VE already discussed that every one of us has a purpose this side of heaven. Our purposes all vary from one another, but we can take promise and celebrate in the special divine purpose and plan God has for our lives. We are here on purpose, for a purpose, and with a purpose. As we come into a greater discovery of what our purpose is, we are better able to figure out the smaller pieces of that journey, and ready to take them on. Doing this gives us a purpose and a place in history, bigger than we can imagine, and helps us to step up and do whatever we are supposed to do, right now.

We are here now, at this time, by no accident. You are reading this book, at this time, by no accident. God has positioned you for something that must be completed through your life and its bigger purpose. It might not seem like a huge, important task, but through a spiritual lens, it is appointed to you because you can do it best. Figuring it out as you navigate from your new life in Christ can seem daunting when you see the current trends of culture, society, or the world. It can seem irrelevant to stay God's path when you see war, famine, political unrest, and difficulties all around you. Is it more desirable to follow a different course? Should you stop pursuing the Kingdom of God and start doing social work? Is it better to be in the Kingdom, or in the world?

These questions are easily answered, even in the most discouraging of outlooks. They come up at different points in time; when we grieve in loss, when we see the problems of this world up close, when things don't go as planned, or when we find ourselves intimidated by problems that don't seem to be resolved with Kingdom confrontation. Yet do not despair, there is hope! God has raised us up to take our place in this time, and as we learn to navigate through our questions and times, we can see why we are here – and how it makes a difference.

ADJUSTING TO CHANGING LANDSCAPES

By the time this book is published, it will be about a year since my late husband died from liver cancer and advanced cirrhosis. Of all the things I've gone through in my over 20 years of ministry, that was, by far, the most challenging. I'd been through many difficulties and trials throughout the years, but this was one I didn't know how I could come back from it. To be fair, grief isn't something we "come back" from, but I didn't know that when I first experienced it. I anticipated I'd be sad for a while, but one day, I'd be the same person I was prior. When that didn't happen, I had to come to a place of acceptance of God's call on my life, all over again. This time, I had to accept it as a totally different person than when I was first called. The change in my life because of my husband's death forced me into a place of new examination, new realities, and new directions, and I now had to see where I, as a person, fit into life, in addition to the call of God that was already there.

When we first discovered my husband was sick, I laid awake all night, thinking about life and about what was going to come next for me. One of the first things I had to face was whether I wanted to do ministry anymore, at all. There were a few reasons why I had this line of thinking. The first was that my late husband was a major source of income for our family, and if he was no longer going to be around, I didn't know how practical it would be to continue to pursue the work. Finances were forever a problem in ministry, and I now was fully responsible for taking care of my household. The second reason was because I had spent much of my marriage pursuing ministry with the goal and hope I could become self-sufficient. My husband resented the fact that I didn't make as much money in ministry as he did at his secular job, and that left me with the drive to make ministry work to prove something not just to him, but to myself. I wanted to feel like I could take care of myself and could be independent, with the hopes I could leave the situation I was in and stand on my own. Without my husband in the picture, I wasn't sure how interested I was in ministry. That pursuit, that drive to make it work wasn't there anymore, because my source of trying to make it work wasn't relevant any longer.

It took about seven months after my husband died for me to start looking at my work in ministry seriously and find the vision and purpose in a place with my newly changed life. There were many changes that would need to take place for ministry to remain part of my life, and those changes wouldn't happen overnight. I also had to look at where I fit into ministry now that my circumstances were different. My outlook and perspective on life was different, and I was a different person than I used to be. The changes of my life made my work – and my approach – to my ministry different, and I needed to see how those new things fit with my already existing spiritual gifts and abilities.

We can start out with a purpose and vision that is from God and as our lives and circumstances change, we can desire to run with it or see it work for totally different reasons. As life goes along, we will reach a point where we are confronted with just what we want to do and how we want to do it for the future. Life is full of change, and change is part of what brings about different perspectives and maturities in our lives. When this happens, we must recommit to our vision and purpose, see how the changes we have gone through now apply to it, and move forward. Sometimes it'll mean God will bring us a whole new vision and outlook, and that it'll be time to do something different. Sometimes it'll mean expanding or doing new things in a different way. All in all, however, the important point is coming to the realization that we do still have a purpose, and God will be just as faithful with us through the next part of the journey as He was through the last part.

For everything there is a season,
  a time for every activity under heaven.
A time to be born and a time to die.
  A time to plant and a time to harvest.
A time to kill and a time to heal.
  A time to tear down and a time to build up.
A time to cry and a time to laugh.
  A time to grieve and a time to dance.
A time to scatter stones and a time to gather stones.
  A time to embrace and a time to turn away.
A time to search and a time to quit searching.
  A time to keep and a time to throw away.
A time to tear and a time to mend.
  A time to be quiet and a time to speak.
A time to love and a time to hate.
  A time for war and a time for peace.

What do people really get for all their hard work? I have seen the burden God has placed on us all. Yet God has made everything beautiful for its own time. He has planted eternity in the human heart, but even so, people cannot see the whole scope of God's work from beginning to end. So I concluded there is nothing better than to be happy and enjoy ourselves as long as we can. And people should eat and drink and enjoy the fruits of their labor, for these are gifts from God.

And I know that whatever God does is final. Nothing can be added to it or taken from it. God's purpose is that people should fear Him. What is happening now has happened before, and what will happen in the future has happened before, because God makes the same things happen over and over again. (Ecclesiastes 3:1-15)

The Bible acknowledges there are many diverse things we go through in this life that we encounter cyclically, going through them over and over again throughout our lives. There will be times when we see birth and death, war and peace, love and hate, grief and happiness, gains and losses, and so on and so forth. The whole of life under the sun is full of these periods, and they cause us to seek out answers to deeper questions in life. The best thing we can do is take what comes, figure out what God is saying to us, and find enjoyment in the product of each and every season of our lives. Odds are good, in some form or another, they will come around again.

Learning to navigate our purpose through these changing seasons is vital for us to leave our mark in this world. As believers, there will forever be a reason not to believe. There will always be a new religion, a new doctrinal fad, someone with a million reasons to say why they think something else is better than Christianity, and someone with a seemingly convincing argument against the faith. There will always be a reason not to do what God has for us to do: lack of money, time, interest, people motivation, or inspiration. Our ultimate encouragement is to press through and press on, and despite any naysayers, difficult times, changes, or differences, to continue focused on the purpose of life we discover through our walk and connection to God.

DOES LIFE HAVE MEANING?

Everyone wants to feel their life has meaning. No one wants to feel like a nobody or a nothing in their lives. We all love the idea of being important to someone, somewhere, even if it's not on the massive level of fame or intrigue. We like to believe the things we do matter, and that is probably because most of the time, we don't feel that way. We just go to the job to get the paycheck, or just clean the house because it's dirty, or we just get married because it's the next thing to do…in this never-ending rat race that almost makes us feel disconnected from our lives. We just do whatever's next on the list, whatever is scheduled, whatever is coming up, or whatever it is we think we are supposed to do.

The book of Ecclesiastes was authored by an individual known as "the Philosopher." The entirety of its contents is about the fact that as we go through life, it's not so much our starting or ending points that should be so notable, but more about the journey we take that teaches us as we go along. This wisdom is what makes our lives notable, but it is unfortunate that we often focus only on our starting and end points, thus missing the lessons of the journey, thus not seeing what gives our life its true meaning. It's not life, all by itself, that has inherent meaning, but what we learn from and do in our lives that gives it meaning and purpose.

Don't let the excitement of youth cause you to forget your Creator. Honor Him in your youth before you grow old and say, "Life is not pleasant anymore." Remember him before the light of the sun, moon, and stars is dim to your old eyes, and rain clouds continually darken your sky. Remember Him before your legs—the guards of your house—start to tremble; and before your shoulders—the strong men—stoop. Remember Him before your teeth—your few remaining servants—stop grinding; and before your eyes—the women looking through the windows—see dimly.

Remember Him before the door to life's opportunities is closed and the sound of work fades. Now you rise at the first chirping of the birds, but then all their sounds will grow faint.

Remember Him before you become fearful of falling and worry about danger in the streets; before your hair turns white like an almond tree in bloom, and you drag along without energy like a dying grasshopper, and the caperberry no longer inspires sexual desire. Remember Him before you near the grave, your everlasting home, when the mourners will weep at your funeral.

Yes, remember your Creator now while you are young, before the silver cord of life snaps and the golden bowl is broken. Don't wait until the water jar is smashed at the spring and the pulley is broken at the well. For then the dust will return to the earth, and the spirit will return to God who gave it.

"Everything is meaningless," says the Teacher, "completely meaningless."

Keep this in mind: The Teacher was considered wise, and he taught the people everything he knew. He listened carefully to many proverbs, studying and classifying them. The Teacher sought to find just the right words to express truths clearly.

The words of the wise are like cattle prods—painful but helpful. Their collected sayings are like a nail-studded stick with which a shepherd drives the sheep.

But, my child, let me give you some further advice: Be careful, for writing books is endless, and much study wears you out.

That's the whole story. Here now is my final conclusion: Fear God and obey His commands, for this is everyone's duty. God will judge us for everything we do, including every secret thing, whether good or bad. (Ecclesiastes 12:1-14)

There are many things in life that can easily get us off track from our journey, from the process of our faith that draws us closer to God and from point A to point B and beyond in our lives. We've all dealt with the sting of disapproval from others or the expectations others had about what we should do or where we should go in our lives. There have even been points in time where those internal discussions come from us: we can't figure out why we wouldn't want to do or have something, so we are going to push for it, because it "looks good on paper."

If we want to discover more meaning in our lives, we must be willing to admit that much of what we desire to take on, from a human perspective, is meaningless. I don't question that, as people living in the world today, we need to have certain things. We definitely need to have transportation, we need a safe, clean place to live, we need to clothe and dress ourselves accordingly, we need the proper skills to sustain our livelihood, and we need people to share it with. We don't need the biggest house on the block, or the designer car or clothes that won't last two hundred years from now. The relationships that don't make it won't be a thought a few generations down the line. All those things that excite us at different stages of our lives, turn our heads and take us far from where we need to be won't be important later. Sometimes, those things won't even be important later in our own lives!

What will matter is our journey, and what we learn from it and take from it. Did we take the time to seek God at each step? Did we hear what God was saying to us? Did we learn something from the journey that helps us grow spiritually? Most importantly, have we applied what we've learned?

<u>Debating the hard questions</u>

One of the things I love most about the Bible is that it doesn't just have one opinion or perspective on many deeper life issues. Some say the Bible contradicts itself, but I don't see this to be the case. I believe the Bible is realistic in the fact that different situations sometimes have different solutions, and that at the heart of what we come to discover should always be God, Himself. This doesn't mean truth changes; it means that it adapts to what we need, when we need it.

Life is full of questions that are difficult to answer because they pose perspectives and issues that can be seen from different angles. We love the idea of absolute answers to human situations, but the longer we live and the more we see God respond to the human condition in the Scriptures, we see that some of these questions don't always have simple, pat answers. We also long to look in the Scriptures and see clear answers for modern-day questions, such as abortion, marriage, suicide, mental illness, relationship questions, who to vote for, and the like, with the reality that some of these issues weren't even a question or a thought in Biblical times, at least not in the way they are handled today. All of us wonder about the answers to the hard questions, especially when they are trendy and burn larger than life in our memory banks, because we find them everywhere. The world we live in has made social issues and political debates life or death issues, and it's easy to feel caught up in the middle of a debate that seems like it is moral, when it really is about control and money.

I, the Teacher, was king of Israel, and I lived in Jerusalem. I devoted myself to search for understanding and to explore by wisdom everything being done under heaven. I soon discovered that God has dealt a tragic existence to the human race. I observed everything going on under the sun, and really, it is all meaningless—like chasing the wind.

What is wrong cannot be made right.

What is missing cannot be recovered.

I said to myself, "Look, I am wiser than any of the kings who ruled in Jerusalem before me. I have greater wisdom and knowledge than any of them." So I set out to learn everything from wisdom to madness and folly. But I learned firsthand that pursuing all this is like chasing the wind.

The greater my wisdom, the greater my grief.
To increase knowledge only increases sorrow. (Ecclesiastes 1:12-18)

The author of Ecclesiastes calls us out when it comes to deep ponderings and the things we seek after, almost compulsively. When it comes to all things, we need to maintain a balanced sense of perspective. That's why there isn't just one solution or answer to some of life's situations in Scripture. Our pursuit in this life can't be the acquiring of things, even those that are intangible (such as acquiring knowledge or wisdom). Our ultimate pursuit needs to consistently be knowing, loving, and serving God, and when we do that, we will find the rest of what we seek. We seek first the Kingdom, and His righteousness, and then God adds the rest to our lives. It's awesome to think about the hard things of life, but we should never pursue it to the point that we forget about our journey or about the things we are able to figure out in life just from living and experiencing God in a profound way through our walk with Him.

So yes, think about what you need to think about, but don't obsess over it to the point where it takes over your entire being. Some things you feel strongly about now, you may change your mind about later. The way we understand the Scriptures comes with growth as well as education, and as we grow and learn more, we might not see things quite the same way as we used to. It's fine to grow, it's fine to acquire more wisdom, and it's great to gain understanding, but these are things we find as we live with God. It's all right that you don't have it all figured out right now or in the way you might like to understand it; just don't get discouraged and think the only way to find it is by making yourself crazy. Feel free to enjoy life; to enjoy the bounty God has given to you; to enjoy your loved ones, be they family, friends, or both; and to take pleasure in life, right now, avoiding the temptation to take life so seriously that you miss the point of this spiritual experience.

Is Human Nature Worse Than Ever?

If you spend time on the internet, you'll hear preachers and wannabe ministers lamenting the fallen nature of humanity and how humanity is worse now than it's ever been. They will point to a number of different incidents, legislations, and trends worldwide (although primarily those that impact the United States) to say that this is the worst humanity has ever been, it will get worse, and we should all respond accordingly, because dealing with the "worse" of this world can take any of us out.

This doom and gloom approach to human nature makes for great drama and fear factor, making us all think if we don't do whatever they are telling us to do, right now, we won't get a second chance to do it again. Whether it's sending someone a lot of money, following their specifics of doctrine, or doing whatever it is they say, if we don't do it right now, we will miss some specific event in time that escapes the ever-increasingly worseness of humanity.

It needs to be said that such propaganda exists to be propaganda. Its intention isn't theological accuracy, nor is it there to help anyone. It's there to be scary, to make us think we live in the worst picture backdrop ever in history, and we should line up with some abstract concept of obedience, immediately. They are there for no other purpose than to mislead for their own purposes, no matter how well-intentioned they may claim to be. It's a scare tactic, plain and simple, and, unfortunately, as the false information is disseminated, it spreads panic, fear, and a misguided sense of spiritual matters.

…But is human nature worse than it was earlier in time? I mean, really, humanity has had thousands upon thousands of years to think up stuff to do and make trouble, and it does seem like a lot of things are going on today…so is there a possibility humanity is worse than it used to be?

Human nature is either fallen into sin, or not. I know that might sound simplistic, but there is no "closer to perfection" in the base of human nature. Today, we are simply closer to the end of the existing system than people were back in the day, but that doesn't mean we are worse than they were. Human beings have always had bad ideas because of sin, and all bad ideas got started somewhere. Most of those bad ideas go back much further than we'd like to admit, although we don't always have all of them spelled out and itemized like we might like. From reading the Scriptures, we can see those issues such as rape, abuse, murder, mistreatment, violence, theft, and the like were all a part of human existence, even in the earliest of times.

*The L*ORD *observed the extent of human wickedness on the earth, and He saw that everything they thought or imagined was consistently and totally evil. So the L*ORD *was sorry He had ever made them and put them on the earth. It broke his heart.* (Genesis 6:5-6)

So the LORD told Abraham, "I have heard a great outcry from Sodom and Gomorrah, because their sin is so flagrant. I am going down to see if their actions are as wicked as I have heard. If not, I want to know." (Genesis 18:20-21)

Then they said, "Come, let's build a great city for ourselves with a tower that reaches into the sky. This will make us famous and keep us from being scattered all over the world."

But the Lord came down to look at the city and the tower the people were building. "Look!" He said. "The people are united, and they all speak the same language. After this, nothing they set out to do will be impossible for them! Come, Let's go down and confuse the people with different languages. Then they won't be able to understand each other." (Genesis 11:4-7)

These three passages are from the book of Genesis, the book of the Bible that records the earliest records of human interaction with God. The people back then were so wicked and so evil, God was sorry He ever created them! They were so insistent on their own way, God had to intervene more than once to stop their advances. This is way before our modern times and way before the modern inventions we have today, so that must mean the base of human behavior has been the same since the fall of mankind into sin. Sin is sin is sin, and people have always sought to do wrong to one another as a result of sin.
Some things to think about:

- Almost immediately after the fall of mankind, Adam lied to God.

- It took one generation from Adam and Eve for someone to murder someone else. Where did Cain get the idea of murdering Abel? He didn't have video games or violent movies to see for an example.

- The people of Noah's day were so wicked, God destroyed them with a flood. Where did they learn how to be wicked? How did they understand wickedness, defying the principles of God?

- The first incidences of rape we see in the Bible are in Genesis 19 and Genesis 34. In Genesis 19, the men of Sodom want to sexually assault the angelic visitors, for no other reason than because they were not part of their tribal culture. In Genesis 34, Dinah was raped by a member of the Hivite tribe. Genesis 19 was long before we ever had consent laws, but these men knew they wanted to violate the bodies and will of outsiders. Genesis 34 was long before the invention of any clothing that people today deem "inappropriate."

- The first incident of a group aspiring to climb back up to heaven to become God is found in Genesis 11. There were no self-help seminars to encourage such behavior.

- Abram thought nothing of deceiving the Egyptians, lying about his marriage to Sarai to benefit himself. He used her beauty to entice them to be good to him in Genesis 12. He had no men's magazines to suggest such was a beneficial idea for him.

- Sarah involved a sexual concubine into her marriage by forcing this woman into a relationship with Abraham, so she could have a child in Genesis 16. There was no reality television to give her this really bad idea.

This short list proves that while there are many things that may not be beneficial today, they are not the cause of human evil. The things we see today – that bother us, or do not bother us – have always existed. Because of the lack of media existence, we didn't hear about them in generations past. They were all still there, however, rearing their ugly heads and causing the same paths of destruction and difficulty that they do, today. That proves to us these issues rest in the beings who do them and are not someone else's provocation or fault. No matter how much we try to figure these things out, we can't figure them out simply or with a systematic approach that will establish a set manner for others who do the same things. Evil is evil, is evil; it enters into the hearts of mankind through sin, and none of us can understand what makes some people do some things. It is without explanation, other than they are active in doing the work of the enemy rather than God.

Instead of romanticizing the people of the Bible, we need to see them for what they were: a brutal, tribal people battling out other tribes for control or dominance. Sometimes, they even fought themselves. In establishing the written law, God had to tell them it was a bad idea to eat a bat, play with dead things, eat or drink blood, share each other's dirty clothes or sit on surfaces while free bleeding during a woman's period.

They were not perfect, nor were they closer to holiness than we are now. Humanity has always had its problems. Despite the things we see in the world today that disturb or bother us, we have the same call people had back once upon a time: to repent, think differently, do differently, and to join the Kingdom of God rather than the kingdom of this world.

No, we can't solve all the world's problems. We can set ourselves aright, however, and follow God's ways for us. That means we can make a difference with the sphere of influence God gives to us. We might not be able to solve it all, but we can certainly do and be exactly who God has for us to become in this lifetime. It is for our learning as much for those around us.

HERE FOR SUCH A TIME AS THIS

Have you ever felt you were born in the wrong era of history? I've met a few people who tell me they feel they would be much better suited as citizens of the world at a different time. They will tell me they don't know why they are even still around today and feel like they can't have purpose because of that feeling. This is often based on perceptions of older times: they like the fashions, they feel the social mores were more in line with their feelings about matters, they believe things were more exciting or interesting than they are today, or they think things were somehow easier.

There's something I often tell my seminarians: "History is written by the victors." When we read historical accounts of different eras, we are reading them through the lens of those who conquered, rather than were conquered. There is almost an enchanted way many write about history, one that distorts the hardships of life people often had. No matter what era of history someone lived in, there were difficulties of some sort.

For example: it's easy to think of the European explorers who were the first to travel to North America, South America, or circumnavigate the globe. We grew up hearing that men such as Christopher Columbus, Marco Polo, and others were brave men who dared to do something no one else was willing to do and believed things scientifically that no one ese was advanced enough to believe. If we genuinely cut through the hype and the "victor" chants, however, we find much darker realities to the work that these men did. They weren't merely explorers; many were slave traders. They brought disease and brutality to the natives in the lands they "discovered." None of them were scientific geniuses, and most, if not all the things we learned they dared to believe on their own were common knowledge in their day and age. It is right to label them as explorers who learned more about the world previously unknown in

Europe at that time, but it is incorrect to label them as voyaging heroes who sought the best for humanity. They were individuals who sought means to increase profits and make more money and did so at the expense of those they encountered who stood in their way or were seen as a potential threat.

No era of history is perfect, just like now is not perfect. Now, however, it isn't any worse than any other time. Every era is different and has had its unique qualities that brought both benefits and challenges. Instead of looking back, we are called to recognize we are here for now, in this time. God could have positioned us at any point in history, even a time when we might think things would have been different or easier for us. God chose now, because there is something we must contribute in the here and now.

In the book of Esther, we learn that Esther was positioned to be Queen of Persia for a specific reason. The wicked Haman was angered and sought to massacre the Jewish people across the empire, as a total misuse of his power and authority. Esther was confronted with the situation and what to do about it, because as a Jew, she was the only person in the entire empire with access to King Xerxes to have this edict overturned.

Then Mordecai told them to return this answer to Esther, Do not flatter yourself that you shall escape in the king's palace any more than all the other Jews.

For if you keep silent at this time, relief and deliverance shall arise for the Jews from elsewhere, but you and your father's house will perish. And who knows but that you have come to the kingdom for such a time as this and for this very occasion?

Then Esther told them to give this answer to Mordecai,

Go, gather together all the Jews that are present in Shushan, and fast for me; and neither eat nor drink for three days, night or day. I also and my maids will fast as you do. Then I will go to the king, though it is against the law; and if I perish, I perish.

So Mordecai went away and did all that Esther had commanded him. (Esther 4:13-17, AMPC)

Esther had the option to waste away her days in the palace, not worrying about the plight of her people. She could have lamented a day and age when the Jews weren't under Persian occupation and she could live freely, without having to be in this position. To do these things would have been the opposite of why she was there, positioned in this time in her life. Esther was there for that time, for handling the situation that was before and resolving this matter, unlike anyone else could.

The same is true for us, in some way in our lives. We are here for such a time as this. We are here to rise against our challenges we face and the situations we encounter to bring about a purposed victory. God doesn't just desire to see us live our lives by reaping benefits. Everything we do and the good we have is to go towards Kingdom productivity. It's not going to always be easy and things aren't always going to go the way we might like, but we are here for now. That means we need to focus our attention on what we are to do now, in this time, and recognize what we are here to do.

Confronting the World in Which We Live

When reality television became a "thing," I never imagined it would still have the force, dominance, and now influence that it has had. I figured reality television would be a passing fad, something that left as quickly as it infiltrated society. I had no idea that reality television would be here, over twenty years later, influencing cultural trends, social media, and yes, even social behavior. Through reality television, we've learned nothing short that if we want to get attention, outrageous behavior is the means to go. We see women catfighting each other, indiscriminate sexual behavior, foul language, inappropriate attire, overconsumption of alcohol and sometimes other drugs, and an overall attitude that if people want to be noticed, they should act as obnoxiously and as crazily as imaginable. The longer reality television continues to pervade culture, the more outrageous – and intense – the behavior becomes.

I would say most Christians look over the landscape of culture today and realize we aren't supposed to be like everyone else. At the same time, I think we aren't sure how to do it or find ourselves approaching this issue in ways that don't do much good. If you turn on the news, it always seems like there is another crazy person trying to make a scene with outrageous behavior. Whether protests, staged events to get people to come to church, improper attitudes or attire, or other things to try and garner attention, it seems like Christians haven't truly embraced what it means to be "counterculture." Being different from the culture in which we originate means more than just copying one another or adopting worldly attitudes and ideals to attract our own attention. Our message isn't enough to make us different – we must also live it and confront the world in which we live through a different means.

Many people (even Christians) fail to realize just how counterculture Jesus was, not just in His message, but how He lived His message. In New Testament times, Jesus lived in a culture that, much like today, was about conformity. He never made a huge fuss to protest; He just did what was right, in the face of a world that had built its principles and precepts on what was accepted, rather than what they should have been doing. Jesus was not just counterculture with his exterior ministry; He was also counterculture in His own personal actions. Some examples include:

- We have no evidence Jesus ever married. Such was downright scandalous in Biblical times, because it was expected all Jewish men (especially teachers) were to be married.

- Jesus spent much of His ministry with people society deemed inappropriate, untouchable, and unredeemable. These included tax collectors, prostitutes, women, Samaritans, those in poverty, soldiers, and adulterers. We can understand this in modern times to indicate Jesus hung out with the people society deemed to be the "wrong" ones.

- Even though Jesus' message did not present an overt protest against the Roman government, preaching and living the Kingdom of God was deemed just as threatening to the powers that be as if He'd launched an all-out rebellion.

- Jesus constantly challenged the authorities of His day who felt they had it all together. They always came around, trying to trick Him, thinking He would fall for their clever word-plays and takes on matters that missed the heart of what God was all about. He was not afraid to speak the truth; because as love come down, He knew truth is part of love.

- Jesus died as a sinner, as a criminal, when He was blameless. We ordinarily balk when we are accused of things we didn't do, let alone bearing a punishment we don't deserve. It doesn't get any more counterculture than the true way that Jesus Christ laid down His life for those He loved (all of us). He was worthy; we were unworthy, and He still did what was best for those who did not deserve it. Talk about going against societal norms and conformities!

Jesus' followers then went on to follow these same non-conforming values as they began and established the church.

Now after [Paul and Silas] had passed through Amphipolis and Apollonia, they came to Thessalonica, where there was a synagogue of the Jews.

And Paul entered, as he usually did, and for three Sabbaths he reasoned and argued with them from the Scriptures,

Explaining [them] and [quoting passages] setting forth and proving that it was necessary for the Christ to suffer and to rise from the dead, and saying, This Jesus, Whom I proclaim to you, is the Christ (the Messiah).

And some of them [accordingly] were induced to believe and associated themselves with Paul and Silas, as did a great number of the devout Greeks and not a few of the leading women.

But the unbelieving Jews were aroused to jealousy, and, getting hold of some wicked men (ruffians and rascals) and loungers in the marketplace, they gathered together a mob, set the town in an uproar, and attacked the house of Jason, seeking to bring [Paul and Silas] out to the people.

But when they failed to find them, they dragged Jason and some of the brethren before the city authorities, crying, These men who have turned the world upside down have come here also,

And Jason has received them to his house and privately protected them! And they are all ignoring and acting contrary to the decrees of Caesar, [actually] asserting that there is another king, one Jesus!

And both the crowd and the city authorities, on hearing this, were irritated (stirred up and troubled). (Acts 17:1-8, AMPC)

The early church certainly ran into its share of issues, but we see they were counterculture in that they came where they went to turn the world upside down. They didn't do it with the expressed intent to be disrespectful or show dishonor. If anything, we consistently see the early church members extend proper respect to authorities, inclusively among Jews and Romans. Still, their radical life of the Gospel – reaching out to everyone, Jew and Gentile alike; not stopping to ask anyone if they were "worthy" of the Gospel as they lived and proclaimed its important message.

The Gospel should turn us into something different than we were before we started. It doesn't mean we suddenly have all new hobbies, but it does mean our perspective of life changes, and what we want to do with our lives is different. We should want to make a difference, have an influence, encourage someone else, and better the lives of others. These are such intense, countercultural acts, they change the entire world. Stepping out to meet with someone society says you shouldn't, influence the life of a group society deems "wrong" through love, acting like Christ, and living this Gospel in full will make you different from others. Embrace it. It is what makes this Christian life fully worth living.

The courage to do what God has called you to do

It takes some major courage to be counterculture and live and do whatever it is God calls you to do. What it takes, in summary, is faith. When you believe that God has called you to do something and that even though the results may not come immediately, it's worth doing, you are applying and walking in your faith that has the potential to change your life.

When we read about those in the Bible who were called or worked for God, we think they were great and noble, and everyone around them must have felt the same way. If we truly study their lives, however, this couldn't be further from the truth. Not only were they not always great and noble, but others also didn't always see what they did from the lens of faith history. Noah smelled like animals and talked about rain for a hundred years, John the Baptist was wild looking with a strange diet, Ezekiel laid on his side for long periods of time, eating his own dung and drinking his own urine, Jeremiah went around crying all the time, Mary was an unwed, pregnant teenage mother...and so on. Yes, we know the other side of the story, but the people of their day didn't have that kind of insight. They looked over the lives of those who did God's work and judged them. Some probably even questioned or doubted their authenticity or whether they even heard from God. I haven't a doubt that the people of God felt judged, misunderstood, defamed, and even lonely, at times. The people of God were still people, and the people who came against them were also people, who can be cruel and unrelenting.

Faith shows the reality of what we hope for; it is the evidence of things we cannot see. Through their faith, the people in days of old earned a good reputation.

By faith we understand that the entire universe was formed at God's command, that what we now see did not come from anything that can be seen.

It was by faith that Abel brought a more acceptable offering to God than Cain did. Abel's offering gave evidence that he was a righteous man, and God showed his approval of his gifts. Although Abel is long dead, he still speaks to us by his example of faith.

It was by faith that Enoch was taken up to heaven without dying—"he disappeared, because God took him." For before he was taken up, he was known as a person who pleased God. And it is impossible to please God without faith. Anyone who wants to come to Him must believe that God exists and that He rewards those who sincerely seek Him.

It was by faith that Noah built a large boat to save his family from the flood. He obeyed God, who warned him about things that had never happened before. By his faith Noah condemned the rest of the world, and he received the righteousness that comes by faith.

It was by faith that Abraham obeyed when God called him to leave home and go to another land that God would give him as his inheritance. He went without knowing where he was going. And even when he reached the land God promised him, he lived there by faith—for he was like a foreigner, living in tents. And so did Isaac and Jacob, who inherited the same promise. Abraham was confidently looking forward to a city with eternal foundations, a city designed and built by God.

It was by faith that even Sarah was able to have a child, though she was barren and was too old. She believed that God would keep His promise. And so a whole nation came from this one man who was as good as dead—a nation with so many people that, like the stars in the sky and the sand on the seashore, there is no way to count them.

All these people died still believing what God had promised them. They did not receive what was promised, but they saw it all from a distance and welcomed it. They agreed that they were foreigners and nomads here on earth. Obviously people who say such things are looking forward to a country they can call their own. If they had longed for the country they came from, they could have gone back. But they were looking for a better *place, a heavenly homeland. That is why God is not ashamed to be called their God, for He has prepared a city for them.* (Hebrews 11:1-16)

Hebrews 11 is often called the "heroes roll" or "heroes hall of faith," but to those of us who live by faith, it offers us a picture of what faith looks like in a way that's easy for us to understand. I've met people who think they don't qualify as having faith if they aren't making strides to evangelize in foreign countries or they don't find themselves able to read the Bible from cover-to-cover in one sitting. This isn't what marks our faith! What marks our faith is our willingness to trust God for everything in our lives, even the calling we have that doesn't always make sense to us or those around us. Faith is those steps, those things we do that change our lives and awaken us to the realities that God is always with us and believing in God does make a difference, even for us, despite our flaws and imperfections.

Faith doesn't look like a bunch of people sitting around, waiting for God to do for them what He told them to do for themselves. Faith looks like action; like courage; like taking the challenge to step out and do exactly what God has for you to do, no matter what everyone around you might think of it. Faith looks like you, like me, like every believer who has walked this earth, from the beginning of faith's history. Faith is manifest through bold steps, steps we make even when we feel afraid, and daring to step out, when we stare them down the face and everything in us wants to flee, rather than follow God. Faith is confronting fears, solving problems, seeing the bigger picture, and focusing right where God has us, right now. It is all of the above, even the parts that seem contradictory or uncertain, and more. It happens as we allow ourselves to be made firm, steady, and strong in the face of a world that doesn't understand your calm assurance and the promise that lies ahead. Faith is trust, faith is love, and faith is the fulfillment of hope. The longer we live, and the more we trust within it, the more we see that there is no way we can live without it.

Despite any flaws they might have had, the people of Bible times who stepped out in their faith were very brave and profoundly moved by their faith to act and move as they did in their day and time. It takes that same faith for us to do the same, now, which is why we have this incredible record of Bible individuals to inspire us. If they could do it, so could we.

Surrounded by So Great a Cloud of Witnesses

We will stand best in our faith when we know and recognize our amazing history as Christians. There is an invaluable amount of insight we gain by examining the biographies, major documents and events, and historical events present in our history as Christian believers. Contrary to popular belief, Christian history is not a boring, monotone thing. It only becomes like this when a historical viewpoint is narrow and gives a limited picture of the entirety of Christian history to try and defend a specific denomination. Christian history is a diverse, cross-cultural experience of God's love and mercy toward people who were flawed, imperfect, confused, and sometimes off kilter. By looking at Christian history, we learn the realities of faith are not as simplistic, nor as neat and tidy, as we might like them to be. Just as we struggle today, people throughout history have agonized over what being people of faith means and just how to have that faith in a way that will touch and transform the world. People have always tripped up on how to best express, describe, and live their faith. Learning from the successes of Christian history, as well as the failures, are what give us the insights, and the focus, to dive in that much more and stay true to our faith, despite the differences of the day.

Therefore then, since we are surrounded by so great a cloud of witnesses [who have borne testimony to the Truth], let us strip off and throw aside every encumbrance (unnecessary weight) and that sin which so readily (deftly and cleverly) clings to and entangles us, and let us run with patient endurance and steady and active persistence the appointed course of the race that is set before us,

Looking away [from all that will distract] to Jesus, Who is the Leader and the Source of our faith [giving the first incentive for our belief] and is also its Finisher [bringing it to maturity and perfection]. He, for the joy [of obtaining the prize] that was set before Him, endured the cross, despising and ignoring the shame, and is now seated at the right hand of the throne of God. (Hebrews 12:1-2, AMPC)

Studying Christian history shows us, much like the Hebrews 11 heroes roll, that we can make it. From the very beginning of the Christian church, believers have been at odds with their surroundings. Early believers faced horrific persecution, torturous deaths, hurts, rejections, and pains, all of which strengthened the resolve of these individuals. It wasn't always easy, but they persevered, nonetheless. We learn from them the importance of following the calling God has for you, no matter the end. Jesus was their focus, and they knew they could handle whatever came along, if they were faithful to the end.

Church history reveals to us the importance of the message we carry as well as the persevering nature of the church, to remain down through the ages, despite the worst efforts of humanity to make the experience of church falter or fall to the wayside. In studying church history, we find people who look not all that different from us. They were flawed, they did the best they could with what they had, and they didn't see everything the same. Yet somehow, despite the differences, the problems, and the issues, we find the enduring power of the Gospel, the message of Christ still present, still living, still active, and still vital. Through all our flaws, Jesus is still there, and Jesus' power still saves.

I believe part of this power is because just as we acknowledge a living Savior, we also acknowledge a living cloud of witnesses, one that surrounds us and gives us hope, encouraging us to go on further, better, and more valiantly than they ever had the ability to do so. Church history anchors us, seeing ourselves not as innovators, but as those continuing a never-ending journey, one that spans this life and the next, time and eternity.

When we aren't sure what to do or what our next step is, take some time and read some biographies of Christian saints from the past. When you aren't sure what God is telling you, look at some of the confusions and difficulties present at different points in church history, when people weren't sure what God was saying to them or directing them to do. They all came through those periods in their lives, in time, in the history of the church, and into a place of spiritual breakthrough. The dark questions rose to light, which rose to encouragement. God has always raised up His people, in His time, even when they had to fight against societies, powers, even institutions we would think they shouldn't have to. They fought so we could be here, we could walk in spiritual power, and we could grow in grace, today.

For the Kingdom of God is not just a lot of talk; it is living by God's power. (1 Corinthians 4:20)

So let's throw off our excuses, reasons, circumventions, avoidances, fears and issues and let's run our race. Let's do this thing of faith, in whatever form God has established it for each one of us. Just as our cloud of witnesses surrounds and encourages from their place present with the Lord, we can encourage one another, down here, to learn from our history and look to our future. We don't have to waste another day or another moment of our lives waiting to do what God has told us to do. Let's do it now, completing our place in spiritual history, fulfilling our duty and inspiring both this generation and the next that faith makes us strong and able to live our faith, right now.

SHARING OUR FAITH WITH OTHERS

Evangelism is a topic that every believer should study and aspire to incorporate in new and different ways throughout their lives. I mention evangelism here, at the end of this chapter, because evangelism is a big part of what we are called to do as believers. If we understand evangelism properly, it is sharing our faith with other people, through every means possible. We do not just share our faith by going door-to-door or giving our testimony to others, however. We evangelize with our lives, whenever we step out in faith, how much we dedicate ourselves to God's precepts and being obedient to Him through our actions, and whenever we genuinely and sincerely help others to see Christ for the amazing Savior that He is.

Sharing our faith with others, however, is a whole measure of faith, in and of itself. Many of us find ourselves shy or intimidated by the idea that we have to tell others about Christ, and that so doing is part of our command as believers. It would seem to be much easier if we went off on our own and got to keep our faith to ourselves, wouldn't it? We could keep our relationship personal and private, and we could endlessly develop our work of faith on our own, without anyone else.

As nice as this might sound, keeping our faith to ourselves stagnates us severely. We won't develop our work of faith without others, because evangelism is just as much for us as it is for those with whom we share our faith. As we talk about our faith, we develop it. Sharing our faith brings us to new realizations and understandings, seeing it for what it is and how it has transformed us. Rather than focusing on how much farther we have to go, we can embrace just how far we've come.

Give thanks to the LORD and proclaim His greatness.
  Let the whole world know what He has done.
Sing to Him; yes, sing His praises.
  Tell everyone about His wonderful deeds.
Exult in His holy Name;
  rejoice, you who worship the LORD.
Search for the LORD and for His strength;
  continually seek Him. (Psalm 105:1-4)

We can see from this passage in Psalms that evangelism, as a cornerstone of our faith, identifies a few very key things. The first is that proclaiming God's greatness is a part of our faith because everyone in the world needs to know the wonders of our God. We share this faith for the reason that people do not know about God, at least not from the perspective we can offer. Anyone can embrace complicated theologies or concepts about God in a doctrinal sense, but coming to know what God has done from a personal perspective is a whole different matter. That's at its heart what evangelism is: proclaiming the heart of Christ, the experience of faith, knowing personally what God has done for us, to others.

The second key aspect of evangelism is the power of rejoicing in what God has done, because we see it for ourselves. We are so happy, so full of the experience of God, we want to talk about it. We want others to know. We want everyone to have this same chance to experience God for themselves. By rejoicing in God and sharing our faith, we are giving others the choice – the option – to choose God for themselves. If we don't share our faith, we don't give others this important and powerful option that has the potential to change their lives, too.

The third key is a continual desire to seek God for ourselves, finding and developing His strength within us. If we are serious about God, others will be able to see that in our character. Sometimes we get so busy trying to tell others about Christ that we forget to live our faith in a way and witness that shows other people just how serious we are about God. That means loving others and meeting them where they are while upholding the necessary boundaries to help you maintain and display your faith in a positive way. You can say no to things you aren't comfortable with while still loving and respecting others and their decisions. It goes a long way when you stick with any conviction or decision you feel strongly about while still respecting it may not be everyone else's choice or decision. It is also awesome for people to see just how much you love God by living whatever you claim to believe. If you can't handle living up to it, then it is probably better not to talk about it. If you don't agree with a stereotype, talk about that with someone else, and introduce the right way. Being relatable, and human with others, shows you aren't too proud or haughty to be real, while still maintaining your faith in all situations.

Sharing our faith doesn't have to be intimidating. It's great to evangelize via a formal program or formula, but the sharing of our faith often comes about just as God moves in us and the Holy Spirit opens that door for us to authentically and sincerely share with others about something that God has done for us. It's so incredible, we just can't keep it to ourselves. It comes down to the way we live and the way people see us live, and how much they want to talk – and share with us – about it in the process.

Evangelism happens whenever we talk about God to another person. It comes about as we share our faith with other believers, and we come to know one another better; as we share ideas (because by doing so, we stir our faith); as we share our testimony and stories; and as we come to a remembrance of just how amazing God is, time and time again. We evangelize when we are kind to someone who doesn't believe, not asking any questions and just doing something for someone else, because that's who we are. It happens every time we believe for someone's healing or victory, and it happens every time we take the time and interest to care about someone else. Our evangelism comes naturally when we know God has been that good to us. He has called and appointed us for now, and He leads us through that call, right through to His Kingdom, and beyond.

Let's make that deliberate intent to see that God's Gospel message is conveyed to the world. Let's live the part, do what He's called us to do, and see an impact in this day and time. Let's do this thing with all that's within us. No more half-hearted commitments; let's do our faith all the way.

If you haven't yet, do the following:

- Be baptized in water.

- Believe for the reception of the Holy Spirit in your life.

- Make the commitment to belong to your church family; get involved in some way and connect with other believers.

- Prepare for and receive communion with your ministry or church family.

- Make a practice to read the Scriptures regularly and take prayer time with God.

- Make an effort to do something good for someone else, at least once every day.

- Develop the calling God has placed on your life. If you are still uncertain about what it is, let God show you more about you so you can find it better.

- Take steps of faith. Do different things you've never done before.

- Love what God is doing in you and see what He is doing in others.

- Tell someone else about God. Let the Spirit move you through that conversation, and let the Lord convey His will through you to someone else.

- Let God love others through you, for real.

⸺ CHAPTER TEN ⸺
JESUS: FIRST, LAST, AND BEST

WHEN it came time to figure out how to conclude this book, I wasn't sure what was most suitable for a tie-together ending. Kingdom-themed writing is always a challenge to wrap up, because we write about a Kingdom that never ends. There is so much we can share, discuss, and examine about the Kingdom of God. Being part of God's Kingdom forever enhances and enriches our lives. The Scriptures teach us that in the time after Jesus returns, the world will be full of the knowledge of God, and we will spend eternity learning about Him. There will be no end to the time of worship, expansion, and experience by which this Kingdom will, once and for all, take over the entirety of the world we know, transform it, and take us into a new dimension.

So, I have saved for the final chapter of this book Jesus Christ, our Savior. In sight of all our Kingdom talk, we can never forget our King, Christ Jesus. It is for Christ because we cannot do all the things discussed in this book if Christ is not in them. If we do all these things without Christ, they are not rightly Kingdom actions and movements. As busy as we get, as much as we want to do, as great as the things we seek to do are, we can't ever lose sight of the reason why we do them. We don't do them to be great or lofty, or just do them to do them, but because Christ has moved within us, transformed us, and is now guiding us. If Christ is not first, and last, and best, we are missing the whole focus of the Kingdom.

Most of us know how important it is to have Jesus when we start out. We usually realize His importance, once again, toward the middle. It is often when we are past these initial phases that we start to phase Christ out, raising up our old flesh with new clichés and sounding the part, without being it within us. The Kingdom of God isn't just a passing fad, something we talk about to look good or to be trendy. We are a part of this Kingdom because of Christ, and that means whether we are first, last, or best, we must always maintain Christ as our center, reaching out to and seeing Him as part of everything. As they say, I have saved the best for last, that we may examine Christ's role in our Kingdom and our lives, in a manner that helps us to focus and keep Him central at all times.

JESUS, BE THE CENTER

A central point indicates it is the same distance away from all the edges, no matter which edge, space, or end one finds themselves on or near. In terms of our faith, I believe having Jesus as our center is a grounding principle that changes and transforms our lives of faith. If we make sure He is in the central place in our lives, He is always accessible, in view, and reachable to us.

I haven't written this book to be particularly theological. We aren't here to debate how you specifically define Jesus in terms of theological definitions, for one simple reason: Jesus isn't a theology. Any way we attempt to define the divine will come with limitations, complications, and other unnecessary things as we try to explain in human terms something that is beyond our limited understanding. What I am here to remind you of, however, is that Jesus needs to be a part of everything you do. We cannot shut Him out and think our lives will produce the level of fruit and purpose we hope they will. We must keep Jesus anchored, purposed and centered, in the whole of our lives, that we may continue to grow in Him.

And now, just as you accepted Christ Jesus as your Lord, you must continue to follow Him. Let your roots grow down into Him, and let your lives be built on Him. Then your faith will grow strong in the truth you were taught, and you will overflow with thankfulness.

Don't let anyone capture you with empty philosophies and high-sounding nonsense that come from human thinking and from the spiritual powers of this world, rather than from Christ. For in Christ lives all the fullness of God in a human body. So you also are complete through your union with Christ, who is the head over every ruler and authority. (Colossians 2:6-11)

As we go through different phases of our Christian walk, we will experience different teachings and theories that compromise the integrity of Christ's centrality in our lives. Some popular ones today encourage us to become our own creators or masters, to save ourselves through consciousness or a false sense of enlightenment, or the idea that we don't need Jesus at all, anymore – we can just replace His presence with our own understanding and we will be just fine. This couldn't be further from the truth! We must remain strong and rooted. When plants are rooted, it is that much more difficult to uproot them. If we keep Jesus as our center, rooting Him there in our lives, it will be that much easier to keep focused on His plans and staying the journey He has us on, throughout life.

We talk about our walk with God as a "journey" because it is something that takes us far from where we start, and in some ways, right back to where we started. It's also something that takes a long time to complete. Our journey with God is spoken of as a "walk" because it's not a plane ride, a car ride, or a train ride. We can't zoom in and out of it. You can't fast-track God with a weekend crash course. We must make the commitment, and find the balance, where Christ becomes more than just the being we use to get what we hope we can have. We must walk this out, day in and day out, and become and discover all He has for us to be.

HAS JESUS LEFT YOUR BUILDING?

In a recent early church history class, my students and I examined different beliefs (and their resulting battles) of the early centuries of Christianity. For several hundred years, the battles of the church divided into east vs. west over matters such as how many natures and wills Christ had, and then further splintered as new questions were added to their already confusing concoction. What should we call Mary? How was Jesus' mother conceived? When can church leaders get married? What do we think of women? Statues, icons, or neither? All these issues continued to divide the church as church matters grew more and more complicated, causing offense and division.

If you take the time to study some church history, the way church matters grew more and more out of control, invasive, and yes, political as the years went by becomes evident. Every fifty to one hundred years or so, someone called a meeting, many leaders came out to attend, and spent the duration arguing, voting, and then arguing again.

After examining these thoughts, one of my students asked the question, "Where is Jesus? It seems like in all this mess, Jesus left the building!"

What happened to the early church is a bigger reality of what can happen in all our lives, if we are not careful. In the mess of early church history were a group of men trying to figure this out without the leading of the Spirit. They were worried about points and concepts and ideas that had no relevance in the development of one's faith and, as a result, the faith of the people went undeveloped. In the process, Jesus was no longer their priority, their center. He was a musing, an idea to debate over, to theorize and develop elaborate ideas and theologies, but He wasn't a Being Who saved and loved them anymore. He was something to be used for fodder, for human debate and stumbling, rather than spiritual knowledge and edification.

How often do we do this same thing? How often is Jesus left out of our picture? We might mention Him from time to time but He is used for a theological debate or battle rather than to reveal His heart or introduce someone to Him. We love our technicalities, our theological base notions that make us feel so smart and evolved, because they are about us – not about Him.

Think about that for a minute. All these ideas we have that introduce endless technicalities to faith are about us, not about Him. Making stipulations that deter people from ever really finding Him – specifications about hairstyles, attire, diet, church rules about what technology one can use, etc. can all make someone feel great about themselves, but by always doing things to make one's self feel better, aren't dealing with the things within them that help draw them to Christ for the process of transformation.

"Not everyone who calls out to me, 'Lord! Lord!' will enter the Kingdom of Heaven. Only those who actually do the will of My Father in heaven will enter. On judgment day many will say to Me, 'Lord! Lord! We prophesied in Your Name and cast out demons in Your Name and performed many miracles in Your Name.' But I will reply, 'I never knew you. Get away from Me, you who break God's laws.' (Matthew 7:21-23)

We love the idea that everyone who acts like we think church people should act will ultimately be saved. It gives us a false sense of hope that our works and appearances can save us. Have we ever considered why the issue of works is so relevant within our faith? It's easy for people to say,

"Well, I do this," or "I did this," or "I'm doing this," and think themselves superior, or ahead of the salvation game, because of what they do. What this would create, though, is an unfair advantage. Someone could enter the Kingdom based on privilege or opportunity rather than an equal, leveling field, one that comes from God, rather than from us. It doesn't matter what we have done; we can trust that as God offers us salvation, we all have that equal chance for a new start.

Thus, Matthew 7 makes it pretty clear the people we think are most saved based on how well they can mimic church behavior or recite doctrine may very well not be the people who really have Jesus for themselves. He could be totally absent from their debates, ideas, and thoughts, much like He was at early church councils. So how do we know Jesus? What does it mean to know Him for ourselves?

KNOWING JESUS

The book of Hebrews was written for Jewish converts to Christianity. Its purpose was to show the essence of Christ as the center of our faith, as the fulfillment of the Mosaic Law and Old Testament prophecy and promise. This might sound weighty and complicated theologically, and with good reason. The book of Hebrews offers us some of the most powerful and basic theological understandings of Christ, all for the purpose of making sure we don't eliminate Christ in the process of developing our faith in a deeper way.

Long ago God spoke many times and in many ways to our ancestors through the prophets. And now in these final days, He has spoken to us through His Son. God promised everything to the Son as an inheritance, and through the Son He created the universe. The Son radiates God's own glory and expresses the very character of God, and He sustains everything by the mighty power of His command. When He had cleansed us from our sins, He sat down in the place of honor at the right hand of the majestic God in heaven. This shows that the Son is far greater than the angels, just as the Name God gave Him is greater than their names. (Hebrews 1:1-4)

Most talk about a "personal relationship" with God, which we've already talked about some. What most don't consider is a personal relationship with God comes about through knowing our Savior. We learn about God and the nature of God as we study and delve into the life of Christ. The more we aspire to know about Christ, the more we see the Father revealed to us. If we want to experience God in our lives, we can do so only through the experience of Christ.

The "theology" we need to understand and know Jesus is contained in the Scriptures and is reasonably plain for us to see. We can see the following when we examine the call, purpose, and nature of Christ:
Jesus Christ was spoken of by the prophets of old. This means when the prophets spoke of a coming Messiah, or ruler, they were speaking of Him. Prophets today, therefore, should also speak of Christ; His nature and being should be the heart of why they proclaim their divine warnings, blessings, and messages. The promise of the Second Coming should also be part of prophecy.

- The Son is a radiation, or reflection of God's glory. He expresses the character and power of God in His being.

- The Son, Christ, was involved in the creation of the world; everything was created through Him.

- If everything was created through the Son, this means the Son has existed with the Father since the beginning, even though we could not see Him in the natural realm.

- The world is sustained through the power of the Son.

- The Son is the reason for our salvation, as through His atonement for sin on the cross, we are now cleansed from all sin. This means the Son came into the created world to accomplish this purpose.

- The Son will receive back all that belongs to Him in this earth when He returns as King.

- Christ sits at the right hand of the Father in heaven, which is the seat of power and authority.

- Jesus is not an angel, in any form; He has power over all angels, just as He has power over the universe that He created. His name, Emmanuel, means "God with us," and is a higher identity than that of the angels.

- Christ is returning again.

In just a few short sentences, we can see the entire foundations of our faith, our very belief and promise in Christ, manifest in a way we can understand and explain if we are asked. Knowing these things about Jesus show us and reveal to us how we are able to have this relationship, and that, most importantly, we can articulate it and somewhat understand it. With what I have presented here, there is no debate for believers. We don't have to sit and argue over the finer points of metaphysical doctrine, because they aren't relevant to the truths we've expressed. Knowing Jesus means embracing this revelation we've received about Him, not something that someone tries to come up with through strange language and technicalities. Our major focus needs to be receiving Christ as He has been revealed and growing and learning from that first place.

Therefore, we don't need to spend a lot of time arguing over strange doctrines. We don't have to be people for whom "Jesus has left the building." Remembering Who He is and what He has done for us can fill our minds, our fascinations until He returns again. Some aspects of the finer things in His being and His life, we will never figure out. What is better for us to do is embrace Jesus as has been revealed to us. The love we have for Him will focus so much more powerfully if we don't trivialize or reduce Him to mere human concepts or ideas. We must know Him for Who He is, not who we might hope – or want – Him to be.

THE REST WE SEEK

If there is one complaint I hear above all others, it is how tired people find themselves. Even though the average person probably doesn't work as physically hard as they did in earlier times (an exception to this would be in agrarian societies), people seem stressed, overworked, and exhausted. Social media abounds with memes that complain about jobs, having to work regular hours, protests about corporate expectations, high costs of living and many expenses. We can barely seem to turn around without hearing how tired someone is or how malcontent they are due to their circumstances.

One of the reasons I believe people find themselves so tired and so unhappy in the long run is because of their lack of spiritual direction in life. When we follow God through Christ, we always have a way made for us. It may not be the way we desire, and it may not take us where we always want to go, but we find ourselves with a higher compass to guide us through the different navigations we will need through this life. Having God changes our world, our perceptions, our ideas about things, and also helps us to step back, slow down, and consider our actions before we proceed.

God's promise of entering His rest still stands, so we ought to tremble with fear that some of you might fail to experience it. For this good news—that God has prepared this rest—has been announced to us just as it was to them. But it did them no good because they didn't share the faith of those who listened to God. For only we who believe can enter His rest. As for the others, God said,

"In my anger I took an oath:
 'They will never enter My place of rest,'"

even though this rest has been ready since He made the world. We know it is ready because of the place in the Scriptures where it mentions the seventh day: "On the seventh day God rested from all His work." But in the other passage God said, "They will never enter My place of rest."

So God's rest is there for people to enter, but those who first heard this good news failed to enter because they disobeyed God. So God set another time for entering His rest, and that time is today. God announced this through David much later in the words already quoted:

"Today when you hear His voice,
 don't harden your hearts."

Now if Joshua had succeeded in giving them this rest, God would not have spoken about another day of rest still to come. So there is a special rest still waiting for the people of God. For all who have entered into God's rest have rested from their labors, just as God did after creating the world. So let us do our best to enter that rest. But if we disobey God, as the people of Israel did, we will fall. (Hebrews 4:1-11)

This passage of Scripture reveals something powerful to us about the person of Christ and about our choice to take refuge in Him. It's not about a literal, physical Sabbath keeping, because such taught us about the importance of setting aside rest in anticipation of the rest we would find in Christ. We learn about the power of Christ to fulfill us, just as He is, and just where we are. Instead of remaining restless and discontent, Christ offers us the perfect and most powerful place to rest our souls, providing us answer for the questions we have and the things we seek. Instead of having to look, figure, conspire, and push, Christ provides us a powerful place to find exactly what we need and what will satisfy.

    How can we experience this "rest" in Christ? We can focus, not so much on resting on a specific, Sabbath day, but taking time in all our days to seek Christ and to keep our focus on Him as our center. We must also be aware of the need for worship and devotion with others, and that we must take time out of our busy lives for that proper honor and worship in our lives.

A High Priest Who Understands

I've met people who are afraid to take their issues, burdens, and thoughts to Christ. They believe what they've done can't stand before His perfection and that He won't understand what they are going through. I can understand why they might think this, especially given the way we often talk about Christ in church. We make Christ sound almost unapproachably angry, hostile, and full of hatred for the people who need Him most. It's easy to think Jesus is unapproachable, with nothing to offer those who are hurting, in need, or just don't measure up to human church standards.

The good news is this isn't how Jesus is, at all. Just because someone at church rejects you or doesn't have a good thing to say to you doesn't mean Jesus feels the same way. In fact, in the Scriptures, we learn the total opposite. Not only does Jesus not reject us, He also always understands our need.

So then, since we have a great High Priest Who has entered heaven, Jesus the Son of God, let us hold firmly to what we believe. This High Priest of ours understands our weaknesses, for he faced all of the same testings we do, yet He did not sin. So let us come boldly to the throne of our gracious God. There we will receive His mercy, and we will find grace to help us when we need it most. (Hebrews 4:16)

Part of the meaning in Jesus' life was that He did inhabit human flesh and did live with the temptations we see and experience in some form. What the author of Hebrews is trying to convey is simple: Jesus had a human experience, and in that human experience, He encountered things we did and do, as well. He knew what it was like to experience temptation, He knew what it was like to be misunderstood, and He knew what it was like to be victimized. We aren't serving a Savior Who is so far off from our needs and our experience that He can't relate to us, and in some way, we can't relate to Him. We have every option to come boldly, because we know He understands. Instead of standing back timidly, unsure of our worthiness, we should run – not walk – to the One we know understands us and our shortcomings. It is at that throne the grace to help will come forth, pouring out, when we need it the most!

The Same Yesterday, Today, and Forever

Change is an inevitable part of our world. At some point in our lives, we will all experience the intense shifting of life's seasons and circumstances. The truth is that change is often a disconcerting experience. We experience new ideas and new thoughts, new times and new cultural changes, or we experience the feeling that our world is changing at a pace we cannot keep. Sometimes the changes we experience are more personal: we lose a job or start a new one, we move to a new area, we have to find a new home, family members move away or people close to us relocate or die, or other changes that cause us to feel like we have no control over our lives.

This is why we discover the importance of the consistency of Christ. When we say Jesus is the same "yesterday, today, and forever," that doesn't mean Jesus doesn't care about what we deal with or about the changes we discover in society as we go along. It also doesn't mean that He doesn't rise to help us face the challenges that are new to us or new to our era. It means Jesus Christ is consistent, solid, and with us, offering us the same truth that He has since the very beginning.

Then the eleven disciples left for Galilee, going to the mountain where Jesus had told them to go. When they saw Him, they worshiped Him—but some of them doubted!

Jesus came and told His disciples, "I have been given all authority in heaven and on earth. Therefore, go and make disciples of all the nations, baptizing them in the name of the Father and the Son and the Holy Spirit. Teach these new disciples to obey all the commands I have given you. And be sure of this: I am with you always, even to the end of the age." (Matthew 28:16-20)

This is a trustworthy saying:

If we die with Him,
  we will also live with Him.
If we endure hardship,
  we will reign with Him.
If we deny Him,
  He will deny us.
If we are unfaithful,

*He remains faithful,
for He cannot deny Who He is.* (2 Timothy 2:11-13)

Jesus Christ is the same yesterday, today, and forever. So do not be attracted by strange, new ideas. Your strength comes from God's grace, not from rules about food, which don't help those who follow them. (Hebrews 13:8-9)

In Biblical times (much as like today), there were many competing groups that taught different ideas and concepts about what it meant to be a believer. Some sought to enforce older dietary laws found in the Mosaic Law, while others still annexed new rules and regulations that they felt would help understanding. Hebrews reminds us that the grace of God is sufficient for us, because Jesus Christ is forever the same. He isn't going to be something new and different tomorrow but will still offer the same consistency in our world of change.

This is why it's important to hear the consistency of Christ in everything we believe. When we are confronted with something we didn't know before, we should hear and see the truth of Christ echoing down to us in a new way. It's not a new teaching; it is just something we never saw before, something we missed. It makes us recognize the transcendence of Christ, from era to era, in everything we do, see, and believe.

WORSHIP

The word "worship" is used casually and freely today, often in ways that diminish its identity and purpose in our lives. When we talk about "worship," we can mean everything from an experience of honor toward God or following our favorite personality on Instagram. This total dichotomy gives us an improper view of just what worship is, and why worship is so important for believers.

The first thing we need to understand is worship isn't as simple as being a genre of music or a section in a church service or even the designation for a service itself. Worship isn't liking someone else or honoring another person with the right behavior and treatment. Worship is the showing of reverence and adoration to the divine: it is humbling ourselves, recognizing God is greater than we are, and God is due something that it is our good pleasure and honor to offer to Him. Worship is expressed to God and God present in Christ alone, not to any other being found in heaven, on earth, or underneath the earth. If we render such worship to another being, any being, we are guilty of idolatry.

As we spoke of earlier, worship is a state of honoring all that God is, for Who God is. This means when we worship Christ, we are worshiping Him in the fullness of His divine nature. It's not something we can ignore, nor is it something that we can substitute. It's an essential part of the Christian experience because it reminds us of Who Christ is as we humble ourselves before Him.

I am speaking of the importance of worship here, in this chapter, because worship is something that is an integral part of the Christian experience in relation to Christ. We worship God because of what Christ has done for us. Down through the ages, even if we weren't happy or excited about anything else at any time in our lives, the work of Christ for our sin is enough to keep us full of worship and devotion to our God for the rest of our days.

Jesus was born in Bethlehem in Judea when Herod was king. After Jesus' birth wise men from the east arrived in Jerusalem. They asked, "Where is the one who was born to be the king of the Jews? We saw His star rising and have come to worship Him."

When King Herod and all Jerusalem heard about this, they became disturbed. He called together all the chief priests and the experts in the Scriptures and tried to find out from them where the Messiah was supposed to be born.

They told him, "In Bethlehem in Judea. The prophet wrote about this:

Bethlehem in the land of Judah,
  you are by no means least among the leaders of Judah.
    A leader will come from you.
      He will shepherd My people Israel."

Then Herod secretly called the wise men and found out from them exactly when the star had appeared. As he sent them to Bethlehem, he said, "Go and search carefully for the child. When you have found Him, report to me so that I may go and worship him too."

After they had heard the king, they started out. The star they had seen rising led them until it stopped over the place where the child was. They were overwhelmed with joy to see the star. When they entered the house, they saw the child with His mother Mary. So they bowed down and worshiped Him. Then they opened their treasure chests and offered Him gifts of gold, frankincense, and myrrh.

God warned them in a dream not to go back to Herod. So they left for their country by another road. (Matthew 2:1-12, GW)

One of my favorite passages in the New Testament is Matthew 2:1-12, which discusses the Wise Men's visit to the child Jesus at His family home. It is one of my favorites because the scenario is one that shows us just how important worship is and what it requires of us to be sincere and genuine. The "wise men" as we call them were really Persian astrologers who knew from studying the stars that something unique and important was happening in the world. They weren't Jews; they were, most likely, either worshipers of a monotheistic Persian religion or pagan individuals. They didn't have the example of the written law to fall back on or to relate to in their own experience. All they knew is there was a star, there was a royal birth afloat, and they needed to learn what they could about it so they could bring the proper items to greet the royal One.

We find these individuals (how many Wise Men there were, we don't know) who didn't know the ins and outs so moved to force themselves to learn, to come, not empty-handed, but with honorable gift, thousands upon thousands of miles to bow down and worship the young King, still just a child. Nothing deterred them, threw them off course, or caused them to question what they knew they needed to do. Whether they got to stay for dinner or just had the honor of offering their gifts and bowing in His presence, they did what they knew they needed to do.

The Wise Men reveal to us a few key things about the heart of worship and the principles of it as we stand before Christ, in this world. The first is that worship is something we absolutely must do, whether it's convenient or not. I meet people who tell me they do not see fit to engage in worship (either corporally or individually) because they don't have the time, they are too tired, they are too busy, or perhaps the real reason, they just don't want to do it. Nothing was going to stop the Persian astrologers from travelling a long distance across land to reach Christ and pay their respects. The trip took so long, in fact, that by the time they arrived, Christ was no longer a baby, but a child! This didn't matter, because their trip was not about convenience. They needed to honor the divine royalty that was Christ, and we need to do the same.

The second thing we learn is that we should never go into a situation of worship empty-handed. When we worship, we are to offer part of ourselves. That is symbolized by our gift, however that gift is given.

Whether it is a monetary offering to the house of worship, some sort of sacrifice or object given, or something we give in our talent, time, gifts, or ability, we should always make sure we are giving something beyond a nice display in our worship.

The third thing we learn is that worship must be sincere. The Wise Men were genuine in their desire. No one forced them to worship, to seek things out, or to do what was right. It was their great desire to honor worship to the King, and it should be ours, as well. No one should have to twist your arm to get you to stand for worship at church (obviously if you are unable to stand, you can be attentive in your heart), to lead prayer, to join in singing, to participate in different ministries that help create an atmosphere of worship, or just to come together as a group (even a small one) and celebrate the Lord of lords. We should be happy and eager to take our time to do such things. There should be no fights for attention from distractions and we should not have to perform in church to get people to focus. Worship is worship, is worship, and worship is our great honor.

The fourth thing we learn is that we don't have to have Christ all figured out – or our spiritual lives all figured out – in order to worship. The Wise Men weren't believers. They had to ask questions and get information in order to understand what was going on. Worship isn't about having everything figured out, it's about recognizing what is real and honoring the One Who has made our spiritual experience possible.

It is my opinion that worship doesn't have to assume a specific physical posture, but rather, we should incorporate many different physical postures into our worship experience. We may want to stand and raise our hands or stand with our hands folded. We may kneel or lie face down on the ground, we may sit or lay down. Some people are moved to dance, many are moved to sing, and some exhibit gifts of the Spirit, such as speaking in tongues. The point of all we do in our spiritual worship is to bring ourselves – ultimately offer ourselves – for divine service. This means worship starts in our services, in our devotions, but finds its full-circle purpose as we walk through this life, displaying our hearts as believers in everything we do. With the Wise Men as our example, we push through, we allow nothing to stop us, and we offer all we are and have for the glory of God present in Christ Jesus.

UNDERSTANDING PROPHECY

Prophecy is a topic on which we could probably write an entire book. No wait, I take that back: we could write several books on prophecy, and still have room left over for something else. We could talk about prophecy before Christ, was born, we could talk about prophecy while He was living, we could talk about prophecy related to His death and resurrection, and we could still, stay here and discipline ourselves, to discuss prophecy related to His return to us. There is so much to say, do, and think about prophecy, it is not reasonable to cover it in one section of a book. But because I just pointed out something very important in relation to prophecy, it is something we will discuss here, albeit briefly. Did you happen to catch what it is that was pointed out?

The reason it is so important – and relevant – to know at least some about the understanding of prophecy is because Christ is at the heart of all prophecy. To understand prophecy is to see Christ at the very heart and center of both human and spiritual existence. If we divorce Christ from prophecy, we find ourselves surrounded by psychics and soothsayers who take random guesses at facts and sometimes get things right but often get things wrong. General, non-specific ideas aren't prophetic, because they don't involve the One Who knows the whole of human history, from start to finish. When we see the prophetic as an integrated part of Christ, and Christ's identity, it changes the way we uphold the necessary standards of prophetic rendering. The standard to which we uphold prophecy should be none less than we uphold the history of Christ and the prophets of old. In everything we do, say, and embrace should be something that either brings us to Christ more fully, confirms the purpose of Christ in one's life, or both.

There's a lot out there about prophecy today. Some of them are good, some of them are not so good, and some of them are downright strange. Sometimes the things people claim are "prophetic" are no such thing at all. Because many people believe the "last days" are a specified period of time rather than a period of time by which we await Christ's return, there are those who have turned fear and propaganda into a so-called "prophetic" art form. Some will shout out general messages about financial or emotional breakthroughs, prefacing the message that they "don't know who it's for." No such actions are properly classified as prophetic. This means when it comes to understanding the prophetic, we need to see just how such is genuine and real as relates to where we are at.

The work of prophecy is to prophesy. To prophesy is to bring the word of God to a situation, coming from a direct, divine revelation. It may come to us through verbal word, a preached or taught message, a spiritual word, a prophetic gift, a written word, or another form of communication. Despite these diverse forms of prophetic messages, the Originator is always the same: God.

Moreover, I will diligently endeavor [to see to it] that [even] after my departure (decease) you may be able at all times to call these things to mind. For we were not following cleverly devised stories when we made known to you the power and coming of our Lord Jesus Christ (the Messiah), but we were eyewitnesses of His majesty (grandeur, authority of sovereign power). For when He was invested with honor and glory from God the Father and a voice was borne to Him by the [splendid] Majestic Glory [in the bright cloud that overshadowed Him, saying], This is My beloved Son in Whom I am well pleased and delight, We [actually] heard this voice borne out of heaven, for we were together with Him on the holy mountain. And we have the prophetic word [made] firmer still. You will do well to pay close attention to it as to a lamp shining in a dismal (squalid and dark) place, until the day breaks through [the gloom] and the Morning Star rises (comes into being) in your hearts.

[Yet] first [you must] understand this, that no prophecy of Scripture is [a matter] of any personal or private or special interpretation (loosening, solving). For no prophecy ever originated because some man willed it [to do so—it never came by human impulse], but men spoke from God who were borne along (moved and impelled) by the Holy Spirit. (1 Peter 1:15-21, AMPC)

From this passage, we can recognize a few important facts about prophecy, and how we can understand it:

- **Prophecy exists to prove God is God, and Christ is Lord:** Even though we might hold our own personal opinions on different matters, the work of prophecy is not the vehicle for our personal opinions. The prophetic word is not about personal understanding, but comes from God, Who moves prophetic word through the Holy Spirit.

- **There is no half-right prophetic word:** If a prophetic message is delivered and is only partially right, it does not qualify as a prophetic word, no matter what someone calls it. This can happen because someone hasn't been properly trained to recognize God, they do not understand prophecy, nor are they hearing from God.

- **Prophecy shouldn't be littered with personal commentary or interpretation:** The purpose of prophecy is to relay God's word, not personal thoughts or ideas. If you cannot discern your personal thoughts from a prophetic message, it will impact the way others receive – or reject – the message. We should never use prophecy to hurt or harm others, to sway certain ideas to our personal thinking, or to use the prophetic medium to exert power and control methods over others.

- **Prophecy is connected to Scripture, because prophecy is connected to Christ:** Prophecy has been involved in Scripture from the very beginning of time; all the way back to Adam and Eve in the garden. Jesus Himself is part of prophecy, both in fulfillment and as the source of it. The prophets of old teach us about prophecy as much as they teach us about Scripture and about Christ, but they do so by telling us what the prophetic looks like, how messages are delivered, the results of prophecy, and why it is important.

- **Prophecy is not an act of human will:** Speaking a word out of personal desire or motive does not qualify as prophecy. We cannot force prophecy to come, nor can we force anyone to be a prophet. Prophecy is divine, from God, pure and simple. Just because a message makes us feel good or feel better than we did when we started doesn't mean it is a message that qualifies to be called prophecy.

- **Prophecy doesn't always make sense at the time it is received or delivered:** When the Prophet Daniel delivered his message about a huge statue with different elements used for specific body parts to represent different nations, it sounded strange to others. It didn't make a lot of sense. Sometimes the elements, symbols, and ideas of prophecy aren't easily understood in foresight, but make sense in hindsight. For this reason, we should always approach the prophetic with an open mind and the desired revelation of the Spirit to guide us.

- **Prophetic instruction is the dedicated commitment to make sure the means of a prophetic word – vision, message, interpretation, or understanding – is properly conveyed:** Prophetic messages should be handled with care, spiritual discernment, and proper guidance and maturity.

Given this information, how do we understand prophecy? We take into consideration the understanding of prophecy doesn't mean understanding every single small detail; it is about a bigger picture, a divine one, if you will. Prophecy comes to us from eternity, so the message of prophecy is about more than just what we can have or experience right now. If the purpose of prophecy is Christ, and finding Christ more deeply, we must see something that points us to Him in our prophetic experience. It might not be always obvious, but through our understanding and meditation on the word we are given, it should do something to help our spiritual relationship with Him.

We also come to understand that prophecy can't be plugged into a media headline. Sensationalism isn't what makes prophecy work; God is! Just because a message is screamed, a Bible verse is attached to a news story, or someone seems to be able to point to a news story to prove the Bible doesn't make it so. Such methods are not new, nor is news or current events new. Life has a way of continuing and trying to identify everything that comes along as some sort of Bible fulfillment will cause you to miss the major picture – Christ – present in prophecy.

We understand prophecy in places that strive for a true understanding of Scripture, beyond what might be current or trendy. Sure, they may not be places that draw massive crowds (it can happen but often doesn't now). It comes as we walk in the Spirit and embrace it for ourselves and test every spirit and every questionable word so we can be sure what we embrace is truly from God. It's walking in discernment and in all the different spiritual gifts for the betterment of the church, because when we do that, we become not just interpreters of prophecy but living participants within it.

That is our ultimate goal: to become living participants with prophecy, active and involved in it. This makes prophecy not some distant, strange, hard-to-understand thing, but something that engages us, calls us, and is real to us. If to know prophecy is to know Christ, the realm of the prophetic is one of the most powerful ways we can know and embrace Him for ourselves. Even if we never have a vision, hear a direct word from God, or have the experience of a multitude of gifts, being a part of the prophetic: nurturing it, loving it, embracing it, and manifesting it will all help us to see Christ living and active, and know when He is present in a prophetic situation, versus when He is not.

Behold, I am coming again!

Our last examination in this book is one of Jesus' final promises to the church. In some ways, I wonder if it is one of the most important for us today, because it stretches our faith the most. We can see the results of salvation, because He died on the cross and rose again. Returning to us, however, is a promise that has yet to be fulfilled. Recognizing He will return to us, He is good to His word even though it has been a long time, and believing it shall happen as He has promised, all stretch our faith, force us to believe in that which has not yet happened, and in great things to come, because we know that no matter how bad it might seem right now, we have not seen the end of the story.

What does it mean that Christ shall "come again?" There are so-called teachers and experts who think they've cornered the market on the Second Coming and just what is to come. They've studied portions of the New and Old Testaments that point to these events and pieced them together, and believe they have the comprehensive answers to all our questions as pertain to the return of Christ.

Problem is, none of them quite agree with one another. Even those who do agree with each other on most points don't agree about some of the nitty, gritty details. There's lots of symbolism present in the literature surrounding the Second Coming and future full reign of Christ, at the time when the kingdom of the world will become the full Kingdom of God. As we just discussed about prophecy, prophetic symbolism doesn't always make a lot of sense to us. It can seem obvious to mean one thing to someone, or something else to someone different, all because God often speaks in symbolism in ways that make sense to the receiver or interpreter, rather than those of us thousands of years later. This means we are reading interpretations of these visions that are sometimes understood later in time, after other events, or in connection with other things, even if they have nothing to do with the original prophecy. As a result, there are about as many opinions as to what these different things mean and how they are pieced together as anything else. There is no one universal consensus, agreement, or idea about what will happen or what this time should look like.

There are a few things, however, we can understand from looking at the words of Jesus Himself in these times. Matthew 24:3-44 offer many details about the period before He will come again, and they help us to understand these issues for ourselves, even now.

Later, Jesus sat on the Mount of Olives. His disciples came to Him privately and said, "Tell us, when will all this happen? What sign will signal Your return and the end of the world?"

Jesus told them, "Don't let anyone mislead you, for many will come in My Name, claiming, 'I am the Messiah.' They will deceive many. And you will hear of wars and threats of wars, but don't panic. Yes, these things must take place, but the end won't follow immediately. Nation will go to war against nation, and kingdom against kingdom. There will be famines and earthquakes in many parts of the world. But all this is only the first of the birth pains, with more to come.

"Then you will be arrested, persecuted, and killed. You will be hated all over the world because you are My followers. And many will turn away from Me and betray and hate each other. And many false prophets will appear and will deceive many people. Sin will be rampant everywhere, and the love of many will grow cold. But the one who endures to the end will be saved. And the Good News about the Kingdom will be preached throughout the whole world, so that all nations will hear it; and then the end will come.

"The day is coming when you will see what Daniel the prophet spoke about—the sacrilegious object that causes desecration standing in the Holy Place." (Reader, pay attention!) "Then those in Judea must flee to the hills. A person out on the deck of a roof must not go down into the house to pack. A person out in the field must not return even to get a coat. How terrible it will be for pregnant women and for nursing mothers in those days. And pray that your flight will not be in winter or on the Sabbath. For there will be greater anguish than at any time since the world began. And it will never be so great again. In fact, unless that time of calamity is shortened, not a single person will survive. But it will be shortened for the sake of God's chosen ones.

"Then if anyone tells you, 'Look, here is the Messiah,' or 'There He is,' don't believe it. For false messiahs and false prophets will rise up and perform great signs and wonders so as to deceive, if possible, even God's chosen ones. See, I have warned you about this ahead of time.

"So if someone tells you, 'Look, the Messiah is out in the desert,' don't bother to go and look. Or, 'Look, he is hiding here,' don't believe it! For as the lightning flashes in the east and shines to the west, so it will be when the Son of Man comes. Just as the gathering of vultures shows there is a carcass nearby, so these signs indicate that the end is near.

"Immediately after the anguish of those days,

*the sun will be darkened,
the moon will give no light,
the stars will fall from the sky,
and the powers in the heavens will be shaken.*

And then at last, the sign that the Son of Man is coming will appear in the heavens, and there will be deep mourning among all the peoples of the earth. And they will see the Son of Man coming on the clouds of heaven with power and great glory. And He will send out His angels with the mighty blast of a trumpet, and they will gather His chosen ones from all over the world—from the farthest ends of the earth and heaven.

"Now learn a lesson from the fig tree. When its branches bud and its leaves begin to sprout, you know that summer is near. In the same way, when you see all these things, you can know His return is very near, right at the door. I tell you the truth, this generation will not pass from the scene until all these things take place. Heaven and earth will disappear, but My words will never disappear.

"However, no one knows the day or hour when these things will happen, not even the angels in heaven or the Son Himself. Only the Father knows.

"When the Son of Man returns, it will be like it was in Noah's day. In those days before the flood, the people were enjoying banquets and parties and weddings right up to the time Noah entered his boat. People didn't realize what was going to happen until the flood came and swept them all away. That is the way it will be when the Son of Man comes.

"Two men will be working together in the field; one will be taken, the other left. Two women will be grinding flour at the mill; one will be taken, the other left.

"So you, too, must keep watch! For you don't know what day your Lord is coming. Understand this: If a homeowner knew exactly when a burglar was coming, he would keep watch and not permit his house to be broken into. You also must be ready all the time, for the Son of Man will come when least expected.

- **The coming of Christ signals the "end of the world:"** The terminology we often translate as the "end of the world" doesn't mean some sort of strange apocalyptic battle between aliens and the government will ensue and kill everyone who is now living. The Jews of the first century believed in three different "eras," or "worlds:" The world that was, which existed before the fall of mankind, the world that is, which was the system they lived under, and the world that would be, in which the Messiah would come and overthrow the powers that be. To talk about the "end of the world" is a period by which the system, powers, and society that we know are winding up, and a new era, or "world to come," will follow. From the point where the church began until now qualifies as the "end times" or "time of the end," that represents the conflict and tumult that would exist in the world until Jesus returns. In the coming era to follow is the official, eternal rule of Christ.

- **Deception is part of the tumult of this "ending system:"** Claiming to be of Christ, Christ Himself, greater than Christ, standing as a false prophet, general deception, or deceiving people into being a Christian are all a part of this world in which we live before Christ returns.

- **Natural disasters, political conflicts, and tumults are not the signs of the end in and of themselves:** Jesus pointed out these things would exist until He returns, but they are the "beginning" of such conflict, not the result of it. We could chase after every disaster, problem, and conflict throughout history, and find there have been so many, we cannot declare them as the "end" on their own. They shall exist, however, in both natural form and supernatural form, until the time when Jesus returns.

- **Persecution of Christians shall come:** Persecution, martyrdom, and harassment of those in the faith exists to this very day, in non-Christian countries worldwide. Such has existed from the beginning of Christianity, and will continue until He returns.

- **Sin is rampant, with major problems arising even in the church (to the point where people feel the urge to flee); things that do not belong in the church are front and center; people shall relocate as exiles between nations and spiritual understandings; and love of others will grow cold:** It's not that sin is new, but it is something experienced everywhere, in many different ways, and while people might claim to love others, true love of others is not found in this world.

- **The Kingdom of God shall be preached in all the world before the end comes:** This means Christians have a mandate of Gospel proclamation, and they best get busy attending to it instead of arguing over everything.

- **Jesus shall appear in the heavens, along with mourning from those who disbelieved in Him. He shall come with power, glory, with angel fanfare, a trumpet blast, and His people shall be gathered, all over the earth:** The Second Coming of Christ shall be as a King, with everyone seeing, processional fanfare, and His people gathered together.

- **We are to be alert and recognizing spiritual signs when they are shown to us:** Just as we understand prophecy, we can understand signs when we look at things from a spiritual perspective.

- **Heaven and earth will disappear:** Heaven and earth will be transformed. What exactly will happen or how this will take place, we do not know, but we do know that what we have and see shall be different after Christ's return.

- **No one knows the exact day or hour when Christ will return:** This includes no one knows the month or the year. We don't know when it will happen, and that is the point. We need to live and believe as if it could happen at any time. This is why it is compared to Noah's day and to any ordinary day when people are living, at work, and engaging in life. It shall come upon us suddenly. We are either ready to meet Christ, or we are not.

To summarize these contents:

- No one knows the day or the hour.
- No one knows exactly what will happen.
- No one knows exactly what it will be like.
- We need to be prepared.

We do not need to fear the Second Coming or the information the Scriptures provide about it. It is there for our information and our preparation, and to give us insights so we can recognize signs. If we are doing what we know we are supposed to be doing, we are continuing in our faith. The difference will be one day, we will walk right into eternity with Jesus.

That's the point of the Second Coming. We look forward to the ultimate Kingdom fulfillment, because we will get to see the Kingdom we already recognize and embrace take its full seat and authority everywhere, before our eyes. We don't learn about the Second Coming to do some sort of special preparation; just to continue in what we already embrace as true and recognize as real, to us. We are going to get to see the Kingdom for ourselves! If we have died in Christ, we will live again in Him, and join in eternity with those now living. Whether it happens in our lifetime or generations from now, we will be able to have this same experience, this same promise, when it comes to be.

It doesn't matter how many years it's been since Jesus promised to return; return, He shall. We know from the fullness of our faith experience how faithful He is to stand among us today, as the leader of the church, as our Savior. Despite two thousand years' worth of human nonsense and mess, He still stands there, loving us, waiting for us, ready for us, and guiding us. We still have the work of the Spirit alive and active, depositing within us today. What Jesus has promised is real, and there for us, now, which is why we know He shall return in this ultimate victory. The Kingdom that shall reign then is alive right now, in us, in the church, today. We live this future promise every time we stand up as Kingdom citizens and do what we know is right, this side of eternity. Every time we gather in worship, every time we speak a prayer, every time we give and sincerely mean it, every time we honor our leaders, every time we study the Scriptures, every time we exercise a spiritual gift, we are living that future time, that one when we will never cease to receive and learn and fulfill a true Kingdom purpose in total perfection. We know it is to come because we live it every time we acknowledge the Kingdom of God for ourselves and mean every action, word, and thought that comes forth from us.

Yes, Jesus is coming again. Yes, Jesus is here, now. Yes, you are His soldier, His servant, His heir, His friend, and one He has redeemed, all living your life and touching eternity as you touch this Kingdom. What holds you back? What can you do better? Where are you ready to go from here? Whatever it is, wherever it is, however it is, Jesus is ready for you to experience His future promise for yourself – right now, right in this way – so you will be that much more receptive when eternity comes through and transforms everything we see, hear, taste, smell, and touch, for good.

He who is the faithful witness to all these things says, "Yes, I am coming soon!"

Amen! Come, Lord Jesus!

May the grace of the Lord Jesus be with God's holy people. (Revelation 22:20-21)

ABOUT THE AUTHOR
Dr. Lee Ann B. Marino, Ph.D., D.Min., D.D.

DR. LEE ANN B. MARINO, PH.D., D.MIN., D.D. (she/her) is "everyone's favorite theologian" leading Gen X, Millennials, and Gen Z with expertise in leadership training, queer and feminist theology, general religion, and apostolic theology. She has served in ministry since 1998 and was ordained as a pastor in 2002 and an apostle in 2010. She founded what is now Sanctuary Apostolic Fellowship Empowerment (SAFE) Ministries in 2004. Under her ministry heading Dr. Marino is founder and Overseer of Sanctuary International Fellowship Tabernacle (SIFT) (the original home of National Coming Out Sunday) and The Sanctuary Network, and Chancellor of Apostolic Covenant Theological Seminary (ACTS).

Affectionately nicknamed "the Spitfire," Dr. Marino has spent over two decades as an "apostle, preacher, and teacher" (2 Timothy 1:11), exercising her personal mandate to become "all things to all people" (1 Corinthians 9:22). Her embrace of spiritual issues (both technical and intimate) has found its home among both seekers and believers, those who desire spiritual answers to today's issues.

Dr. Marino has preached throughout the United States, Puerto Rico, and Europe in hundreds of religious services and experiences throughout the years. A history maker in her own right, she has spent over two decades in advocacy, education, and work for and within minority spiritual communities (including African American, Hispanic, and LGBTQ+). She has also served as the first woman on all-male synods, councils, and panels, as well as the first preacher or speaker welcomed of a different race, sexual orientation, or identity among diverse communities. Today, Dr. Marino's work extends to over 150 countries as she hosts the popular *Kingdom Now* podcast, which is in the top 20 percentile of all podcasts worldwide. She is also the author of over 35 books and the popular Patheos column, *Leadership on Fire*. To date, she has had five bestselling titles within their subject matter: *Understanding Demonology, Spiritual Warfare, Healing, and Deliverance: A Manual for the Christian Minister; Ministry School Boot Camp: Training for Helps Ministries, Appointments, and Beyond; Discovering Intimacy: A Journey Through the Song of Solomon; Fruit of the Vine: Study and Commentary on the Fruit of the Spirit;* and *Ministering to LGBTQ+ (and Those Who Love Them): A Primer for Queer Theology* (and its accompanying workbook).

As a public icon and social media influencer, Dr. Marino advocates healthy body image (curvy/full-figured), representation as a demisexual/aromantic, and albinism awareness as a model. Known to those she works with, she is a spiritual mom, teacher, leader, professor, confidant, and friend. She continues to transform, receiving new teaching, revelation, and insight in this thing we call "ministry." Through years of spiritual growth and maturity, Dr. Marino stands as herself, here to present what God has given to her for any who have an ear to hear.

For more information, visit her website at kingdompowernow.org.

www.ingramcontent.com/pod-product-compliance
Lightning Source LLC
LaVergne TN
LVHW051112080426
835510LV00018B/2006